AF782528

CONTENTS

Page

WITNESSES

LETTERS, STATEMENTS, ETC., SUBMITTED FOR THE HEARING

APPENDIX

THE SITUATION IN HAITI

HEARING

BEFORE THE

SUBCOMMITTEE ON THE WESTERN HEMISPHERE

OF THE

COMMITTEE ON INTERNATIONAL RELATIONS HOUSE OF REPRESENTATIVES

ONE HUNDRED EIGHTH CONGRESS

SECOND SESSION

MARCH 3, 2004

Serial No. 108–93

Printed for the use of the Committee on International Relations

Available via the World Wide Web: http://www.house.gov/international_relations

U.S. GOVERNMENT PRINTING OFFICE

92–343PDF WASHINGTON : 2004

For sale by the Superintendent of Documents, U.S. Government Printing Office
Internet: bookstore.gpo.gov Phone: toll free (866) 512–1800; DC area (202) 512–1800
Fax: (202) 512–2250 Mail: Stop SSOP, Washington, DC 20402–0001

COMMITTEE ON INTERNATIONAL RELATIONS

HENRY J. HYDE, Illinois, *Chairman*

JAMES A. LEACH, Iowa
DOUG BEREUTER, Nebraska
CHRISTOPHER H. SMITH, New Jersey, *Vice Chairman*
DAN BURTON, Indiana
ELTON GALLEGLY, California
ILEANA ROS-LEHTINEN, Florida
CASS BALLENGER, North Carolina
DANA ROHRABACHER, California
EDWARD R. ROYCE, California
PETER T. KING, New York
STEVE CHABOT, Ohio
AMO HOUGHTON, New York
JOHN M. McHUGH, New York
ROY BLUNT, Missouri
THOMAS G. TANCREDO, Colorado
RON PAUL, Texas
NICK SMITH, Michigan
JOSEPH R. PITTS, Pennsylvania
JEFF FLAKE, Arizona
JO ANN DAVIS, Virginia
MARK GREEN, Wisconsin
JERRY WELLER, Illinois
MIKE PENCE, Indiana
THADDEUS G. McCOTTER, Michigan
KATHERINE HARRIS, Florida

TOM LANTOS, California
HOWARD L. BERMAN, California
GARY L. ACKERMAN, New York
ENI F.H. FALEOMAVAEGA, American Samoa
DONALD M. PAYNE, New Jersey
ROBERT MENENDEZ, New Jersey
SHERROD BROWN, Ohio
BRAD SHERMAN, California
ROBERT WEXLER, Florida
ELIOT L. ENGEL, New York
WILLIAM D. DELAHUNT, Massachusetts
GREGORY W. MEEKS, New York
BARBARA LEE, California
JOSEPH CROWLEY, New York
JOSEPH M. HOEFFEL, Pennsylvania
EARL BLUMENAUER, Oregon
SHELLEY BERKLEY, Nevada
GRACE F. NAPOLITANO, California
ADAM B. SCHIFF, California
DIANE E. WATSON, California
ADAM SMITH, Washington
BETTY McCOLLUM, Minnesota
CHRIS BELL, Texas

THOMAS E. MOONEY, SR., *Staff Director/General Counsel*
ROBERT R. KING, *Democratic Staff Director*

SUBCOMMITTEE ON THE WESTERN HEMISPHERE

CASS BALLENGER, North Carolina, *Chairman*

RON PAUL, Texas
JERRY WELLER, Illinois
KATHERINE HARRIS, Florida
JAMES A. LEACH, Iowa
ILEANA ROS-LEHTINEN, Florida

ROBERT MENENDEZ, New Jersey
WILLIAM D. DELAHUNT, Massachusetts
GRACE NAPOLITANO, California
ENI F.H. FALEOMAVAEGA, American Samoa
DONALD M. PAYNE, New Jersey

CALEB MCCARRY, *Subcommittee Staff Director*
JESSICA LEWIS, *Democratic Professional Staff Member*
TED BRENNAN, *Professional Staff Member*
JEAN CARROLL, *Staff Associate*

THE SITUATION IN HAITI

WEDNESDAY, MARCH 3, 2004

HOUSE OF REPRESENTATIVES,
SUBCOMMITTEE ON THE WESTERN HEMISPHERE,
COMMITTEE ON INTERNATIONAL RELATIONS,
Washington, DC.

The Subcommittee met, pursuant to call, at 2:35 p.m. in Room 2172, Rayburn House Office Building, Hon. Cass Ballenger (Chairman of the Subcommittee) Presiding.

Mr. BALLENGER. First of all, let me apologize to the people who sat and waited. It really was not 45 minutes; it was only about 40 minutes.

Before we get started, I want to ask unanimous consent that all Members of Congress in attendance today be permitted to join the Members of the Subcommittee up here on the dais. Without objection, it is so ordered. Okay, thank you.

I wish to announce some of the ground rules upon which both Ranking Member Mr. Menendez and I have agreed. First, Members of the Subcommittee will be allowed to offer an opening statement. Second, all Members of the House will be allowed to insert their written statements into the record. Third, all Members, time permitting, will be given 5 minutes to ask questions of the witnesses, and I would like to say to those of you who are here, we are going to be pretty strict on that 5 minutes, or we will be here all day. Accordingly, I ask unanimous consent to allow all nonmembers of the Subcommittee to speak when they are recognized by the Chair to question witnesses.

Without objection, it is so ordered.

Alternating by party, priority will be given first to the Members of the Subcommittee; then, as time permits, to the Members of the full International Relations Committee; and, finally, to Members who do not serve on the International Relations Committee.

Fourth, in the interest of time, I am going to be pretty strict on the clock so that each Member will have the best chance of being able to say something.

Before I begin with my opening statement, I wish to remind everyone that this hearing will be lively and emotional, since we all want a full debate, and I also ask that everyone remain cordial and respectful throughout, if possible, and we have an obligation to uphold the dignity of our offices and this Subcommittee. While we may disagree on some issues, we remain obligated to work together to discuss the important issues which face our Nation and those of Haiti. In my considered opinion, we can and must work together in good faith to meet the challenges that we now face.

And now, my opening statement.

This afternoon we will examine the situation in Haiti. This situation in Haiti is, as has been for some time, extremely challenging. The needs of the Haitian people for democracy, jobs, education, and health care, and for basic necessities such as food and clean water are as great as they have ever been. One can lay out terrible statistics, but they cannot even begin to describe the situation of Haiti's impoverished citizens.

The efforts of the some of the world's most experienced diplomats to resolve the political stalemate in Haiti all ended in frustration. The Deputy Secretary General of the Organization of American States made 20 trips to Haiti to try to work out a solution. President Aristide resigned and left Haiti. Presidents in other countries, including our own, have resigned for the good of the people.

Let me be clear. I fully support the steps taken by the Bush Administration to give the people of Haiti a chance to build a better future. Our government has acted with the backing of other governments, particularly France and Canada, and has secured the unanimous vote in the United Nations Council for a resolution that supports actions to help Haiti.

There is something else I would like to say. There have been accusations that officials of the U.S. Government have committed a felony punishable by death, and that is kidnapping. The head of the Steele Foundation, which was responsible for President Aristide's security, told me, personally, that if U.S. forces or any other forces had tried to kidnap or otherwise harm President Aristide, his men had orders to resist and were authorized to do so with lethal force, if necessary. The accusation that President Aristide was kidnapped is clearly false.

It is my hope that the hearing can support an initiative that I agreed with several Members to come together on a bipartisan basis to see how we can help Haiti. I have personally committed to deliver humanitarian assistance to Haiti with private funds as soon as the situation there permits.

There is a new provisional President in place in accordance with the Haitian Constitution. American Marines are now on the ground in Haiti, and it is time to move forward to help the Haitian people.

With that, I yield to the Ranking Member.

Mr. MENENDEZ. Thank you, Mr. Chairman.

Our Members are well-informed and very passionate about the issue, but they have every intention of pursuing both the truth as well as their policy points of views, and I do not expect anything less.

Today the Americas are watching. The people of our hemisphere watched this Administration turn its back on democracy and walk out on a democratically-elected President. They were watching in Bolivia where massive protests forced President Sanchez de Lozada to resign last October. They were watching in Argentina where riots overturned numerous Presidents in 2001. They were watching in Ecuador when a massive protest overturned a President in 2000.

But let us be clear that in Haiti, President Aristide was confronting a violent, step-by-step takeover of his country by rebel leaders and not simply protests in the street. They watched, and they got the clear messages that this Administration sent: This Administration will not stand up for a democratically-elected Head of State they do not like, and this Administration will stand idly by as rebels, thugs, and prisoners topple a democratically-elected government.

Now, we should watch out. That is an incredibly dangerous and irresponsible message to send reverberating throughout this hemisphere, particularly at a time when many democracies are teetering on the verge of chaos, crisis, and conflict. Let us be clear: We do not get to choose who gets elected in other countries. We may like them. We may hate them. And certainly it is our responsibility to question their policies and to shape our own policy toward them. But it must be clear to the world and to all the countries in the Americas that we respect and support democratically-elected Heads of State, period. In fact, I have serious concerns myself about President Aristide's policies and actions, but that cannot dictate our support for democracy.

This Administration has tried to suggest that when a gang of thugs was on the President's doorstep, that his only choice was either nonintervention and subsequent death, or resignation. Imagine if millions of Americans had stormed the White House after the 2000 elections. Would we have said that the President's only choice was to leave office or face the mob? Absolutely not. We would rail that that action would cause the beginning of the end of our Constitution and our democracy.

As Andreas Oppenheimer said in his column in the Miami Herald last Sunday, and I quote:

> "These are dark days for the cause of democracy in Latin America. The fact that a few rebels in Haiti could sway major countries to demand the resignation of an elected President should sound alarm bells throughout the hemisphere. It happens at a time when violent antigovernment groups are spreading in several Latin American countries with politically weak elected leaders, and where some elected governments seem more tolerant of dictatorship than their predecessors."

And we must look clearly at what this Administration's policies have wrought. Yesterday Guy Philippe declared himself military chief, and Louis-Jodel Chamblain, a convicted killer and accused F-squad leader, says he is now in command of operations. According to today's *Washington Post*, rebel leader Guy Philippe declared on Tuesday that he was in control of Haiti's security forces, and then watches as followers looted a downtown museum to the roaring approval of thousands of supporters outside the National Palace. And as violence escalated in Port-au-Prince, bodies laid at intersections and downtown warehouses, and unclaimed at the morgue.

And so we say to the people of the Americas, at least in this hearing, we in Congress are watching, too, and we will not abdicate our responsibility to democracy in this hemisphere. That is why I am here today, to ask serious questions about the Administration's policy in Haiti. How could this Administration allow so-called rebel leaders, known thugs and convicted murderers to violently take over Haiti, piece by piece, city by city? How could the Administration turn a deaf ear to Aristide's call for help, while passively supporting his resignation and strongly urging him to reconsider whether his Presidency should continue?

There are, of course, the allegations of President Aristide himself. They need to be explored and responded to. We must also fully understand the Administration's involvement with opposition groups and whether violent nondemocratic groups received funding or support. And the Administration must account for its decision not to send peacekeepers in without a political solution when it was obvious that there would be no political solution without those peacekeepers.

Finally, as we turn to our witnesses, I remind them that the words, actions, and deeds of this Administration in Haiti must be judged not only for their impact in Haiti, but for their consequences throughout this hemisphere. The Americas are watching, and so are we, gentlemen, and we look forward to your testimony and the answers to the questions that we pose to you.

Mr. BALLENGER. I thank the gentleman.

I would like to say, I hope your telephones are ringing the way mine are. I have gotten 45 phone calls from Florida, and everybody there, every phone call I have gotten so far, is in favor of what happened.

Next is Congressman Weller.

Mr. WELLER. Thank you, Mr. Chairman, and thank you for conducting this important hearing today and for the opportunity to give my statement as a Member of this Subcommittee.

Mr. Chairman, in recent days the Congress and the American people have heard plenty of rhetoric from supporters of President Aristide regarding the situation in Haiti. I believe it is now time to move away from political rhetoric and talk about the facts. I think it is important to remember that every American, including the President and every Member of Congress, sincerely wants to help the people of Haiti.

We continue to hear outrage from some that Aristide is no longer in power, and that the United States should have stepped in to let him keep his or help him keep his power over the Haitian people. We even hear unfounded accusations that the United States kidnapped Aristide and his family and forced them out of the country. But what are the facts that we have known about Aristide and his government?

Fact number 1: Under Aristide, Haiti blatantly became a hub of narcotics trafficking. Where is the outrage to the fact that Barry McCaffrey, President Clinton's own drug czar, said with regard to Aristide and his role in narcotrafficking that:

> "It is hard to imagine that Aristide himself isn't taking part in this enormously lucrative form of criminal activity. It makes one wonder why Aristide became very quickly Haiti's wealthiest man."

What do we hear Aristide supporters saying about the fact that the United States State Department *International Narcotics Control Strategy Report for 2003* revealed that top officials under the government of Aristide were directly involved in narcotics trafficking? Where is the outrage that under Aristide's government, aircraft filled with drugs have been allowed not only to land on roads in Port-au-Prince, but have received assistance from Haitian National Police officers in blocking traffic, offloading the drugs, and ground transport?

And one of the most important assertions made by Aristide's supporters is that this is a coup against democracy. Let us make sure and get the facts on the record today about what kind of democracy Haiti experienced under Aristide. The 2000 elections were noteworthy not for their democratic nature, but for the fraud and violence that accompanied the elections. The Organization of American States Electoral Observation Mission condemned the 2000 legislative election as rigged, and noted that 1.2 million ballots for senatorial candidates were discarded.

Here are the facts on the presidential election. The November 2000 presidential election was held with no OAS observation, an illegally constituted commission, boycotts by the observation, and no domestic observation. Less than 10 percent of eligible voters participated in those national elections in Haiti. The Clinton Administration refused to provide aid to support the elections, and, most importantly, the United Nations saw right through Aristide's brand of democracy. Secretary General Kofi Annan recommended that the United Nations close its mission to help build democracy in Haiti, saying U.N. efforts were useless considering the government's questionable legitimacy and increasing isolation.

Let us be clear on the role of the Administration in trying to solve Haiti's crisis. The Bush Administration was actively involved, both independently and through the OAS and CARICOM nations, in working to bring President Aristide back from the precipice he placed himself and his country upon. Countless delegations from the United States visited, counseled and urged Aristide to fix the flawed elections that brought him to power and to renounce corruption, but nothing could dissuade Aristide from rejecting reform and rejecting building public institutions. Aristide squandered the opportunity he had to lead Haiti in favor of personal gain.

Roger J. Daley, U.S. General Consul in Haiti from 1998 to 2002, summed up democracy under Aristide:

> "To support Aristide's continued tenure as President is to focus on the shadow of democracy and not on its substance."

Finally, Mr. Chairman, I am extremely concerned about the harm that continued unsubstantiated allegations that Aristide was kidnapped and forcibly removed from the country may do to our armed services and diplomats currently in Haiti today. In fact, recently, a senior United States diplomat in Haiti, a Latino-American, has been specifically targeted by name, putting both he and his family at risk. They are already in a dangerous situation, and irresponsible comments may not only serve to add gasoline to the fire of mob violence in Haiti, but I respectfully urge everyone to consider the safety of our Armed Forces before making statements that may endanger their lives.

Mr. Chairman, this is an important hearing for our Western Hemisphere, and I want to commend you for your leadership in arranging this hearing, and thank you for the opportunity to make a brief statement.

Mr. BALLENGER. Now, Congressman Delahunt.

Mr. DELAHUNT. Thank you, Mr. Chairman. I would have to respectfully disagree with the last speaker in terms of his version of the facts, but maybe we can illuminate that during the course of the questions and answers. Let me just say up front, too, I am no defender of President Aristide. I told him at a meeting that I considered him a profound disappointment, and I think at least two members of the panel have heard me say that on other occasions.

But let us reflect where we are today. Haiti has been taken over by assassins, drug dealers, thugs, and terrorists. Guy Philippe is a former Police Chief who fled the country after allegedly planning a coup. He is reportedly under investigation by U.S. authorities for involvement in drug trafficking. His cohort, Mr. Chamblain, is a convicted killer, the number 2 man of the death squad commonly referred to as the FRAPH (Front for the Advancement and Progress of Haiti), which brutalized Haiti during the junta years. By the way, the leader and founder of FRAPH, Emmanuel Toto Constant, a terrorist of the worst sort who is responsible for the deaths of thousands, he is not part of this new junta yet because he is in the United States, purportedly selling real estate in New York City.

So now we hear that the leaders of this so-called democratic opposition, including Evans Paul and Charles Baker, have been meeting with Philippe and Chamblain. Joining them was the notorious Dany Toussaint, well-known to anyone who is conversant with Haiti. He is suspected of drug dealing and the murder of the country's most prominent journalist, and today our Ambassador apparently had a meeting with Philippe.

Call it what you will, a coup, an alteration in the constitutional order, a resignation, the fact is that this Administration did nothing to save democracy in Haiti, and people who represent the very worst in that society are in the process of taking it over. It is obscene and a stain on our national honor. It goes against everything that we in America embrace, and it did not have to happen. Haiti did not have to be delivered into the hands of people who are, to put it in terms familiar to many of us, pure evil.

The fact is that for the past 10 years, the Majority in this Congress and the current Administration did nothing to nurture democratic institutions in Haiti. Instead, aid was blocked or not requested for the police, for the judicial system, the human rights observers for election monitors. And remember, in September 2002, an independent electoral council was accepted by Aristide, but it could not function because the so-called Democratic Convergence refused to name its representative to the council.

In late 2003, Aristide accepted a plan put forth by the Haitian Bishops and supported by Secretary Powell in which he would have shared power, but it was rejected by the opposition. And in January, the Caribbean community secured Aristide's agreement to a coalition government and the disarmament of violent thugs, but the opposition refused to negotiate unless Aristide resigned. At any of these moments, the message from the Administration should have been sent loud and clear that it was time for the opposition to put the Haitian people above their petty desires and negotiate in good faith. I see no evidence that that occurred.

Just a few days ago, Secretary Noriega said that some in Congress are disappointed because the U.S. did not send in troops, and I am using his quote, "to bail out Aristide." I reject that premise. Our troops would not have been going into Haiti to bail out Aristide; they would have been going in to protect the Haitian people from some of the worst butchers and thugs in that nation's history.

Let me conclude that recent events portend a very bad sign for the future of democracy and human rights in this hemisphere.

I yield back what time I may have left.

Mr. BALLENGER. Congresswoman Ros-Lehtinen.

Ms. ROS-LEHTINEN. Thank you so much, Mr. Chairman. I would like to thank you for holding this important hearing and allowing all of us the opportunity to speak on an issue that is of vital importance, especially to my south Florida community, but, indeed, to the international community in their efforts to support true democratic and political reform in Haiti. So I commend you for having this hearing and for addressing your commitment to the current situation and improvement in Haiti.

I would also like to welcome our witnesses today. Ambassador Noriega has advised the President and Secretary Powell with a true sense of professionalism and understanding of the region, and we welcome him back to our neck of the woods, here in our Subcommittee.

To Administrator Franco, I would like to thank him for his ongoing efforts and commitment to the humanitarian situation in Haiti. I know that you have been following it closely, and it is important to note that this Administration's contributions have even exceeded congressional funding.

Adolfo, I am thrilled to see that one of my former staffers, Jose Fuentos, is sitting behind you and working with you and USAID on these important issues. In concert with Assistant Secretary Dewey, I am positive that your offices and the staff of all of these fine gentlemen are working extremely hard to make the current situation in Haiti less painful for the people of Haiti.

That is why we are here, Mr. Chairman, to discuss and learn about the current situation in Haiti and, more importantly, about the future of Haiti and a future that we hope is a bright one and a positive one.

The state of affairs in Haiti is changing and updated not only on a daily basis, on an hourly basis, but indeed every minute it seems to alter. Most recently the United Nations laid out its plan for Haiti where Resolution 1529 called for a multinational interim force to work with Haitian political forces and the international community to restore a true, a lasting, and a transparent democracy in Haiti. Additionally, CARICOM nations are working on the CARICOM Action Plan. Under this plan, civil society, political opposition, and the government each appoint one member to this council.

Recent accounts, as we know, are troubling. Our own DEA agents indicate that Haiti has been a major transit point for narcotics into the United States. Statements by elusive narcotraffickers are shedding light on Haiti's turning a blind eye to drug trafficking. These drugs, which infest the streets and the playgrounds of our neighborhoods, only bring tragedy to American families. So at all levels, the United States has taken a leadership role in eliminating this danger and in working in tandem with our regional and international allies to create a stable and working government for the people of Haiti, a government responsible to its people and to the needs of the Haitian people.

With a population exceeding 7 million, we must come together to help the people of Haiti overcome the transition it is currently experiencing. The women and the children of Haiti sit in despair awaiting assistance, be it military or humanitarian. But let us not take our eyes off the target and remember that at the end of the day, the children of Haiti are looking for international help, and the United States will be there to help them.

Secretary Powell summarized our objective while addressing EU ministers earlier this week, and I quote:

> "And now we are there to give the Haitian people another chance, and we will be working with Haitians to help Haitians put in place a political system, and we will support it to the best of our ability. I am pleased that the international community has responded so quickly with a unanimous U.N. resolution."

Those are the Secretary's words.

So as I sit here today with my colleagues discussing the current situation in Haiti, I cannot help but ponder upon the suffering of a people and on the current situation of an island not too far from Haiti, my homeland of Cuba. But I strongly encourage this Administration to work on promoting the security situation in Haiti, in supporting an independent government that enjoys true popular support and restores respect for the rule of law in Haiti.

The United States has been and probably always will be Haiti's leading provider of economic aid. I encourage our colleagues here today to continue their support for the international financial loans. Our country has been the shining beacon for freedom and liberty for our Western Hemisphere neighbors. Haiti is currently in a situation where assistance is warranted, and I call on my colleagues to make all efforts to bring stability and transparency to a people who for so many years have longed for it.

Thank you again, Mr. Chairman, for this opportunity to hear from so many others.

Mr. BALLENGER. Now Congressman Payne.

Mr. PAYNE. Thank you very much. I, too, express my appreciation for this hearing to finally be held. I know that Chairman Menendez as our Ranking Member has called repeatedly for a hearing, and our colleague Barbara Lee on the International Relations Committee, not on this Subcommittee, has also done that, and, of course, my voice. But I guess it took the situation that we currently have in Haiti to talk about now what can we do, whereas if we had a meeting before, perhaps some of these areas could have been addressed before, and we could have prevented what happened.

It is always interesting to hear the people from the other side. My colleague from Illinois talked about how tremendous this drug-dealing state of Haiti has been. And I, you know, get amused because President Aristide asked the DEA to bring him more support. He allowed the U.S. to have overflight responsibilities where our aircraft could fly over and have surveillance over its country, could use our Coast Guard at their ports, but we did not take advantage of it. So the easy way to do it is to say, well, you know, he allowed drug-dealing to happen. So we need to take a look, I guess, at Panama, Mexico, Peru, Bolivia, Colombia, Afghanistan, Iraq, Iran, all of those places that we are spending tremendous amounts of funds supporting in some instances the new leadership, while we still have this tremendous thing. And so I really kind of question a person to say there is drug-dealing going on. It is going on even in the State of Illinois, and we do not, therefore, condemn the Governor to say that he has turned his back.

So I would just like to say that, you know, you can have a self-fulfilling prophecy. If you wait and wait and wait until the last minute, there is no other option but to leave. And when the thugs were coming down, town by town—and, as Mr. Delahunt mentioned, these are convicted killers: Chamblain, former sergeant, accused of killing businessmen and others; Philippe, who was actually convicted of killing Antoine Izmery and Guy Malary. These are people our government evidently feels more comfortable in sitting down with, negotiating with, because I guess that is what they are going to do because those are the new people who will be in charge of this government.

It makes no sense at all to take people who have been in the DR, people who are in New York, the former FRAPH that stood on the docks and turned the country of Harlem around. Do you remember that? The same people now are in this new government. This is a disgrace.

Then we have our great Colonel, David Berger—and I know that he is concerned since there are so few Marines—said that, "I am not a police officer, and I have no instructions to disarm." So as the American Marines sit by, protecting U.S. properties, this band of thugs and gangsters and killers simply can do whatever they want to do.

If, in fact, we are going to do nothing, then we ought to leave and just let the place go down like it is happening. How can we send in people and just allow the killings to go on, to look the other way? You would do better maybe with the Haitian Police Department. They might at least try to apprehend the criminal.

So I think several weeks ago when the French made it pretty clear that they were willing to go in with 4,000 Marines, but I suspect that somehow they were discouraged—I was told by Secretary of State Powell that it was a misinterpretation. They really did not want to go in. However, they not only said they would go in, they said they didn't necessarily need Americans to go in. They said they would appreciate it if we would participate in the costs. I can see one thing being blurred by interpretation, but not a specific kind of a plan like that, that all of a sudden we find that it was totally misinterpreted. We should allow countries that have some goodwill toward a situation, that when they see right over wrong, to do their thing and not necessarily say that is in our sphere of influence, which I would suppose occurred.

So I am very—it is a sad day for democracy. This regime change is who we want to see elected and who we do not. If we do not agree with them, they are out. If we do, they are okay, regardless to—it reminds me of the Cold War, the Mobutus that we created for 30 years in Zaire. The people who rob and kill their own people are those that we would rather negotiate with. It makes no sense. It is a flawed policy. It is a dark day in our history.

I think that when a President—why not take him out and then come up with that diplomatic solution that Secretary of State Colin Powell was trying to negotiate? Why do we have to resign in order for him to leave? He could have left the country and come back once order was restored. But since he resigned, I guess then we can deal with the country because a coup d'etat did not occur. He just quit, retired, had enough, decided to resign and go somewhere else. Therefore, legally, I guess, the international communities could then deal with this coup d'etat, which even in the Africa Unions say that if a country is taken over by military forces in Africa, countries do not have diplomatic relations, and that country is isolated and boycotted, and sanctions go out on that country. However, the convenient resignation of President Aristide, therefore, precludes even the AU's, African Union, laws to preside.

So as you can tell, we are very—many of us are very frustrated. We appreciated the President finally meeting with us last Wednesday, but we have seen nothing positive really come about. I would hope that we would have a plan. I would hope that we would—if we don't want to intervene with disarmament, why don't we let someone else go in, those who may be willing to have disarmament reintegration, so that the killings can stop right now? It is simply a lawless place, and I believe that we can do better.

Mr. BALLENGER. Pursuant to the previous order, Members, other Members, may submit their written testimony for the record. Without objection, so ordered.

Let me go to the first panel now. What I plan on doing is introducing all members of the panel first, and all will testify before any questions will be asked.

First of all, Roger Noriega. Roger Noriega serves as Assistant Secretary of State for the Bureau of Western Hemisphere Affairs. He is a frequent visitor of this Subcommittee, and we always enjoy having him here.

Second is Arthur Gene Dewey. Gene Dewey serves our Nation as Assistant Secretary of State in the Bureau of Population, Refugees, and Migration. He is responsible for overseeing U.S. policies regarding the refugees and international migration. He is a graduate of West Point and served two combat aviation tours in Vietnam. I would like to thank him for coming.

Third is Adolfo Franco. Adolfo Franco is the Assistant Administrator for Latin America and the Caribbean of the U.S. Agency for International Development. Mr. Franco previously served as a counsel to the Majority on the International Relations Committee, and it is a pleasure to see you again, Adolfo.

Let me please request of you if you could reduce your testimony to 5 minutes, and we will enter your total statement for the record, if that is satisfactory. And if that is okay, Secretary Noriega.

STATEMENT OF THE HONORABLE ROGER F. NORIEGA, ASSISTANT SECRETARY OF STATE, BUREAU OF WESTERN HEMISPHERE AFFAIRS

Mr. NORIEGA. Thank you very much, Mr. Chairman. It is a pleasure to appear before you and to have an opportunity to speak to this Subcommittee today on the topic of Haiti.

Mr. Chairman and distinguished Members, one chapter in the history of Haiti has just come to a close, a very sad chapter, and the Haitian people are preparing to write a new one. The resignation of President Aristide on February 29 marked the end of a process that in its early days held out a bright promise to free Haiti from the violence, authoritarianism, and confrontation that has plagued that country since its independence 200 years ago. Sadly, that hope remains unrealized today. While responsibility for this failure resides largely with former President Aristide himself, the task before the United States, working with the international community, is to help the people of Haiti break the cycle of political misrule that has caused so much misery.

As we move ahead, it is important that we understand where the problems lie. The Haitian people are not to blame for the country's poverty and lack of development. Those of us who have Haitian friends and colleagues know that they are an especially creative and particularly industrious people. Those who have made the United States their home are a blessing to our community and to our economy. Rather, the absence of good governance, even the absence of the will to govern fairly and effectively, lies at the heart of the problem.

President Aristide's legacy of frustrated hopes was caused as much by what he did not do as by what he did do. At the end, even his supporters in the international community realized that his rule had undermined democracy and economic development in Haiti, rather than strengthened it.

Let us be very clear. United States policy in Haiti and throughout the Western Hemisphere, indeed throughout the world, is to support and strengthen democratic institutions. On September 11, 2001, the United States joined the 33 other members of the Organization of American States, including Haiti, in signing the Inter-American Democratic Charter. The creation of the Democratic Charter owed much to the hemispheric concern against the undermining of democratic institutions by elected governments themselves. It acknowledges that the essential elements of representative democracy go well beyond merely holding elections, and that governments have the obligation to promote and to defend democratic principles and institutions.

A commitment to constitutional democracy was what led this government to demand that Jean-Bertrand Aristide be restored to power after he was deposed by a military coup in 1991. By the fall of 1994, the United States led a multinational force to restore President Aristide to power, as a matter of fact. From the outset, Mr. Aristide's supporters began committing systematic acts of violence that undermined the confidence of the Haitian people in our international mission. Many Haitians began wondering whether we were in Haiti to strengthen democracy or merely keep one individual in power.

Looking back, it is fair to say that had the international community been more rigorous in holding President Aristide to his commitments to respect human rights and the rule of law, his rule might not have ended with his resignation and his self-imposed exile 10 years later.

Killings of President Aristide's opponents began within months of his return to power, but no persons were ever arrested or convicted for these crimes. The undermining of the democratic process was demonstrated by the highly flawed Parliamentary elections of July 1995, badly run local elections in April 1997, and the fraudulent Parliamentary elections once again in May 2000. This series of farcical electoral exercises and the Haitian Government's unwillingness to govern justly opened the door to the many subsequent acts of political violence and the intimidation by President Aristide against his opponents. Incidentally, his election at the end of November 2000 was pronounced by the international community as not meeting international standards.

Since 1994, the United States has provided $850 million in assistance to Haiti. However, our aid programs failed to produce sustainable growth because of the corruption and the inaction of the Haitian Government. An impressive investment of money and technical assistance to create a 5,000 Haitian national police force was squandered as President Aristide deliberately politicized and underfunded the organization. Instead, Aristide and his successors undermined the rule of law by relying on criminal gangs and failing to confront narcotraffickers.

Mr. Delahunt has referred to Danny Toussaint as being one of the thugs that is pretending to run Haiti today. Danny Toussaint was an aide to President Aristide. He was a security aide to President Aristide. He was one of his principal advisers. He is a creature of President Aristide, and you are right, he is a very bad man. You are wrong, though. He is not running Haiti.

Despite the justified frustration of the international community, we never gave up on Haiti or the Haitian people. Our approach in encouraging respect for constitutional processes and good governance of Haiti focused on working with our hemispheric partners through the OAS and with the other friends of Haiti. In June 2001, the OAS General Assembly approved Resolution 831 calling on the Government of Haiti to take steps to create an environment conducive to free and fair elections as a means of resolving the political crisis created by the tainted, corrupted elections of 2000.

On December 17, 2001, only a few months later, the Government of Haiti instead lashed out at its opponents with a series of brutal attacks by pro-Aristide thugs on persons and property. This led to the OAS Resolution 806, which called for the creation of an OAS Special Mission to strengthen democracy in Haiti and for the Aristide regime to take vigorous steps to restore a climate of security.

When the Government of Haiti failed to comply with the terms of Resolution 806, the OAS responded with another resolution, 822, in September 2002. In this resolution, the Government of Haiti again committed itself to take a series of actions to promote a climate of security and confidence leading to free and fair elections in 2003. I was Chairman of the OAS Permanent Council when Resolution 822 was approved, and the U.S. delegation did the heavy lifting in negotiating that document. Resolution 822 is an important resolution because it took the key step of calling for the normalization of economic cooperation between the Government of Haiti and the international and financial institutions as a means of providing Haiti with further a incentive to develop its institutions and promote sustainable development.

Mr. BALLENGER. Mr. Secretary, if you could bring it to a close; if I am going to be tough on everybody else, I guess I have to be tough on you, too.

Mr. NORIEGA. Well, I guess I could stop right now if you do not want to hear the rest of this.

Mr. BALLENGER. Well, I would love to hear it, but I just—could you——

Mr. NORIEGA. Well, then, I will keep going.

In the face of the Haitian Government's noncompliance with the terms of these resolutions, the Caribbean community, CARICOM, and the OAS sent a high-level delegation, which included President Bush's Special Envoy for Western Hemisphere Affairs to Haiti in March 2003. In September 2003, the United States facilitated the OAS effort to send another special envoy to Haiti, Ambassador Terence Todman, to help broker a breakthrough in the political stalemate. While all of this was taking place, the United States donated another $3.5 million to the OAS Special Mission in Haiti to support its work.

These determined efforts came to naught. Rather than taking steps to build political consensus, reign in the rampant corruption that robbed Haitians of their already meager resources, or promote an atmosphere of security, Aristide continued to recruit and arm gangs of thugs to be unleashed against his opponents.

Mr. BALLENGER. Mr. Secretary, they are checking your statement up here, and you have a couple more pages to go.

Mr. NORIEGA. Sure.

Mr. BALLENGER. If you don't mind, could you bring it to a close, please, sir?

Mr. NORIEGA. Well, let me tell you what I need to tell you about the future, sir.

I want to talk about several key points regarding United States policy and how we go forward with our international partners to help the Haitian people.

The United States has been and will continue to be a firm supporter of democracy in Haiti. That is the cornerstone of our policy. President Aristide's departure was never a demand by the United States. We continuously worked with our international partners to break through the political impasse and allow democracy to have a chance. The United States has been and will almost certainly remain Haiti's leading provider of economic assistance. This aid was never suspended or cut off, as some have claimed. Between 1995 and 2003, the United States provided $850 million in assistance.

Looking forward, our goal is to further stabilize the security situation and provide emergency humanitarian assistance to Haitians, promote the formation of independent government that enjoys broad popular support, and work with the government to restore the rule of law and other key democratic institutions in Haiti, while encouraging steps to improve the difficult economic condition of the Haitian people.

The United States is not alone in this process. Under the terms of the U.N. Security Council resolution, United States forces are on the ground in Haiti, participating in a Multilateral Interim Force to contribute to a secure and stable environment. And, Mr. Menendez, the countries of the Americas are doing more than watching what we are doing in Haiti, they are helping. And, quite frankly, to compare them in any way to the way President Aristide has governed Haiti is, as a matter of fact, an insult to the Latin American leaders.

As the Multinational Interim Force ends its mission, we will continue to support a U.N. stabilization force, and key countries in the hemisphere are going to participate in that process and will build up a Haitian national police. These are the people who will be protecting Haitians from killers.

President Bush has called for a break from the past in Haiti. Indeed, there must be a break from the past if Haiti is to move forward. That break will not come in the form of a new autocrat or demagogue, but by unleashing the incredible potential of the Haitian people in positive and productive directions. Nowhere is it written that the Haitian people must be ruled by tyrants. They deserve leaders worthy of their trust and respect who favor the common good over personal gain.

Mr. Chairman, you are going to hear from Pierre-Marie Paquiot in a few minutes. This is the legacy of President Aristide, the Director of the University of Haiti whose legs were pulverized by Aristide's gangs when he dared to wander into the middle of a demonstration in December 2003 and try to break up the violence, beaten to where his legs were pulverized, and he has to go through rehabilitation. This is the legacy of violence of President Aristide. He is also part of the future, and you will be able to hear his message, because that is the voice of the Haitian people.

Thank you very much, Mr. Chairman.

[The prepared statement of Mr. Noriega follows:]

PREPARED STATEMENT OF THE HONORABLE ROGER F. NORIEGA, ASSISTANT SECRETARY OF STATE, BUREAU OF WESTERN HEMISPHERE AFFAIRS

Mr. Chairman, it is a pleasure to appear and to speak before this Subcommittee today on the topic of Haiti.

Mr. Chairman, distinguished Members:

A chapter in the history of Haiti has just come to a close and the Haitian people are preparing to write a new one. The resignation of President Aristide on February 29 marked the end of a process that in its early days held out a bright promise to free Haiti from the violence, authoritarianism, and confrontation that has plagued that country since its independence two hundred years ago. Sadly, that hope remains unrealized. While responsibility for this failure resides largely with Aristide himself, the task before the United States, working with the international community, is to help the people of Haiti break the cycle of political misrule that has caused so much misery.

As we move ahead, it is important that we understand where the problems lie. The Haitian people are not to blame for the country's poverty and lack of development. Rather, the absence of good governance, even the WILL to govern fairly and effectively lies at the heart of the problem. Aristide's legacy of frustrated hope was caused as much by what HE DID NOT DO as by the steps he took. At the end, even his supporters in the international community realized that his rule had undermined democracy and economic development in Haiti rather than strengthened it.

Let's be very clear. U.S. policy in Haiti and throughout the Western Hemisphere—indeed the world—is to support democracy and the strengthening of democratic institutions. On September 11, 2001, the United States joined the 33 other members of the Organization of American States—including Haiti—in signing the Inter-American Democratic Charter. The creation of the Democratic Charter owed much to the hemispheric concern against the undermining of democratic institutions by elected governments. It acknowledges that the essential elements of representative democracy go well beyond merely holding elections and that governments have the obligation to promote and defend democratic principles and institutions.

The commitment to strengthening democracy has been the cornerstone of our policy in Haiti since the restoration of Aristide to power—by the international community led by the United States—in 1994. This process was set back by the highly flawed parliamentary elections of June 1995, badly run local elections in April 1997, and fraudulent parliamentary elections once again in May 2000. This series of bogus electoral exercises and the Haitian government's unwillingness to govern fairly opened the door to many subsequent acts of political violence and intimidation by Aristide against his opponents. Our approach in encouraging respect for constitutional processes and good governance in Haiti focused on working with our hemispheric partners through the OAS and with other friends of Haiti. In June 2001, the OAS General Assembly approved Resolution 1831 calling on the Government of Haiti to take steps to create an environment conducive to free and fair elections as a means of resolving the political crisis created by the tainted elections of 2000.

On December 17, 2001, the Government of Haiti lashed out at its opponents with a series of brutal attacks by pro-Aristide thugs on persons and property. This led to OAS Resolution 806, which called for the creation of an OAS Special Mission to Strengthen Democracy in Haiti and for the Aristide regime to take vigorous steps to restore a climate of security.

When the Government of Haiti failed to comply with the terms of Resolution 806, the OAS responded with another resolution—822—in September 2002. In this resolution, the Government of Haiti again committed itself to take a series of actions to promote a climate of security and confidence leading to free and fair elections in 2003. I was Chairman of the OAS Permanent Council when Resolution 822 was approved and the U.S. delegation did the heavy lifting in negotiating the document. Resolution 822 took the key step of calling for the normalization of economic cooperation between the GOH and the international financial institutions—as a means of providing Haiti with further incentive to develop its institutions and promote sustainable development.

In the face of the Haitian Government's non-compliance with the terms of these resolutions, the Caribbean Community—CARICOM—and the OAS sent a high-level delegation, which included President Bush's Special Envoy for Western Hemisphere Affairs, to Haiti in March 2003. In September 2003, the United States facilitated the OAS effort to send another special envoy to Haiti, Ambassador Terence Todman, to help broker a breakthrough in the political stalemate. While all this was taking place, the United States donated $3.5M to the OAS Special Mission in Haiti to support its work.

These impressive efforts came to naught. Rather than taking steps to build political consensus, reign in the rampant corruption that robbed Haitians of their already meager resources, or promote an atmosphere of security, Aristide continued to recruit and arm gangs of thugs to be unleashed against his opponents. In the process, he undermined what little legitimate law enforcement capacity remained in the already corrupted and weakened Haitian National Police. U.S. law enforcement assistance was essentially limited to support of the Haitian Coast Guard, a rare and largely autonomous police unit that continued to have professional and competent leadership.

Further undermining the rule of law and the effectiveness of his government, Aristide turned a blind eye to the rampant corruption and drug trafficking of those within his circle of power.

It is no wonder, therefore, that when one of the largest pro-Aristide gangs turned against him and rose in open rebellion in the city of Gonaïves last month, the Government of Haiti had no effective, let alone legitimate means with which to respond. The rapid collapse of Government authority throughout Haiti bore testimony not to the strength of the thugs and gangs who sought to bring him down, but to Aristide's own failures. By gutting respect for the rule of law and reverting to authoritarian practices, he undermined his own legitimacy and demeaned the word "democracy."

Under these circumstances, Aristide agreed to what he had steadfastly rejected before, a plan that would open the door to consensus government and a way forward to resolve Haiti's political crisis. This was, of course, the CARICOM Prior Action Plan, with its own Plan of Action and endorsement by the United States, France and Canada. For Aristide, this change of heart came too late to save his government. Nor did his eleventh-hour appeal for foreign military intervention garner support in the international community. No country, the United States included, was inclined to send forces to sustain the failed political status quo in Haiti. In what may eventually be considered his finest hour, Aristide decided to resign, initiating a constitutional process that transferred power to the President of the Supreme Court.

There are several key points that I wish to make regarding U.S. policy toward Haiti—as we move forward with our international partners to help the Haitian people:

1. the United States has been and will continue to be a firm supporter of democracy in Haiti. That is a cornerstone of our policy.
2. Aristide's departure was never a U.S. demand. We continuously worked with our international partners to break through the political impasse and allow democracy to have a chance. Even France, while calling on February 25 for Aristide's ouster, remained supportive of our efforts to find a negotiated solution. While we were convinced that Aristide was a key obstacle in these efforts, we sought to work with him up until the very end. These efforts were conducted at the highest levels of the United States Government, with Secretary Powell in the forefront.
3. The United States has been and will almost certainly remain Haiti's leading provider of economic aid. This aid was never suspended or cut off, as some have claimed. Between 1995 and 2003, the United States provided over $850 million in assistance to Haiti.
4. Our leadership at the OAS in negotiating Resolution 822 in September 2002 helped to open the door to normalized relations between Haiti and the IFIs and since then IDB loans have begun to flow. We will continue to support IFI loans to Haiti based on their technical merits.

Looking forward, our goal is first to stabilize the security situation and provide emergency humanitarian assistance to Haitians, promote the formation of an independent government that enjoys broad popular support, and work with that government to restore the rule of law and other key democratic institutions in Haiti, while encouraging steps to improve the difficult economic condition of the Haitian people. The United States is not alone in this process. Under the terms of a UN Resolution approved unanimously by the Security Council on February 29, U.S. forces are already in Haiti, participating in a Multilateral Interim Force to contribute to a secure and stable environment. The key elements of the CARICOM prior action plan are, as we speak, being carried out to name a new Prime Minister who will in turn form a consensus government to lead Haiti forward. As the Multinational Interim Force ends its mission, we will support the UN stabilization force called for by the Security Council and will work with the UN and OAS to help the Haitian people rebuild their institutions, starting with the Haitian National Police.

President Bush has called for a "break from the past" in Haiti. Indeed there MUST be a break from the past if Haiti is to move forward. That break will not come in the form of a new autocrat or demagogue but by unleashing the incredible potential of the Haitian people in positive and productive directions. Nowhere is there written that the Haitian people must be poor or ruled by tyrants. They deserve leaders worthy of their trust and respect, who favor the common good over personal gain. The rule of law must be upheld. Those responsible for crimes and abuses must be punished. Gangs and thugs cannot be allowed to hold sway. Support from the United States and the international community can help—and they will have it—but the long-term job of building Haitian democracy is up to the Haitians themselves. They, above all people in our Hemisphere, deserve some success.

Mr. BALLENGER. Secretary Dewey. Witnesses are not supposed to be regulated by the 5-minute rule, but I made that statement to begin with, so I have to stick with it. Sorry about that.

STATEMENT OF THE HONORABLE ARTHUR E. DEWEY, ASSISTANT SECRETARY OF STATE, BUREAU OF POPULATION, REFUGEES, AND MIGRATION

Mr. DEWEY. Mr. Chairman, Members of the Subcommittee, I, too, appreciate this opportunity to discuss recent developments in Haiti as they pertain to refugee and migration affairs.

I am thankful first that the number of Haitians taking to the sea in overcrowded, unseaworthy vessels was not of the order of those who had departed during previous migrations. Had there been a mass migration by sea, we would almost certainly have seen people drowned or otherwise lost at sea. We continue to encourage Haitians not to take to sea.

During the course of the last week, the U.S. Coast Guard rescued some 900 migrants at sea. Once aboard cutters, they were given medical attention and food and cared for while awaiting repatriation in coordination with the Haitian Coast Guard.

If at any time during the course of interdiction and repatriation efforts a migrant in any way expresses or indicates a fear or concern regarding returning to Haiti, that migrant is interviewed by a trained Department of Homeland Security protection officer to determine whether the migrant requires protection against repatriation. During last week's repatriations, migrants who expressed the fear of return were promptly transferred to a separate vessel for protection screening.

Among those interdicted, only a handful expressed fear of returning home. They were promptly transferred to a separate vessel. They were not immediately returned to Haiti with the other migrants. And after a thorough screening, these migrants were found not to have a credible fear of persecution and were repatriated.

The U.S. Coast Guard effected these repatriations with superb assistance from the Haitian Coast Guard and from U.S. Embassy staff in Port-au-Prince, who were on the scene for as much of the repatriation process as possible. My own bureau, the Bureau of Population, Refugees and Migration at the State Department, is now making emergency funds available to the Embassy to cover food, transportation, and similar expenses to assist repatriated migrants as they return to their homes.

We are working closely with the Department of Homeland Security, including the U.S. Coast Guard and the Department of Defense, in this endeavor, as we have worked closely together throughout the recent events in Haiti.

In addition to these efforts, we contacted the Office of the United Nations High Commissioner For Refugees well before the onset of the crisis to discuss, among other issues, what could be done to assist Caribbean countries like Jamaica, the Dominican Republic and the Bahamas in the event of a large outflow from Haiti.

With our full support, UNHCR dispatched a team of specialists to the Caribbean to draw up a comprehensive regional response to any crisis that might emerge. They have provided guidance to Caribbean governments throughout the crisis. Consideration of an international appeal for assistance is now on hold pending new developments.

Our goal in this endeavor has been to mobilize the international community through the High Commissioner For Refugees to ensure that the United States, and the United States taxpayer, do not bear sole responsibility for responding to this crisis, and that we can count on our international partners to shoulder responsibility as well. Application of international burden-sharing to rebuild Haiti will also minimize motivations in the future for Haitians to attempt to flee their homeland.

Thank you, Mr. Chairman.

Mr. BALLENGER. Thank you, Mr. Dewey.

[The prepared statement of Mr. Dewey follows:]

PREPARED STATEMENT OF THE HONORABLE ARTHUR E. DEWEY, ASSISTANT SECRETARY OF STATE, BUREAU OF POPULATION, REFUGEES, AND MIGRATION

Mr. Chairman, members of the subcommittee, I appreciate this opportunity to discuss recent developments in Haiti as they pertain to migration and refugee affairs.

I am thankful, first, that the number of Haitians taking to the sea in overcrowded, unseaworthy vessels was not of the order of those who departed during previous migrations. Had there been a mass migration by sea, we would almost certainly have seen people drowned or otherwise lost at sea. We continue to encourage Haitians not to take to sea.

During the course of the last week, the U. S. Coast Guard rescued some 900 migrants at sea. Once aboard cutters they were given medical attention and food, and cared for while awaiting repatriation in coordination with the Haitian Coast Guard.

If at any time during the course of interdiction and repatriation efforts a migrant in any way expresses or indicates a fear or concern regarding return to Haiti, that migrant is interviewed by a trained Department of Homeland Security protection officer to determine whether the migrant requires protection against repatriation. During last week's repatriations, migrants who expressed a fear of return were promptly transferred to a separate vessel for protection screening.

Among those interdicted, only several expressed fear of returning home. They were promptly transferred to a separate vessel. They were not immediately returned to Haiti with the other migrants. After thorough screening, these migrants were found not to have a credible fear of persecution, and were repatriated.

The U. S. Coast Guard effected these repatriations with superb assistance from the Haitian Coast Guard and from U.S. Embassy staff in Port-Au-Prince who were on scene for as much of the repatriation process as possible. My own bureau, the Bureau of Population, Refugees and Migration, is now making emergency funds available to the Embassy to cover food, transportation and similar expenses to assist repatriated migrants return to their homes.

We are working closely with the Department of Homeland Security, including the U.S. Coast Guard, and the Department of Defense in this endeavor, as we have worked closely together throughout the recent events in Haiti.

In addition to these efforts, we contacted the office of the United Nations High Commissioner for Refugees (UNHCR) well before the onset of the crisis to discuss, among other issues, what could be done to assist Caribbean countries like Jamaica, the Dominican Republic and the Bahamas in the event of a large outflow from Haiti.

With our full support, UNHCR dispatched a team of specialists to the Caribbean to draw up a comprehensive regional response to any crisis that might emerge. They have provided guidance to Caribbean governments throughout the crisis. Consideration of an international appeal for assistance is now on hold pending new developments.

Our goal in this endeavor has been to mobilize the international community through UNHCR to ensure that the United States—and the United States taxpayer—do not bear sole responsibility for responding to the crisis, and that we can count on our international partners to shoulder responsibility as well.

Application of international burden sharing to rebuilding Haiti will also minimize motivations in the future for Haitians to attempt to flee their homeland.

Mr. BALLENGER. Adolfo, it is your turn.

STATEMENT OF THE HONORABLE ADOLFO A. FRANCO, ASSISTANT ADMINISTRATOR FOR LATIN AMERICA AND THE CARIBBEAN, U.S. AGENCY FOR INTERNATIONAL DEVELOPMENT

Mr. FRANCO. Thank you, Mr. Chairman and Members of the Committee. It is always a pleasure to return home to the House International Relations Committee, and today is a very timely hearing, discussing the unfolding humanitarian situation in Haiti and USAID's continuing efforts to assist the Haitian people to realize their dream of peace, prosperity and democracy. I have submitted a complete statement for the record, and I ask that it be made a part of the record.

Mr. BALLENGER. Without objection.

Mr. FRANCO. I used to be the guy who monitors those lights, so if it goes yellow, just let me know, and I will wrap it up. I appreciate it.

Although we might have differences of opinion, I know that President Bush, this Congress, and the American people are all fully committed to the well-being and prosperity of the Haitian people. Just as Secretary Noriega has noted, the United States is and has been the largest bilateral donor in Haiti, and this Administration will not shirk its responsibilities to the Haitian people.

With the situation regarding the humanitarian efforts at hand, Mr. Chairman, since the conflict began in early February, there has been some restriction of movement of commercial goods and relief supplies, including food, fuel, and medical stocks. This has hindered AID's ability to distribute food assistance to those populations it normally serves. Access and distribution remain our major obstacle for both humanitarian deliveries and regular commercial activity in the country. USAID is implementing with its nongovernmental organizational partners, but has, however, reported that the primary concern of humanitarian assistance is lack of security, and this impedes the safe passage for the transportation and distribution of relief supplies, fuel, water, and food commodities.

However, Mr. Chairman, as I stated last week, I want to make clear that based on the best information available to USAID, and we are in constant communication with Port-au-Prince, we have staff there and our partner organization, Haiti has enough food to feed its population, although insecurity and disruptions in transportation and distribution could potentially cause a deterioration in the availability of food, particularly in urban areas.

Despite overall availability of food, however, it is true that certain pockets of particular need exist, and these are certain populations, particularly in the north, with the elderly and some orphanages that have reported to us difficulties in receiving food supplies. I will travel to Haiti this weekend to personally assess the situation on the ground with our staff and our partners in Port-au-Prince.

To meet the needs of Haiti, Mr. Chairman, we have 20,000 metric tons of food available in Louisiana for immediate transport to Haiti if that would become necessary, and we have stocks of 11,000 metric tons of food. This is just USAID food in country. You may have read that some of this food was looted in the unrest on February 29, but I am very pleased to report to the Committee today that the subsequent investigation by our personnel on the ground reveals that most of our USAID emergency food supplies remain intact and are under secure storage in Port-au-Prince.

I want to state, Mr. Chairman, that prior to this, we were preplanning, and I reported this to the committee last week, if necessary, drops throughout the country that were not using the Port-au-Prince facility, use of helicopters, certainly any other means that we would in a complex emergency to deliver food. So we have been on top of this since well before February 18.

The interruption of basic health services in the north is a serious concern, and due to hazardous and very difficult road conditions, this represents a point of concern for us. We have sent a large amount of medical supplies to Haiti in the last few days and provided a grant to the Pan American Health Organization for additional supplies. In addition, the International Committee of the Red Cross has increased the number of staff to meet these shortages of medical personnel in clinics and hospitals, particularly in Port-au-Prince.

Currently there are no reports of an outbreak of the six major childhood vaccine-preventable diseases in the country. However, we do have reports of increased cases of diarrhea and fever in the towns of Gonaives, particularly due to the lack of water. According to the Pan American Health Organization, there is a shortage of tuberculosis, TB, drugs, and the disruption of TB programs in the north of the country. We are working with Pan American Health Organization currently, and we hope to bring the situation under control as soon as possible, and I will report to the Committee on the progress being made.

Again, Mr. Chairman, USAID is responding quickly to the potential for humanitarian crisis in Haiti. When Ambassador Foley declared a disaster emergency on February 18, our Office of Foreign Disaster Assistance provided $50,000 to transport and distribute emergency relief supplies, including 12 medical kits and 3 surgical kits that serve 10,000 people each for the next 3 months. In addition, we provided $400,000 that I mentioned to the Pan American Health Organization to purchase additional medical supplies immediately and to conduct emergency relief activities in Haiti. They have an extensive and very good network in the country.

On February 24, we deployed a three-person team to Port-au-Prince, including a senior regional team adviser, a health officer, and an information liaison officer with our partner organizations to coordinate our humanitarian activities in the country. USAID has also contracted several small aircraft to transport staff throughout the country to conduct an assessment of the conditions, and I can report to you that airplanes took off early this afternoon to conduct those assessments. These planes also, in addition to the assessments, carry cargo, including relief supplies, to remote areas as needed.

Our Office of Foreign Disaster Assistance is currently awarding a $400,000 grant to Catholic Relief Services for procurement of what we call cash grants, and these are providing small cash so people can buy food on the commercial markets, and this serves particularly the most vulnerable populations, such as orphanages and hospitals. We are also—our Embassy in Port-au-Prince is conducting a security plan to address the protection of our staff and our implementing partners as they transport goods and needed services to people throughout the country. We work with CSR, Catholic Relief Services, World Vision, CARE, and Save the Children.

In conclusion, Mr. Chairman, we have been, for some time, engaged in Haiti, so we were well prepared for this potential emergency. We have been monitoring the situation well before the disturbances of February 18, and as Secretary Noriega has said, our commitment and our resolve is to provide the necessary assistance to the people of Haiti, and we will continue to do so. Thank you.

Mr. BALLENGER. Thank you, Mr. Franco.

[The prepared statement of Mr. Franco follows:]

PREPARED STATEMENT OF THE HONORABLE ADOLFO A. FRANCO, ASSISTANT ADMINISTRATOR FOR LATIN AMERICA AND THE CARIBBEAN, U.S. AGENCY FOR INTERNATIONAL DEVELOPMENT

Mr. Chairman, Members of the Committee, it is a pleasure to appear before the House Committee on International Relations to discuss with you the unfolding humanitarian situation in Haiti and USAID's continuing assistance with helping the Haitian people realize their dream of peace, prosperity and democracy. The central focus of my remarks will be on what USAID is doing through our humanitarian assistance programs to mitigate the effects of the social and political unrest on the most vulnerable segments of Haiti's population.

FOOD SECURITY

The ongoing political turmoil and economic deterioration in Haiti have created the potential for a humanitarian crisis, and have affected numerous aspects of development such as food security, health and nutrition, and water and sanitation. While sufficient food stocks are currently in-country and no immediate food crisis exists at present, this could change quickly in coming weeks, especially in the north, due to insecurity and disruptions in the transportation and distribution system. USAID currently has in storage, more than 11,000 metric tons of P. L. 480 Title II food commodities. The bulk of these commodities are monetized and the proceeds are used for delivering health care, education, and agricultural production services to Haiti's most food-insecure population. The rest is used for direct food distribution to Haiti's indigent populations and children's orphanages throughout the country. Most of the food stocks are under secured storage in Port-au-Prince. The World Food Program and European Union also have available for distribution, stocks of at least 5,000 metric tons, and 3,100 tons respectively.

HUMANITARIAN PROGRAM

The U.S. Government through USAID is Haiti's largest bilateral donor. In FY03, USAID contributed $71 million. Through fiscal years 1995–2003, USAID provided a total of $850 million in direct bilateral assistance. Prior to the outbreak of violence, USAID had planned $52 million in assistance in FY04 to programs ranging from health, democracy and governance, education and economic growth. We are currently analyzing additional assistance options. To ensure that quality service delivery continues to benefit those Haitians who are most in need, USAID assistance is channeled principally through NGOs. USAID is also the lead donor in addressing critical transnational issues such as HIV/AIDS and other debilitating infectious diseases, a seriously degraded natural resource base, respect for human rights and the rule of law, and trafficking in persons.

USAID uses food aid both to supplement its humanitarian program and as a truly development tool. PL 480 Title II funds account for more than one-half of USAID/Haiti's funding. This food-assisted program promotes improvements in household food security, nutrition, and the welfare of women, children, and poor, marginal farmers in six out of the nine districts of Haiti—affecting the lives of 640,000 poor Haitians. Emergency response is also critical. Last year, over $3 million in emergency assistance was provided to communities affected by drought and flooding.

CIVIL UNREST AND THE USAID PROGRAM

Civil unrest reached a peak in Port-au-Prince over the past week, and although not as intense, lawlessness continues and the situation remains fluid following the resignation of Aristide. There have been violent conflicts between opposition protestors and government supporters, accompanied by widespread looting, and robberies of civilians at roadblocks throughout the capital. On February 27–29, several warehouses in Port-au-Prince were looted. Reports indicate that 800 metric tons of European Union food commodities may have been taken. The manager of the food storage facilities in Port-au-Prince where USG-funded stocks are located reported that approximately five percent of the food stocks there have been looted. One of four USAID-supported Cooperating Food Sponsors, Catholic Relief Services (CRS) reported on March 1 that looters stole 30 pickup trucks from the CRS garage. In Port-au-Prince, looters also stole medical supplies.

Increasing conflict since early February has severely restricted movement of commercial goods and relief supplies, including food, fuel and medical supplies, creating difficult conditions in some areas, and for those normally dependent on food assistance. Access and distribution remain major obstacles for both humanitarian deliveries and regular consumption. USAID and its implementing partners continue to report that the primary humanitarian concerns at present stem from limited access, security, and unsafe passage for transporting and distributing relief supplies, fuel, water, and food commodities. There appears to be no massive shortages of food or other essential commodities at this time as Haiti benefited from good harvests over the last two agricultural seasons. However, an accurate assessment is difficult at present due to lack of secure access to vulnerable areas throughout the country.

Food Availability: USAID's NGO development food aid partners and the U.N. World Food Program (WFP) currently have approximately 15,000 metric tons (MT) of food stocks in country. The European Union (EU) has 2,500 MT at a warehouse and 600 MT at the port in Port-au-Prince. There is also an additional 2,000 MT available from other donors. Thus the total amount of food assistance available from all donors is approximately 20,000 MT.

Due to poverty and chronic malnutrition in Haiti, some segments of the Haitian population are vulnerable to severe malnutrition. However, daily reports from USAID's four partners in Haiti-CARE, Save the Children Foundation (SCF), World Vision International (WVI), and CRS-indicate that none believe the situation requires re-programming of planned food assistance. Region-specific reports from food aid organizations are summarized as follows:

- WVI does not anticipate a food crisis erupting in its targeted areas of Central Plateau and Île de la Gonâve, even if distributions stop for a few months because of the strong coping mechanisms among the populations and the good December harvest. WVI is currently operating at 100 percent on Île de la Gonâve.
- CRS reported that food supplies for orphanages in Haiti are limited and some orphanages may begin to run out of food early March. CRS is considering using existing funds to purchase food on the local market for vulnerable orphanages.
- On February 22, looters broke into a WFP warehouse in Cap-Haïtien and took 800 metric tons (MT) of food stocks, mainly vegetable oil and pulses. Despite the loss of food stocks, WFP estimates that it still has sufficient stocks either in Haiti or en route to the country to provide assistance to 373,000 people.
- WFP reported that the shipment of 1,200 MT of rice scheduled to arrive at the Cap-Haïtien port is on hold until the security situation improves. According to WFP, a total of 268,000 people are in need of food in the north and northeast, where prices have increased by 20 to 30 percent since early February. However, the prices of these commodities have decreased after the February 22 looting of the WFP warehouse in Cap-Haïtien.

Fuel Availability: Fuel is vital not only for transport, but also for the continued operation of facilities and equipment such as hospitals, bakeries, and freight moving equipment at ports. Reports regarding fuel supplies in the capitol are conflicting. According to the fuel companies, there is currently enough fuel in storage in Port-au-Prince to supply the country, but the International Federation of Red Cross and Red Crescent Societies (IFRC) are concerned that fuel shortages may lead to the shutdown of the capitol's electrical plant and water treatment station. Further exacerbating the situation is the destruction of at least one fuel station in Port-au-Prince during the civil unrest. CARE reported that there is a potable water crisis in Gonaives due to a lack of fuel. Although CARE has food stocks in Port-au-Prince, the organization lacks fuel for transportation, particularly for food distributions in the north.

Medical Supplies: A major humanitarian concern at present is the interruption of basic health services, particularly in the north. The ability to purchase and transport drugs and fuel to health facilities nationwide has been disrupted in major population centers due to the sporadic access to banks and insecure travel on the roads. The ICRC has been organizing regular convoys to both Gonaives and Cap-Haitien in cooperation with the Haitian Red Cross, and ICRC medical teams have also been stationed at facilities in these cities.

It is not clear at this time how many medical facilities have been affected by the recent unrest. Reports from the Hospital Communaute Haitienne in the capitol indicate that there is an increase in the number of trauma patients at the hospital and care is hindered by fuel shortages for generator power and lack of surgical and medical kits. Negotiations for a planned expansion of ICRC operations in the Canape Vert Hospital in Port-au-Prince ended without agreement and ICRC has reported that there are no doctors remaining at Canape Vert following the withdrawal of ICRC staff. Similar disruptions of supplies are occurring in Gonaives and other areas.

Currently there are no reports of an outbreak of the six major childhood vaccine-preventable diseases. However, increased cases of diarrhea and fever have been reported in the town of Gonaives due to a lack of potable water. The Expanded Program on Immunization (EPI) has sentinel sites in Haiti, of which 30 percent to 40 percent are still functional and operating.

A Pan American Health Organization (PAHO) epidemiologist recently arrived in Haiti to reactivate the health surveillance system, as Haiti lacks adequate surveillance data from health facilities throughout the country. PAHO will monitor data on measles outbreaks, polio, diphtheria, typhoid, and violence, as well as acute malnutrition. According to PAHO, there is a shortage of tuberculosis (TB) drugs and a disruption of TB programs in the north. Médicins Sans Frontières-Belgium is requesting TB drugs from PAHO.

Displaced Populations: USAID and its NGO partners continue to report very limited displacement and no “sites” with concentrations of internally displaced persons (IDPs). According to the U.N. Office for the Coordination of Humanitarian Affairs (UNOCHA), numbers of IDPs cannot be accurately assessed at present. However, UNOCHA notes that significant numbers of residents are moving from insecure cities to other areas or returning to their places of birth in the mountains. Movements have also been reported from rural areas to main cities. According to a well-known and trusted source, he has never been aware of the existence of IDPs in Haiti.

On February 23, the Government of the Dominican Republic (GODR) indicated that the Dominican Republic does not have structures in place to manage a migratory wave of refugees. The GODR also noted that Dominican authorities have reinforced the border with Haiti along critical points. On February 24, the GODR sent 1,200 additional troops to patrol its border with Haiti. The GODR has declined to state the total number of troops along the 225-mile border. According to the U.N. High Commissioner for Refugees, approximately 400 Haitians have fled to the DR, Jamaica, and Cuba since early February 2004.

U.S. GOVERNMENT HUMANITARIAN RESPONSE TO HAITI’S POLITICAL CRISIS

- On February 18, U.S. Ambassador to Haiti James B. Foley issued a disaster declaration due to the ongoing complex emergency in Haiti. As an initial response to the situation, OFDA has provided $50,000 through USAID/Haiti to support the transport and distribution of emergency relief supplies, including 12 medical kits and three surgical kits, valued at approximately $87,000. Each medical kit is equipped to serve 10,000 people for approximately three months. On February 26, the medical kits arrived in Port-au-Prince. In addition, OFDA approved $400,000 in funding for PAHO to purchase additional medical supplies and to conduct emergency relief activities in Haiti.
- On February 24, OFDA deployed a three-person team to Port-au-Prince, including a Senior Regional Advisor as Team Leader, a Health Officer, and an Information Officer.
- OFDA has contracted with Airserve for two to three aircrafts to move relief personnel and light cargo around Haiti if required in the coming days and weeks.
- USAID/Food For Peace has significant amounts of additional food stocks which can be transported to Haiti by sea for food assistance within 7–14 days if needed
- OFDA is currently awarding grants in the amount of $400,000 to CRS for local procurement and emergency cash grants to institutions serving vulnerable populations such as orphanages and hospitals.
- The U.S. Embassy in Port-au-Prince is currently developing a security asset plan that will address protection of people and USG buildings, transport of goods and people, and security of NGO partners, such as CRS, WVI, CARE, and Save the Children. A top priority of the security asset plan is to secure and protect the airport and port in the capital.
- There are approximately 15,000 MT of USG-procured food commodities immediately available for distribution in Haiti. USAID will continue to work with other members of the donor community to mobilize the additional resources required for the Haiti post-conflict effort.

CONCLUSION

USAID is closely monitoring the humanitarian impact of the current political crisis in Haiti. With the presence of international forces in Haiti, we expect the security situation to improve significantly. This will facilitate the delivery of humanitarian assistance. USAID/Haiti and OFDA personnel will continue to assess the unfolding humanitarian situation, and develop appropriate responses for the Haitian post-conflict period. USAID is working closely with other agencies and implementing partners to develop a post-conflict program strategy that will ensure the continued provision of emergency relief and improved basic services, and generate productive employment over the immediate, short- and medium-term. In addition, USAID is working with other donors to jointly identify long-term priorities in Haiti.

Mr. BALLENGER. I yield myself 5 minutes, and yield my time to the gentleman from Indiana Mr. Burton, who has to leave early.

Mr. BURTON. Well, I want to thank the Chairman for yielding to me. I was the Chairman of the Subcommittee on Western Hemisphere in 1995 and 1996, and I had a chance to go to Haiti on a couple of occasions. I think Mr. Noriega was with the Foreign Affairs Committee at that time. I would like to just go through a few points that we found that we thought was very important.

First of all, regarding the murders and the horrible atrocities that were taking place down there, in 1995, one of the leading opponents of Mr. Aristide was Mariel Burtan. She was surrounded and shot to death at Port-au-Prince right on the main street in broad daylight, and we questioned the FBI—Mr. Dobbins was before the Committee—about whether or not Aristide was involved, and Mr. Dobbins lied to the Committee. And we subsequently followed up, and we found out that there was no question that Mr. Aristide had to know and be involved in the murder of Ms. Burtan.

In about that time period, when Mr. Aristide was coming back into power, we had clips of Mr. Aristide giving speeches, and they were translated, and in his speeches he was talking about the value of putting a tire around people's necks that didn't agree with him, filling them with gasoline, and burning them to death.

There is a real democrat kind of fellow for you—democratic person.

In 1994 Mr. Aristide, according to a drug cartel informant, received a sackful of money in order to let the drug cartel move drugs through Haiti. And the State Department has reported that high officials all the way up to the top of the government are involved in drug trafficking. According to the State Department's *2003 International Narcotics Control Strategy Report*, it is a major transshipment point for narcotics.

On February 25, 2004, one of Haiti's most flamboyant drug traffickers told a Miami Federal Court under oath that he couldn't thrive in Haiti without paying millions of bribes to his close friend, the President, Mr. Aristide. So he was involved in drug trafficking according to testimony in Federal Court.

On February 26 of 2004, Barry McCaffrey, as has been stated earlier, who was the drug czar under President Clinton, said it was hard to imagine that Aristide himself wasn't taking part in drug trafficking.

The human rights records I think are legion. After the election—I want to talk about the election that took place. Everybody talks about it being so democratic. The Lavalas Party conducted the counting of the ballots. They said Aristide received 91 percent of the vote and there was a turnout of 61½ percent. But according to reports from others who were there from the international community, the turnout was about 10 percent, and it was flagrant voter fraud.

In fact on November 29, 2000, after Aristide was reelected, U.N. Secretary Kofi Annan recommended that the U.N. Close its mission to help build democracy in Haiti, saying U.N. Efforts were useless, considering the government's questionable legitimacy and increasing isolation.

Now, regarding human rights—and this is something that really bothers me. In the government—in our government's June 1, 2003 *Trafficking in Persons Report*, the Haitian Government does not fully comply with the minimum standards for the elimination of human trafficking and is not making significant efforts to do so. And the reports said Haiti is a source country for trafficking of children for forced labor and sexual exploitation. And between 90 and 300,000 poor rural children age 4 to 14 serve as unpaid domestic laborers in slave-like conditions.

This is the kind of government that was going on under Aristide in Haiti. He was a brutal dictator who had no problem of putting tires around people's necks and burning them to death.

The gentleman who is going to testify later was beaten and had his legs broken down there. They were allowing children to go into slave labor. He was a major source point for drug trafficking and was taking money from drug traffickers in the millions of dollars, and this is the kind of person we were supposed to go in there and defend and protect?

If we hadn't gone in there, and if Aristide had stayed, I believe he would be dead today because I think the people there would have killed him. I think the rebels would have taken the capital and he would have been killed. So, Mr. Aristide is alive today because he chose to leave when he did. As far as this kidnapping charge is concerned, anybody that knows, knows that America does not work that way

Mr. BALLENGER. Mr. Menendez.

Mr. MENENDEZ. Thank you Mr. Chairman.

Let me first, Mr. Noriega, tell you that I don't appreciate your insolent mischaracterization of my remarks. Either you did not listen to them, or you in fact purposely mischaracterized them. Either way I resent it, and I don't intend to take it.

I have a series of questions and I would like the first two to give me a yes or no answer. Did the Government of the United States formally recognize President Aristide as the duly elected President of Haiti, yes or no?

Mr. NORIEGA. I don't think it is that simple. We treated him as a constitutional President.

[Chairman Ballenger asked that Assistant Secretary Noriega provide an expanded response to the question posed by Congressman Menendez. Mr. Noriega's response follows:]

I don't think it is that simple. We regarded Aristide as a constitutional President. Aristide was elected, but he did not govern democratically and the presidential election of November 2000 did not truly reflect the will of the Haitian people. Opposition parties did not participate in that election, nor was it observed or supported by the international community, which estimated voter turnout at 5–15 percent. This happened because Aristide and his ruling party refused to reconsider the results of the legislative elections in May 2000, after international observers uncovered fraudulent vote tabulation.

Mr. MENENDEZ. Did our Ambassador present credentials to President Aristide?

Mr. NORIEGA. Yes.

Mr. MENENDEZ. Did the United States seek to invoke the Democratic charter that you talked about at the OAS as it related to Haiti?

Mr. NORIEGA. We didn't and neither did the Republic of Haiti. Aristide did not use the self-help mechanism——

[Chairman Ballenger asked that Assistant Secretary Noriega provide an expanded response to the question posed by Congressman Menendez. Mr. Noriega's response follows:]

We didn't, and neither did the Republic of Haiti. Aristide did not use the self-help mechanisms that were available to his country under the Charter. This was Haiti's decision to make, not that of the United States or other OAS member states. Haiti did consent to OAS action in Haiti, such as the establishment of the OAS Special Mission in Resolution 806, but only after the Permanent Council called upon it to do so.

Mr. MENENDEZ. I asked you for a yes or no, and it is no.

Mr. NORIEGA. Sometimes these issues are a little more complicated.

Mr. MENENDEZ. I fully understand that, but there are some questions that can be answered yes or no so you don't eat up all of my time. The reality is the United States, the Democratic charter that you referred to inferentially in your statement to try to paint the brush, the United States did not pursue that Democratic charter at the OAS as it related to Haiti.

Mr. NORIEGA. None of the 34 countries——

[Chairman Ballenger asked that Assistant Secretary Noriega provide an expanded response to the question posed by Congressman Menendez. Mr. Noriega's response follows:]

None of the 34 member countries of the OAS did. Aristide's government could have invoked the Charter directly in any number of ways to restore democracy, but it chose not to do so. The Aristide government did co-operate with OAS initiatives, such as creation of the OAS Special Mission to Strengthen Democracy in Haiti, but only after the OAS Permanent Council asked it to do so. One last comment - the implication that the United States did not support efforts to settle Haiti's political crisis democratically and peacefully is entirely false. The Administration fully supported OAS efforts, both financially and diplomatically, while at the same time pursuing vigorous diplomacy directly with Aristide and the opposition to achieve a political settlement.

Mr. MENENDEZ. I didn't ask you about the 34 countries, I asked you about the United States, Mr. Secretary. And if you want to play games with us here——

Mr. NORIEGA. No, sir, I am telling you that none of them did.

Mr. MENENDEZ. Let me ask you this. On February 13, Secretary Powell said "the Administration was not seeking Mr. Aristide's resignation." On February 17, Secretary Powell went even further and said, "we cannot buy into a proposition that says the elected President must be forced out of office by thugs."

And yet that is exactly what the Administration did when, on February 26, 9 days later, Secretary Powell suggested Mr. Aristide "examine the situation that he is in and make a careful consideration of how best to serve the Haitian people at this time and subsequently suggest that he leave." So all of those statements, including your own, Mr. Noriega, on October 21 of this past year, before this very Subcommittee where you said "as it relates to Haiti, violence has no place in settling political dispute in a democracy."

Well, if violence has no place in such a set of circumstances, if I tell the thugs that are at the presidential gate that we won't go in until there is a political solution, and the inherent fact in that statement is that you can go ahead and pursue violent overthrow because I am not going to send anybody in until you have a political solution, that ultimately encourages that type of action. And it is that type of action, whether it exists in Haiti or whether it exists in other countries in this hemisphere, that I was referring to.

So how is it that this Administration says that violence has no place in settling political disputes, that we cannot buy into a proposition that says an elected President will be forced out of office by thugs; that we, in fact are not seeking that resignation especially under those set of circumstances, and then we allow those who would by violent effort overthrow a government?

Mr. NORIEGA. Thank you very much, Mr. Chairman and Congressman Menendez.

And if I can give you more than a yes or no to that question, it is extraordinarily important to bear in mind that we do not have an obligation to put American lives at risk to save every government that may ask us for help, whether it is democratically-elected or not. We do not have an obligation to do that. We have to make decisions about where we will put American lives at risk.

In the case of Haiti, I think it was a difficult decision, but we made the right one. The erratic, irresponsible behavior of President Aristide in the last 48 hours demonstrated that he was not a reliable person or reliable interlocutor. That does not mean by any means that we support the violent overthrow of that man. However, it did mean that he was not a sustainable political solution.

Mr. MENENDEZ. In the 20 seconds that I have left, I will simply say that we made a very clear message. Yes, we don't have to send troops each and every time, but we sent a very clear message: You can go ahead and pursue your violent activity because, unless there is a political solution, we don't seek to intervene either ourselves or through any international effort.

And that is a risk for democracy in this hemisphere.

Mr. BALLENGER. Congressman Weller.

Mr. WELLER. Thank you, Mr. Chairman, and Mr. Secretary and Mr. Secretary and Mr. Administrator, and I thank all of you for participating today.

And we have heard some terms such as thugs, killers, and narcotraffickers being used in comments before this Committee today, but they also describe the government of President Aristide. And I would note that over the last several years, the Bush Administration has bent over backwards, time after time, to help the people of Haiti; in particular, where President Bush waived other considerations to continue providing aid and assistance to Haiti.

And let me give you an example of where that is. There is probably no greater threat to democracy than the corruption that comes from narcotrafficking as well as the threat to our own Nation's security. According to the State Department in March 2004, serious allegations persisted that high-level government and police officials were involved in drug trafficking. And in 2001, 2002, and 2003, the Bush Administration said Haiti was not certified as having fully cooperated, or had failed demonstrably to comply with the United States drug control efforts.

All 3 years, President Bush determined however that it was in the national interest in the United States to continue providing aid to Haiti despite its lack of effort and counternarcotics, but also expressed concern regarding the human rights record of the Aristide administration and, it appears, which human rights were of no concern to President Aristide. In fact, it appears that President Aristide instigated violence against his political opponents.

In June 2001, Mr. Aristide announced a zero tolerance policy on crime which many Haitians interpreted as an imitation vigilante justice. That December, the pro-Aristide organization called Sleep in the Woods, took matter into its own hands and hacked to death radio journalist Brignol Lindnor in the town of Petit Goave. Lindnor had done radio broadcasts critical of Mr. Aristide.

Little more than a month ago, Mr. Aristide pardoned 42 violent criminals, commuting the sentences of 66 others, provided amnesty to an additional 90 accused whose cases were still under investigation. So it is wondering whose side some of the thugs were on.

We talk about the election, Mr. Secretary, and of course, you know, it appears in many cases that the elections of Mr. Aristide were very, very tainted. It is often cited, his reelection in November 2000 is proof that he was a freely elected democratic leader. However, international observers, not just American observers, refused to observe this election. The head of the Provisional Electoral Council Leon Manus fled Haiti because he was threatened by Aristide for failing to endorse fraudulent election results. And after Manus fled, the ruling Lavalas Party installed a one-party electoral council and held the November 2000 presidential elections. The Clinton Administration even refused to provide support of any kind for that election process.

Public disenchantment with the sham election process was expressed by a voter turnout estimated less than 10 percent of eligible voters by foreign diplomats and journalists. The question is: Can this really be termed a free and fair election?

One of our senior United States diplomats who was in Haiti during the November 2000 presidential election stated that there was more enthusiasm and participation in the elections that gave Charles Taylor the presidency of Liberia, and who the United States Government told last year to step down when civil war reached Monrovia. And did anyone seriously advocate sending U.S. troops to prop up Charles Taylor's regime? That is an ironic question here, because some of those who called for the removal of Charles Taylor are those who say that we should have sent troops in to keep President Aristide in. And when you had greater election participation in Liberia for Charles Taylor than you did in Haiti, you wonder about the legitimacy of the Haitian elections.

So the question is: Why is Charles Taylor out, good; versus Aristide out, bad? What is the difference when Liberia had a greater level of participation in the election?

I guess, Mr. Secretary, the question I have for you is did we treat Charles Taylor in Liberia any differently than we treated Aristide, or have we treated Aristide any differently than we did Charles Taylor and Liberia in similar circumstances?

Mr. NORIEGA. Thank you very much, Congressman. The decisions we made regarding President Aristide for the last several years have been tied to support for a diplomatic negotiated solution to get Haiti back on a democratic course. I explained during my testimony that we did not achieve that objective, but we tried.

We didn't achieve that objective because of the lack of political will by President Aristide, in part. The fact that other political actors in Haiti didn't want to participate and didn't have confidence in President Aristide's ability to keep his promises was also another problem. But for example, when we asked for steps to improve the security climate, we asked that a new police chief be appointed. He was appointed and within a couple of days, showed up in the U.S. Embassy seeking political asylum.

Mr. BALLENGER. I hate to cut you off. It is our mistake up here. Generally speaking, we don't cut our witness' time off, but my big mouth got us in trouble. So I apologize for the difficulty. If you need a second, 10, 15 seconds, go ahead, without objection.

Mr. NORIEGA. In the last few weeks we saw the Haitian National Police without arms, but had reports that the government was distributing arms to its gangs. We saw most of the looting and violence against persons and property in Haiti and Port-au-Prince committed by those gangs of President Aristide. We saw these gangs attack their own Coast Guard installation, which was clearly intended to prevent the United States from being able to return migrants, so it would provoke perhaps a migrant crisis.

We saw that President Aristide in those final days was not a reliable person and he would not be part of a sustainable political solution. We were prepared to send some forces in to support a sustainable process that kept Aristide in power, but we were not prepared to put American lives on the line merely to do that.

MR. BALLENGER. Thank you. Mr. Delahunt.

Mr. DELAHUNT. Thank you, Mr. Chairman.

Why didn't you use your influence with the opposition, Mr. Noriega, to get them to agree to the various accommodations that Aristide made? Be really brief about it; I don't want a long answer now.

Mr. NORIEGA. We made a strong effort to do that. We spent 4 hours a couple of Saturdays ago trying to convince them to do that.

Mr. DELAHUNT. But it didn't work.

Are you currently supporting the government, as it exists now, of Prime Minister Neptune.

Mr. NORIEGA. Yes, sir. Prime Minister Neptune is the head of the government until a new government is formed.

Mr. DELAHUNT. And what plans do you have for the formation of a new government?

Mr. NORIEGA. There is a Tripartite Commission which will include a representative of the Lavalas Party, a representative of the international community, and a representative of the Democratic Platform.

Mr. DELAHUNT. That is the only answer. It is sufficient for me.

Mr. NORIEGA. It is not the answer, sir.

[Chairman Ballenger asked that Assistant Secretary Noriega provide an expanded response to the question posed by Congressman Delahunt. Mr. Noriega's response follows:]

It is not the answer, sir. That is, it is not the only answer. The new government is being formed in accordance with the CARICOM plan. Under that plan, the Tripartite Commission appoints a seven-member Council of Eminent Persons. That Council nominates a new Prime Minister, and Interim President Alexandre appoints the Prime Minister, who then chooses a cabinet. We are giving our full support to this transition process. A permanent government will be formed after elections are held.

Mr. DELAHUNT. It is sufficient for me, Mr. Noriega. I am asking the question, so I would ask you to desist.

What are our plans as far as Toto Constant is concerned? Are we going to allow him to stay in this country?

Mr. NORIEGA. Mr. Chairman and Congressman, I don't know much about his situation. I will tell you that I asked several weeks ago, when this recent violence happened, that U.S. law enforcement be notified because we didn't want this individual to show up in Haiti.

Mr. DELAHUNT. The answer is you don't know much about it.

Mr. NORIEGA. I don't know particularly.

Mr. DELAHUNT. Your information would be the same as mine, that the former head of the FRAPH, who is responsible for thousands of deaths during the period from 1991 to 1994, is currently here in New York City and is free? Is that your information?

Mr. NORIEGA. I think he came here about 6 years ago.

[Chairman Ballenger asked that Assistant Secretary Noriega provide an expanded response to the question posed by Congressman Delahunt. Mr. Noriega's response follows:]

I think he came here about 10 years ago. In 1995, the Department of State revoked his visa and an Immigration judge issued a deportation order. In late 1995, Constant sued the U.S. Government seeking damages. In 1996, that suit was settled. In 1997, an assessment was done evaluating the threat to Constant if he were returned to Haiti. Based on that assessment, reviewed by various U.S. Government agencies, Constant was not returned to Haiti. In 1998, Constant tried to reopen his asylum case, but an Immigration judge denied the motion. Constant appealed, and the Board of Immigration appeals upheld the denial in September 2003. At the moment, I do not believe there are any pending appeals or other legal impediments to Constant's removal. The Departments of State and Homeland Security are evaluating whether Constant can be deported now, in light of current country conditions.

Mr. DELAHUNT. I want to point out because you make references to international support and maybe this is a statement that has been rescinded, but CARICOM, through the Prime Minister of Jamaica, recently issued this statement:

President Aristide has submitted his resignation as the President of Haiti and left the country for an undisclosed destination. We are bound to question whether his resignation was truly voluntary, as it comes after the capture of sections of Haiti by armed insurgents and the failure of the international community to provide the requisite support despite the appeals of CARICOM. The removal of President Aristide in these circumstances sets a dangerous precedent for democratically-elected governments anywhere and everywhere, as it promotes the removal of duly elected persons from office by the power of rebel forces.

It was a statement that has been issued by CARICOM. Is that accurate?

Mr. NORIEGA. That was a statement they issued a few days ago, and they are meeting today and we hope we can encourage them to be part of the solution.

Mr. DELAHUNT. In terms of the fraudulent elections that we talked about, and you alluded to the OAS report. Let me read the report as I have it before me. And I happened to be a volunteer, an election observer, and unfortunately there was no one other than some Members on the Democratic side of this Committee and staffers and no one from our colleagues on the other side. So I was there, Mr. Noriega.

> "Election day proceedings on May 21 represented the high point of the electoral process. An estimated 60 percent of registered voters went to the polls. Very few incidents of violence were reported. Haitian National Police responded efficiently and professionally to situations that could have deteriorated into violence. While voters had to wait in long lines, especially at the beginning of the day, they were eventually able to cast their ballots free of pressure and intimidation. Most voters were able to find their polling with relative ease."

This is really about the tabulation. Let us really understand what the fraudulent elections are all about so the American people understand them. The elections themselves were relatively well done, given the situation in Haiti at the time. It was about whether a certain runoff of 7 Senate seats would occur. Is that a fair statement?

Mr. NORIEGA. Yes, it is an accurate statement.

Mr. DELAHUNT. Thank you. You indicate in your written testimony:

> "Under the circumstances, Aristide agreed to what he had steadfastly rejected before, a plan that would open the door to consensus government."

You are referring to the CARICOM plan.

Was I under a misunderstanding that Secretary Powell endorsed a plan put forth by the Catholic Bishops of Haiti that Aristide agreed to?

Mr. NORIEGA. We were promoting—

[Chairman Ballenger asked that Assistant Secretary Noriega provide an expanded response to the question posed by Congressman Delahunt. Mr. Noriega's response follows:]

We were promoting the CARICOM plan. The Secretary endorsed CARICOM's plan on February 13, after his meeting with CARICOM foreign ministers, Canadian Foreign Minister Bill Graham, and OAS Secretary General Cesar Gaviria. There were two Bishops plans—one was withdrawn in November 2003 and the other was never presented because the CARICOM plan evolved at the same time. To the best of my knowledge, the Secretary did not endorse any plan put forward by the Bishops, although he and other Administration officials were urging the parties to settle their political differences throughout this period of time. Aristide agreed to the CARICOM plan.

Mr. DELAHUNT. Answer my question. Did Aristide agree and the opposition reject the plan that was put forward by the Catholic Bishops of Haiti where he would share power?

Mr. NORIEGA. Yes, that is correct.

Mr. BALLENGER. Ms. Ros-Lehtinen.

Ms. ROS-LEHTINEN. Thank you very much and thank you, gentlemen. I wanted to ask questions related to refugees and migration as well as to the level of U.S. and international aid.

When I first got elected to Congress, I had the high honor of representing the area in Miami known as little Haiti, and I was able to establish great communication with the leaders and the common folk in that community and have found them to be hardworking, law-abiding, a wonderful addition to the fabric that makes up our south Florida communities. And it breaks my heart to see our—the U.S. policy being one that repatriates individuals to a very difficult condition in their homeland, and that is why some of us have been advocating for TPS status for Haitian nationals living in the United States, Temporary Protected Status, so they are not set back to a country that by all accounts, wherever—whether you are pro-Aristide or anti-Aristide, all of us can agree it is a tumultuous situation of civil strife, no respect for the rule of law. We don't know when true democratic elections will take place. We are not sure who the leader is, although we have a constitutional leader there and it breaks our hearts to see continued divisions of families.

I wanted to ask you about if there would be any change in the United States policy toward either repatriation and/or conferring TPS status to Haitian nationals who are otherwise very law-abiding, wonderful citizens of our community.

And my second question has to do with the level of U.S. and international aid. How much military aid do you see forthcoming in the coming weeks, in the coming months; how much humanitarian aid; what will be the level of the international aid with CARICOM or the U.N.; how will it be supervised; who will be there to make sure the distribution is done in the correct way and will not be stolen by whoever happens to consider himself or herself the chief of the town?

So I am concerned about the free flow supervision of humanitarian aid so that it does get to the people themselves.

Mr. NORIEGA. Mr. Chairman, if I may, I will answer the first part on the security component and the current security mission, and I will ask Mr. Dewey and Mr. Franco to address the specific points you raised.

The security presence that we have on the ground is primarily United States and French forces. The Chileans are arriving very soon, and other countries will be joining. This is part of the initial phase of the Multinational Interim Force to establish a certain amount of order so we can have a constitutional succession and begin to reestablish the institutions of government, starting with the Haitian National Police and the formulation of a civilian government.

The initial troop presence will be on the order of 3,000 or more soldiers in the follow-on mission under another U.N. Mandate and a more traditional peacekeeping-type operation which contemplates the presence of several thousand.

We have had a good number of countries in the Hemisphere indicating their willingness to participate in that follow-on mission, and it will carry out its work as U.N. Missions generally do for these peacekeeping missions. I will ask Mr. Dewey to address the migration issue.

Mr. DEWEY. We understand your concern on that issue and it is fortunate also we are concerned in watching that issue of Temporary Protected Status very closely. The Secretary of the Department of Homeland Security makes the determination on Temporary Protected Status in consultation with the State Department.

We are also checking people that we feel can give us good advice and input in terms of our advising DHS. We talked to the Office of the High Commissioners for Refugees, for example. And there is concurrence now at this point that it is not time to recommend that status, and the reason is because the situation is just too fluid. It varies day by day and I think you can appreciate that. But we are not relenting our vigilance in watching it.

Mr. BALLENGER. Mr. Payne.

Mr. PAYNE. Thank you very much.

Once again for Mr. Weller, I want to make a couple things clear, and he seems to be an expert on Liberia. We did not call for the removal of Charles Taylor, for your information.

Secondly, when you compare President Aristide to Charles Taylor, for your information, there was a special court in Sierra Leone that was sponsored by the United Nations that indicted Charles Taylor. So I want you to get some of your information correct.

Let me just say—let me ask you, Mr. Noriega, as you know, the CIA paid and protected the FRAPH-squad people in the old days. And I would like to know what you know about Guy Philippe. Mr. Philippe was trained by the United States military in Ecuador. Do you know anything about that?

Mr. NORIEGA. No.

[Chairman Ballenger asked that Assistant Secretary Noriega provide an expanded response to the question posed by Congressman Payne. Mr. Noriega's response follows:]

No. The U.S. has never trained Philippe in Ecuador, or any other country.

Mr. PAYNE. Let me say, do you have any knowledge of why—the DR, the Dominican Republic, they haven't been having any outside problems with foreign countries in quite awhile, right?

Mr. NORIEGA. No, sir.

Mr. PAYNE. They weren't invaded by Iraq, right?

Mr. NORIEGA. Right.

Mr. PAYNE. Let me ask you another question. Why would, then, the U.S. ship 35,000 weapons, 20,000 guns that were sold to the DR recently? Do you have any idea why there would be so much weaponry—and I am asking the question because, as you know, the rebels have a lot of U.S.-made weapons. I think they have a lot of M–16s, M–60s. They have rocket-propelled launchers. And we know that 20,000 weapons were sent by the U.S. to the DR. I don't know the date. But you don't know anything about it. You honestly don't know anything about—you are in charge of Latin America and you don't know about these 35,000.

Mr. NORIEGA. No.

[Chairman Ballenger asked that Assistant Secretary Noriega provide an expanded response to the question posed by Congressman Payne. Mr. Noriega's response follows:]

No. Your information is inaccurate. The U.S. has agreed to sell reconditioned M–16s to the Dominican Republic, but has not delivered any of them. The last U.S. Government arms sale to the Dominican Republic took place in 1991, when we sold side arms to the Dominican military.

Mr. PAYNE. And never heard of any training in Ecuador, Mr. Noriega?

Mr. NORIEGA. I heard the accusation and I heard the reference, and I don't know that it is true.

[Chairman Ballenger asked that Assistant Secretary Noriega provide an expanded response to the question posed by Congressman Payne. Mr. Noriega's response follows:]

I heard the accusation and I heard the reference, and I don't know if it is true. I believe Philippe attended the Ecuadoran Army Academy for about one year in the 1990s as part of a bilateral exchange program between Haiti and Ecuador. As I understand it, the United States was not involved in any way in that exchange program, and did not at any time provide support or training for Philippe.

Mr. PAYNE. Let me ask you, when you worked as the chief aide to Jesse Helms, at that time there were allegations that President Aristide was mentally unbalanced. Do you remember your report on that?

Mr. NORIEGA. I was working here for Ben Gilman at the time.

Mr. PAYNE. Did you work for Jesse Helms?

Mr. NORIEGA. I sure did. I am proud to have worked for Jesse Helms for 4 years.

Mr. PAYNE. And you weren't proud to work for Ben Gilman? I know Ben Gilman. Let me——

Mr. NORIEGA. Let the record show, I love Ben Gilman.

Mr. PAYNE. Well, I am just saying that you said you were proud to work for Ben Gilman but evidently not so proud—I mean of Jesse Helms, not so proud of Ben Gilman.

Will the Haitian military be reactivated?

Mr. NORIEGA. That is a decision that will have to be dealt with by the next elected government of Haiti.

Mr. PAYNE. And under their Constitution, I thought that the Chief Justice of the Supreme Court took over the government.

Mr. NORIEGA. He is the new President now. He is the Head of State.

Mr. PAYNE. He will be the Head of State until the next elections?

Mr. NORIEGA. Until there is a new election.

Mr. PAYNE. The question about the fact that Mr. Aristide—as you may recall, we asked for intervention into sending the troops into Haiti, the same way for Mr. Weller's information. We asked for United States troops to also be sent to Liberia; same thing as we did for Haiti. We didn't do either one. We sent them after the Nigerians went in Liberia, but did not send anything in until Mr. Aristide left.

But could you explain the resignation as well as you know it?

Mr. NORIEGA. President Aristide resigned. I don't know if I have a copy of the letter here or—one of my people probably does have a copy of the letter. All I have is a translation of it. I have seen the actual letter. He submitted his resignation on the evening of the 29th, I believe.

[Chairman Ballenger asked that Assistant Secretary Noriega provide an expanded response to the question posed by Congressman Payne. Mr. Noriega's response follows:]

President Aristide resigned. I don't know if I have a copy of the letter here or—one of my people probably does have a copy of the letter. All I have is a translation of it. I have seen the actual letter. He submitted his resignation on the evening of the 29th, I believe. The resignation letter itself is revealing. Aristide wrote that if his resignation could prevent a bloodbath, then he agreed to leave in the hope that there would be life and not death. Aristide knew full well that if he tried to remain as president, many people would die in the impending clash between his armed partisans and the advancing insurgents. At no time did the U.S. force this conclusion on Aristide or even suggest it. The evening before Aristide left, he passed a message to Ambassador Foley through his private security guards, asking what the U.S. thought would be in the best interest of the Haitian people—staying or resigning. After consulting with Secretary Powell, the Ambassador replied to Aristide: You have to decide what is best for Haiti. Hours after this, Aristide told the Embassy that he was ready to go that night. The U.S. helped Aristide get to the airport and arranged air transportation out of the country for him, his wife, and his private security detail.

Mr. PAYNE. Thank you, Mr. Chairman.

Mr. BALLENGER. Mr. Foley.

Mr. FOLEY. Let me first extend to Mr. Noriega my personal appreciation for going down to Haiti and attempting to negotiate a settlement to the crisis. You went in the middle of turmoil. You did so at some risk and peril to your own life, and I want to applaud you on behalf of Congress, or at least this Member of Congress, for endeavoring to seek a peaceful settlement to the crisis. Congressman Wexler and I have neighboring districts and we have a newspaper, *The Palm Beach Post*, the most liberal probably of any newspaper in Florida. They have never printed a kind word about President Bush or his brother, Governor Bush.

Let me read you today's editorial:

> "A Delusional Aristide. Jean-Bertrand Aristide can accuse the United States of many things, but depriving him of an opportunity to bring democracy to Haiti isn't one of them. The United States, in conjunction with France and the Organization of American States, helped Mr. Aristide to leave the country. Though his destination wasn't clear when the plane took off, the action protected Mr. Aristide and his family. It might have prevented a blood bath.
>
> "His departure decreased the chance that armed criminals masquerading as rebels will take control and increased the chance that an international effort can move Haiti toward democratic elections."

Now, that is by an observer, *The Palm Beach Post*.

I hear a lot of things about a gentleman being kidnapped, spirited away in the middle of the night, and we will have plenty of time to ferret those issues out. But there is one thing for certain: Haiti needs our help. And this Administration has stepped up to the plate.

Now I can read testimony, Randall Robinson and I were on CNN the other day and he is making wild accusations about this kidnapping. Mr. Robinson's wife was paid some $300,000 by the Haiti Government to represent them in matters of public relations. This is what he said about President Clinton:

> "Civil rights lobbyist Randall Robinson said he opposed President Clinton because he had exhausted all patience with President Clinton's failed, insensitive, and ultimately racist policy in Haiti."

And it goes on about the President's flip-flop on Haiti, indifference, sending in troops; no, maybe I won't.

So we can continue to have this political dialogue and see who we can blame. I personally take the word of Secretary Colin Powell over this man. He has had ample opportunity to help his people with aid from this country and others. France, Canada, would not invest one nickle or one body to save this man's failed presidency.

The State Department's *International Narcotics Control Strategy Report of 2003, 2002*, and *2001* established that senior officials throughout the Haitian Government, including the Haitian National Police, presidential security unit, and Aristide's palace guards, were actively involved in drug trafficking. These reports established that light aircraft, landing with drug cargoes on Route 9 in Port-au-Prince, are actively helped by Haitian National Police who block traffic and help with offloading the drugs and providing ground transportation.

Let me read you another thing that is very important and I would like you to comment on:

> The 2003 State Department *Human Rights Report* for Haiti confirms that there were credible reports of extrajudicial killings by members of the Haitian National Police, municipal national government officials, and civilian attaches associated with the Haitian National Police. In 1994, the United States used military force to restore Aristide to office. One of the compelling reasons for using force to restore Aristide to office was that the military regime was using civilian attaches to terrorize the population, particularly Aristide supporters. Aristide, it turns out, has been using civilian attaches to terrorize the population, particularly his political opponents.

What does this use of attaches say about the Aristide's government's commitment to the rule of law?

Mr. NORIEGA. Thank you very much, Congressman Foley, and I will pass on to our staff the statements of gratitude for the work they are doing to help Haiti. The report and the references to the human rights violations are written by professionals at the State Department, and they make a compelling point, which is, we do not choose who runs various countries. We don't choose who we recognize as constitutionally-elected leaders, but we do have an obligation to choose where we put American lives at risk. And in this case, we made the decision based on what we know about President Aristide after years of trying, that it was not an effective, sustainable, political solution to merely prop him up.

Mr. BALLENGER. Now for the other Members, we are going to call on you. Since it is all going to be Democrats, we are going to call on Members of the Committee by seniority and then finish up with whoever is left. And you have my condolences, Charlie, as you may be last.

Mr. BROWN. Thank you, Mr. Chairman. And, Mr. Noriega, for joining us.

This hearing has been intriguing, to say the least, with some of the charges thrown around. And it just seems—I have been involved in working on issues regarding Haiti for 3 or 4 years and have just been amazed at how the Bush Administration has simply set Aristide up for failure. The $154 million that Ms. Lee and many in the Congressional Black Caucus, Mr. Wexler and others have tried to spring loose the $154 million the Administration blocked for water, for sewer, for health, for roads, for sanitation, for all the things that would have made this regime a lot more successful simply wasn't available.

It is hard to look at this situation and think that the Bush Administration really wanted the experiment of democracy in Haiti to succeed.

But let me move to a question about the Constitution. I have heard Mr. Noriega refer to the Constitution many times. President Bush, I would like to quote, said on Sunday:

> "The Constitution of Haiti is working. There is an interim President, as per the Constitution, in place."

The White House described Aristide's exile as "peaceful, democratic, and constitutional." I don't think the President and, unfortunately, the President or his Administration frankly took the time to read the Constitution of Haiti, or they simply chose to ignore it. I would like to read article 149 of the 1987 Constitution of Haiti:

> "Should the Office of the President of the Republic become vacant for any reason, the President of the Supreme Court of the Republic or, in his absence, the Vice President of that Court or, in his absence, the judge with the highest seniority,"

and so on by order of seniority,

> "Shall be invested temporarily with the duties of the President of the republic by the National Assembly, duly convened by the Prime Minister. The election of a new President for a new 5-year term shall be held at least 45 and no more than 90 days after the vacancy occurs pursuant to the constitutional electoral law."

The Administration's assertion that Haiti's Constitution is working simply doesn't mesh with the facts. In urging President Aristide's resignation, without a legislature to ratify the interim President, the Bush Administration played a role in subverting and effectively nullifying the Constitution to which you consistently point.

If the opposition had chosen to join in diplomatic solutions to the crisis, democracy could have been preserved. Instead, the U.S. stood by as a rebel minority forced him out of power.

Now, the Haiti Constitution calls for the election of a new President at least 45 and no more than 90 days after the vacancy occurs. To the best of my knowledge, after urging President Aristide to resign, the Bush Administration offered no insight and no plan as to how this will be accomplished.

Please explain to me how the Constitution was followed as President Bush promised, and how it is possible to move forward constitutionally without a legislature.

Mr. NORIEGA. Well, there is no Parliament because the Parliament's term expired because there were no elections held in a timely fashion. We have——

[Chairman Ballenger asked that Assistant Secretary Noriega provide an expanded response to the question posed by Congressman Brown. Mr. Noriega's response follows:]

Well, there is no Parliament because the Parliament's term expired because there were no elections held in a timely fashion. We have had to deal with this political reality in offering advice on how Haiti could reconstitute its government while respecting the 1987 constitution. When President Aristide resigned, Boniface Alexandre, President of Haiti's Supreme Court, became Haiti's president under Article 149 of the constitution. Under Haiti's Constitution, the Prime Minister is the head of government. Article 165 of the constitution says that if the Prime Minister resigns, the government remains in place until the appointment of a successor, in order to transact current business. Article 165 does not specify how or when a successor Prime Minister should be chosen, but a reasonable interpretation would require the President to choose a new Prime Minister from the majority party in Parliament, as stipulated in Article 137. But what does the constitution say about appointing a new Prime Minister if there is no Parliament? It is silent on this point. Whatever the reasons were for Parliament's expiration, Haiti needed a government after Yvon Neptune, Aristide's Prime Minister, resigned. Doing nothing, because the constitution is silent, was not an option. Since the legislature did not exist, Haiti used the provisions of the CARICOM action plan to provide a mechanism for the appointment of a new Prime Minister. In my view, this does not make Haiti's transitional government unconstitutional. To the contrary, the transitional government was formed with full respect for the constitution under the circumstances prevailing at the time. And we need to recall that this is a transitional government, to be replaced when elections are held within a year or so.

Mr. BROWN. Because the opposition didn't block any elections and the administration didn't force the opposition to move forward and conduct those elections.

Mr. NORIEGA. We didn't force them to do it, but our ability to do that would be limited. But the reason they didn't want to do it was because they didn't trust the process. And every time they raised their head in the political process——

[Chairman Ballenger asked that Assistant Secretary Noriega provide an expanded response to the question posed by Congressman Brown. Mr. Noriega's response follows:]

We didn't force them to do it, but our ability to make them do this would be very limited. The reason the opposition didn't want to participate in elections was because they didn't trust the process. Every time they raised their head in the political process, all they saw was President Aristide evading his commitments to the OAS to create a secure climate for elections. Aristide partisans, at times armed and acting with the complicity of the Haitian National Police, violently suppressed many of the opposition's peaceful demonstrations. In December 2001, there was a concerted, nation-wide attack against the opposition. Many offices were torched and some residences of opposition leaders as well. Going back to the May 2000 elections, Aristide's government refused to fix fraudulent election results for the Senate, despite an OAS finding that the vote results were tabulated in a fraudulent manner and despite requests from opposition leaders, the U.S., and other members of the international community. Little wonder, then, that opposition and civil society leaders would not engage in an electoral process without good faith action from Aristide to ensure their security—action that Aristide never took despite his many promises that he would act.

Mr. BROWN. Whenever our policy as a government—whenever there is an opposition that objects to an election, we say well, then, that is okay not to have an election?

Mr. NORIEGA. That isn't what I am saying, and I don't have much time to give an answer. The process is going to have to be worked out by the new government, which will be a government that is formed by a consensus, by a group of wise men that is being formed by a Tripartite Commission that will advise on the appointment of a new Prime Minister. President Aristide's party will be represented as well as other representatives of civil society and the international community. They will form this new government, appoint a new Cabinet.

[Chairman Ballenger asked that Assistant Secretary Noriega provide an expanded response to the question posed by Congressman Brown. Mr. Noriega's response follows:]

That isn't what I am saying and I don't have much time to give an answer. The process is going to have to be worked out by the new government, which will be a government that is formed by a consensus, by a group of wise men that is being formed by a Tripartite Commission which will appoint a seven member Council of Eminent Persons, which will in turn advise on the appointment of a new Prime Minister. President Aristide's party will be represented as well as other representatives of civil society and the international community. The Council of Eminent Persons will advise on nominations for a new Prime Minister, President Alexandre will appoint the new Prime Minister, who will appoint a new Cabinet. This is the process for the formation of the transitional government, a process that follows provisions of the Haitian constitution. This is the first step toward free and fair elections that will put a new permanent government into power. The international community, including the U.S., will be heavily involved in making sure that these elections are conducted in a secure environment, so that all political parties, including Mr. Aristide's party, can participate without fearing for their personal safety. Before Aristide left, neither we nor anyone else could force the opposition to agree to elections when it was plain that Aristide would use violence and intimidation to retain power. That is not democracy. Such an election would not be free, fair, or democratic.

Mr. BROWN. Is this in the Constitution that President Bush has asserted that we are following?

Mr. NORIEGA. This is based on an international plan that was posed to President Aristide, which he accepted, and we are trying to follow that process to the best of our ability.

Mr. BROWN. The opposition didn't accept it.

Mr. NORIEGA. The opposition didn't accept it because they didn't trust President Aristide, and we have heard a few reasons why. Regarding your statements that this Administration linked the delivery of assistance—or blocked the delivery of assistance is not accurate. And your statement that we—well, I will stop.

Mr. BROWN. If your statement is about to be that if you didn't block it, you can't count the number the phone calls that many of us made to try to free up that money for roads and sewers and for clean water, where their water is some of the worst drinking water in the world.

Mr. BALLENGER. Your time is up. You are out of order, Mr. Brown. Mr. Wexler, please proceed.

Mr. WEXLER. Thank you, Mr. Chairman.

Mr. Noriega, I found the collective response to Ms. Ros-Lehtinen's question with respect to the Temporary Protective Status, with respect to many Haitians that are in the south Florida community mostly, the response is an incredulous one. And I guess it is sort of a twisted sense of reality where, on the one hand, you take rightful point in introducing the gentleman who is sitting in his wheelchair in the front row—and I am very happy that he is here—as a personal example of the tragic circumstances that not only himself but thousands of other Haitian people have found themselves in, and understanding that Mr. Aristide no longer is the President.

But on the one hand, we have sitting in the front row a gentleman, who in your own language, had his legs crushed. And now, for months, we have been deporting Haitians back to Haiti. We continue to deport Haitians back to Haiti today. We have asked on a bipartisan basis that through the turmoil, we just take a timeout. We are told it is not ripe yet to take a timeout deporting people. And apparently our boats that are circling Haiti don't have on those boats people who can speak Creole, so that when we take these people into custody, they can't even articulate, because nobody on our side of the equation understands them, what fears they may in fact have.

Well, the gentleman in the front row seems to be the personification of the fears. So it seems to me on the one hand, you can't parade people. And I am thrilled with an enormous amount of respect that this gentleman is here, but you can't have people sitting here in the front row that had their lives ruined, and at the same time say that we are continuing the current policy of sending Haitians back so they too can have their lives ruined.

Which are we supposed to believe? Either there is a crisis or there isn't. But we can't claim a crisis to justify our inaction or our feelings toward the previous President and then continue to send others back so they can get mauled like this gentleman in the first row. Which is it?

Mr. NORIEGA. Now that President Aristide is no longer President of Haiti, perhaps it is safe for this man to go back to Haiti.

Mr. WEXLER. Is that the policy? Is that the American policy now?

Mr. NORIEGA. On the other hand, if there are people, for example, persons who are from the Aristide government who were to come to the United States and have a credible fear of persecution, that would be weighed today. We have to make decisions based on individual cases. If there is a credible fear, then we have an obligation to run that fear to ground, to give them an opportunity to substantiate a political asylum claim. So that process does exist. It has to be done on an individual basis.

Mr. WEXLER. What circumstances would need to occur in Haiti in order for the State Department to recommend to the Department of Homeland Security that Temporary Protective Status be provided for Haitians? What hasn't occurred that needs to occur?

Mr. DEWEY. The conditions for Temporary Protective Status are an acute situation and widespread violence throughout the country, or a natural disaster, as has been the case for some of the countries in Central America. It doesn't meet that test, and the Department of Homeland Security makes that decision.

Mr. WEXLER. How many more Haitians will have to die in order for the chaos to be great enough so we can grant a Temporary Protective Status? Is there a level that needs to be established that we have to reach?

Mr. DEWEY. If we have evidence that Haitians are dying. There have not been any that have been repatriated after the departure.

Mr. WEXLER. Do you recognize the dichotomy? On the one hand, Mr. Noriega spends his entire testimony documenting all the tragedies that have occurred in Haiti. And up until 2 days ago that same gentleman was in charge, and now we are saying there is no documented problem.

Mr. NORIEGA. May I address that point very briefly? May I note that in the days——

Mr. BALLENGER. Without objection.

Mr. NORIEGA. In the days before President Aristide's departure, we had about 900 people that had taken to the seas. Since the days of Aristide's departure, we have three intercepted on the seas. So I think the situation may be improving and we hope it gets better every day.

Mr. BALLENGER. Mr. Meeks.

Mr. MEEKS. I find it incredible. I look at today's news. I understand that the United States is shifting its policy, where Staff Sergeant Timothy Edwards said that at airports, the Marines' mission now is aimed to protect Haitians from reprisal attacks. I mean, it is clear what is going on. We are shifting our policies now. This is just in today's paper. I don't know whether you read it today. But there are problems that we have to shift it because of the reprisals, and they are talking about bodies laying in the street.

I watched CNN the other day. But they have had bodies just recently that they were putting in and taking to the morgue. So people are dying every day. I think that is well documented.

I wonder, is Venezuela next? I wonder, because we tried that once and it didn't work, and maybe we ought to go back again because we believe in democracy. I wonder if Venezuela is next.

Let me ask you, I think that it is clear—and I wonder what is the most important thing here. It is clear to me, and I think it is clear to all, that you and the Administration for whatever the reason, you don't like—didn't like Aristide. Now, I wonder what becomes more important. Is it an individual or an institution of government that is important in the lives of the people, the 8 million people that happen to live in Haiti, the most important thing, the saving of lives of Haitians?

Now if, in fact, you have a policy that is just based upon who you like and dislike in regards to who heads the country, and you make those decisions, then I wonder why we even went through the charade of saying that we agree with, first, the Bishops. When they came together, they had an agreement and they wanted to sit down and get both parties together so we can stop atrocities. Why would we even say we agree with that? Why would we even say that we agreed with the CARICOM agreement, if in fact we weren't serious about trying to get two sides to the table to negotiate an agreement?

We know an agreement cannot be had but one side. You need two sides at the table. And if fact—why would we say we want a diplomatic relationship? Based upon everything I heard here, you are saying that your minds were made up before CARICOM and you were saying you didn't want a diplomatic conclusion to this problem. You just wanted to get rid of Aristide. That was the objective, not to preserve this democracy. The objective seems to me to get rid of a Head of State.

You indicated in your testimony we don't put American lives at risk to save a government. But by now, right now, by not trying to save a government, we are going to put American lives at stake, because we have rebels and criminals and hoods that are controlling the streets. And our own admission when we look at individuals—and I am not a conspiracy theorist at all, but when, in fact, you have these allegations, I think some of them have been fairly well documented, and I will ask you that when you have allegations that the CIA had been connected to the FRAPH, whose leaders went through Aristide originally, and most recently over the weekend, and the FRAPH death squad leader Toto Constant, who not only lives in Queens, lives in my district and is causing heck in my district as we speak, causing people—and we are separating Haitians in the streets of New York and Brooklyn, Queens and Brooklyn from each other, but Constant is there and he is going to come back.

Then you have Guy Philippe, who is a leader of the current movement, was trained by the United States military in Ecuador. We have M–16s that were found and M–60s and rocket-propelled grenade launchers in the hands of the rebels appear to be weapons sent by the United States to the Dominican Republic, and now they end up in Haiti. You have a situation, as I said, where the U.S. did not really back the CARICOM peace plan at all, but they claim they backed it after the Congressional Black Caucus—I would ask—and I can go on and I could bring up allegation after allegation, but I would like to know—and then you also have all sorts of figures who are coming out of the woodwork to rule in Haiti—Guy Philippe and I hear Baby Doc is coming back, Danny Toussaint.

What is our current plan for Haiti and will these people be allowed to take office? There are criminals that have been released. Prisons were broken into. The people that broke laws, people that went to the DR, some people serving a life sentence, all is forgotten about and these people can now come back, and are these going to be the ones that are going to negotiate a peace agreement for a democratic government in Haiti?

Mr. NORIEGA. Thank you, Congressman. Congressman, the Bishops that you referred to, the Bishops' plan that you referred to, was actually withdrawn by the Bishops. We tried to get them to propose another plan, and Secretary Powell encouraged them to propose another plan. But the Bishops' consensus was that Aristide had to leave, and we were told they would not put forward a plan that would leave Aristide in place.

With respect to the question of whether we like the man or not, that isn't the issue. It isn't even the issue of whether we like what he did when he was in office over a 10-year period. But we do have to make some judgments about whether we want to put American lives at risk merely to keep him in power for a little bit longer.

We were not asked and are not expected to put American lives at risk to keep in power good men in Bolivia or in Argentina or in Ecuador. And it is not merely a question of whether we like a person; it is whether we think it is a sustainable, viable investment for American foreign policy. It is a reasonable assessment that we are obligated to make.

[Chairman Ballenger asked that Assistant Secretary Noriega provide an expanded response to the question posed by Congressman Meeks. Mr. Noriega's response follows:]

Thank you, Congressman. Congressman, the Bishops that you referred to, the Bishops' plan that you referred to, was actually withdrawn by the Bishops. We tried to get them to propose another plan, and Secretary Powell encouraged them to propose another plan. But the Bishops' consensus was that Aristide had to leave, and we were told that they would not put forward a plan that would leave Aristide in place.

With respect to the question of whether we like the man or not, that isn't the issue. It isn't even the issue of whether we like what he did when he was in office over a 10-year period. But we do have to make some judgments about whether we want to put American lives at risk merely to keep him in power a little bit longer. We were not asked and are not expected to put American lives at risk to keep in power good men in Bolivia or in Argentina or in Ecuador. And it is not merely a question of whether we like a person; it is whether we think it is a sustainable, viable investment for American foreign policy. It is a reasonable assessment that we were obligated to make.

It is worth remembering that Haiti's political crisis had festered for more than two years by the time the rebels began armed attacks in the north. Intervening with troops in the middle of an armed insurgency caused by the unresolved political crisis was not, in our judgment, a prudent policy. The armed insurgents opposing Aristide would have viewed the intervention as supporting Aristide, substantially increasing risk for American troops. When President Aristide resigned and left the country, it became possible for troops to conduct stability operations without being in between two armed factions.

Let me address some of the other questions you raise in your statement. You said that we didn't like Aristide, that our minds were made up before the CARICOM plan, that we did not want a diplomatic conclusion to the problem. The facts, I think, show something far different. We were observers at the meetings where CARICOM came up with its plan, and offered our advice and counsel when asked. We knew what the plan involved from the very beginning, and were it favor of it. The Secretary himself publicly endorsed the CARICOM plan on February 13. After Aristide accepted the plan in Kingston, we engaged in intensive diplomacy to convince opposition and civil society leaders to accept the CARICOM plan, including that part of the plan that called for Aristide to serve out the remainder of his term. So we did engage in diplomacy to achieve a political solution, and this settlement included President Aristide remaining in office.

As I said earlier, the U.S. Government has delivered no M–16 rifles, or any of the other weapons you mention, to the Dominican Republic. The last U.S. weapons sale to the Dominican Republic was 1991, when we delivered side arms. I have also testified that Guy Philippe's military training in Ecuador was not funded or sponsored by the U.S., but was part of a bilateral program between Haiti and Ecuador.

On our current plans for Haiti, the U.S. intends to support efforts to rebuild Haiti's governmental institutions, including a professional, independent police force. We will support free and fair elections as soon as the interim Haitian government determines it is practical to hold them. One of the guiding principles of our engagement in Haiti is that political power will not be turned over to persons who have participated in political violence, including irregular armed groups.

Mr. BALLENGER. Again, sorry, Mr. Secretary. Ms. Lee.

Ms. LEE. Thank you, Mr. Chairman, and let me thank you and the Ranking Member for this hearing. It is long overdue, but now I understand why.

It is very clear to me, Mr. Noriega, that, first of all, we have been involved in the process of destabilizing and undermining the government of Haiti over the last 3, 4 years. It is also very clear to me that—and it is this Administration's policy that regime change is a central component of its foreign policy and it manifests itself in a variety of ways. It just so happens in Haiti, it was planned in this way, working with the murderers and the thugs and those paramilitary groups to achieve what you had planned from day one, and that is a coup and overthrow of the government of President Aristide, the duly elected President of a black nation of 8 million people, the poorest in the Western Hemisphere. I think your testimony confirmed that for me.

Let me also indicate that it is very important for me to just ask you about the safety and security of President and Mrs. Aristide, because we have called the State Department just to ask them to put us in touch with them, and it is my understanding there is no

United States Embassy in the Central African Republic. Or is there a way to at least know what is transpiring? I want to make sure from your point of view that you are ensuring their safety and their well-being.

Next I would like to know just, really, Mr. Noriega, when did you decide that Mr. Aristide had to go? And what did you do to make sure that that happened? And I ask you that because I wrote to Secretary Powell on February 12 and said in this letter—let me just read one paragraph. I said—and this was February 12:

> "I must say, Mr. Secretary, that our failure to support the democratic process and help restore order looks like a covert effort to overthrow a government. There is a violent coup d'etat in the making, and it appears that the United States is aiding and abetting an attempt to violently topple the Aristide government. With all due respect, this looks like regime change."

There were a series of questions I asked the Secretary of State. He has not responded yet. Maybe you can.

Does the State Department support the democratically-elected government of Haiti, and what tactical steps is our government taking to support the democratic process?

Secondly, is our country supporting and sanctioning an overthrow of the Aristide government by giving a wink and nod to the opposition? And I said to the Secretary, there are reports that we are covertly funding the opposition.

Thirdly, does the United States support the CARICOM proposal and will we work through the OAS to broker a peaceful solution and not an overthrow of the Aristide government?

Finally, I asked, is it true that Haitian opposition parties and leaders have received USAID funding? Mr. Secretary, I think it is very important that these questions be answered truthfully because many would like to believe the Secretary of State.

I know he said recently some of our statements are nonsense. There have been reports that we are buying into conspiracy theories. But I also think it is very important to ask these questions, given the facts that the Secretary of State made and the presentation he made at the United Nations with regard to the weapons of mass destruction, with regard to Iraq. It is important we know the truth. And it is important to answer some of these questions that we have been asking today, because certainly your testimony to date begs the question, just when did we plan this and how did we see this being executed? And I would like to hear from you on that.

Mr. NORIEGA. Well, Congresswoman, on the safety and well-being of President Aristide and his party, he is not the responsibility of the United States Government. We facilitated his safe departure from the country at his request. He is free to leave the Central African Republic at any time.

[Chairman Ballenger asked that Assistant Secretary Noriega provide an expanded response to the question posed by Congresswoman Lee. Mr. Noriega's response follows:]

Well, Congresswoman, on the safety and well-being of President Aristide and his party, he is not the responsibility of the United States Government. We facilitated his safe departure from the country at his request. He is free to leave the Central African Republic at any time.

On your next question, we never decided that Aristide had to resign office—he decided that himself when he realized that continuing in office would mean death and suffering in the conflict between his armed partisans and the insurgents. And as I responded a moment ago to Congressman Meeks, we supported the CARICOM plan, which among other things called for President Aristide to remain in office for the balance of his term.

While Aristide was in office, we acknowledged him as Haiti's elected president and supported the democratic process by working with all parties to achieve a settlement of the political crisis. This included urging Aristide on several occasions to end his undemocratic suppression of legitimate political dissent and free press. We also asked him to do something to create a climate of security for elections, as he promised the OAS he would, but never did. We engaged in an intensive effort to obtain the opposition's agreement to the CARICOM plan, which initially they did not accept because it allowed Aristide to remain in office.

Opposition parties and leaders in Haiti have never received direct funding from USAID. Opposition parties and their leaders have participated in political party training given by USAID grantees, the National Democratic Institute and the International Republican Institute.

Ms. LEE. Mr. Secretary, let me just say my office was in touch with the State Department throughout this process, and we were told that President Aristide and Mrs. Aristide were going to a destination of their choosing. We heard that President Aristide had no idea where he was going until 20 minutes before they landed.

Mr. NORIEGA. That is accurate. He had chosen a destination which decided it would not be able to accept him. We then had to find a place that would accept him. We did, and the Central African Republic has graciously accepted to do that.

They also now say that he is free to leave any time he wants, and the public statements I have seen, I think that they would welcome his leaving whenever he wants.

Ms. LEE. And wouldn't we get a letter in response to the questions that we asked of the——

Mr. NORIEGA. I think you certainly are owed an answer, Congresswoman.

Ms. LEE. And this was February 12, mind you, before the coup took place.

Mr. BALLENGER. Okay. Could I request, just to assist you all, we have quite a few more people, and let us be honest, I think they are more interested in making a statement than asking questions. But if you could record the questions that we do not have time to answer, it would be greatly appreciated.

Sooner or later, the gentleman with the leg problem is supposed to come up and, at the rate we are going, it may be midnight. So let me ask the people that are going to ask questions, either make your statement and don't ask questions, or ask questions and give them time to answer.

So it is now.

Ms. WATSON. I am going to read you a statement and then would you tell me if it is true.

> "The United States State Department, which never negotiates with terrorists, has sufficient cozy contact with the Haitian rebels to convince them to delay their onslaught on Port-au-Prince. Even after the rebels rejected terms of settlement acceptable to President Aristide, in a matter of hours, the State Department acceded to the rebel demands, which was the removal of President Aristide."

Would you say that is a true statement, or would you say it is not?

Mr. NORIEGA. That statement is false.

Ms. WATSON. All right.

Now, does the State Department deal with those who plan coup d'etats or overthrow of legitimately elected democratic governments?

Mr. NORIEGA. No, we do not.

Ms. WATSON. What kind of conversation did you have with the leaders or leader of the rebel groups?

Mr. NORIEGA. None.

Ms. WATSON. All right.

How, then, did you know they would not accept the proposal that was offered and agreed to by President Aristide?

Mr. NORIEGA. The conversations we had were with the civilian democratic opposition, representatives of political parties and civil society, not with the so-called "rebel groups," which I would prefer to refer to as "criminal gangs."

Ms. WATSON. Apparently, it is a criminal gang member, Philippe, that has threatened other duly elected officials if they do not attend a meeting. I understand less than 24 hours ago this statement was made, and I understand this person has been responsible for the deaths of hundreds, if not thousands, of Haitians in the past.

Mr. NORIEGA. I did not see the statement you are referring to, ma'am, but we have communicated to the so-called "rebels," "criminal gangs," that they should lay down their arms and leave the city.

Before they reached the city, we had public statements that said that they would be held responsible, if they came into the city, for the violence that ensued, and the international community would hold them responsible for that. They said that they saw those statements, among other things, on the Internet and said that they were not coming into the city.

They immediately proceeded to come into the city. So they were not responding to these public statements.

But as the international community is able to put more security forces on the ground, these folks will have no choice but to respond and to comply and to pull out of the city.

Ms. WATSON. Is it true or not true that our Ambassador, Ambassador Foley, met with the rebel leader today?

Mr. NORIEGA. That is not true.

Ms. WATSON. He did not meet with him today?

Mr. NORIEGA. No, he did not.

Ms. WATSON. Maybe before?

Mr. NORIEGA. I don't think he has ever met the man.

Ms. WATSON. Okay. Maybe the Associated Press got it wrong. I know they do get some things wrong. But it is in the Associated Press today, and I will see that you get a copy:

> "A day after declaring himself Haiti's new military chief, rebel leader Guy Philippe met briefly with U.S. Ambassador James Foley at the envoy's residence on Wednesday. Neither side would comment about the content."

Mr. NORIEGA. That is false. The meeting that I know Ambassador Foley had was with Yvon Neptune, who was President Aristide's Prime Minister, and with the interim President of Haiti, Boniface Alexandre. As far as I know, Ambassador Foley has never met with a guerrilla leader.

The leader of the U.S. military contingent met with Philippe briefly this morning to tell him that he should lay down his arms.

Ms. WATSON. What did you just say? Repeat what you just said, the last sentence.

Mr. NORIEGA. The head of the U.S. military contingent met with Philippe this morning to tell him to lay down his arms and to leave the city.

Ms. WATSON. Under whose authority? Was that under the Ambassador's authority?

Mr. NORIEGA. No. That man does not work for the Ambassador.

Ms. WATSON. Who directed?

Mr. NORIEGA. What he is doing, in the interest of the security of U.S. forces, is to tell this man to leave the city to prevent any sort of a confrontation. If he does not leave the city, he will have to respond to the force of the international community; and that was the simple message to him.

Ms. WATSON. Well, I would suggest strongly that the State Department immediately contact the Associated Press to clarify this, that is going out over e-mail.

Mr. BALLENGER. If I may, I have the latest quotation of 2:57 this afternoon from the Associated Press, so it saves you the trouble of finding out:

> "Rebel leader Guy Philippe said Wednesday his forces laid down their arms as United States Marines fanned out through the capital, rifles at ready, to help restore some order amid Haiti's bloody uprising."

And now—I mean, it is the same Associated Press that you agreed was not too smart.

Ms. WATSON. Mr. Chairman, if you will allow me just to finish my question, and it probably is more like a statement.

I have listened for the last hour or so to an assault on a President that was duly elected in a democratic process.

Mr. BALLENGER. I hate to be impolite, but we did not let anybody else have additional time.

Ms. WATSON. Well, you kind of took some of my time, but you are the Chair, you can do that. But there is definitely a double standard.

Mr. BALLENGER. Your time had already expired.

Ms. WATSON. Thank you, Mr. Chairman.

Mr. BALLENGER. Mr. Rangel.

Mr. RANGEL. Thank you so much, and thank you, Mr. Noriega, for sharing your views with us.

You had indicated that you would not deal with these rogues and thugs that were part of the militia, and I guess the noncivilian part of the opposition, but there did come a time where these rogues and thugs were approaching the palace and that our government thought that President Aristide was in danger of his life and his family's.

Mr. NORIEGA. Pardon me, sir? I didn't hear the last part of that.

Mr. RANGEL. Did there come a time that the United States Government thought that these rogues, these thugs, these criminals were approaching the palace and that President Aristide and his family would be in danger?

Mr. NORIEGA. Yes.

Mr. RANGEL. And as you said, that we did not think it was appropriate to put our military in harm's way to shore up his safety?

Mr. NORIEGA. That was a decision we made.

Mr. RANGEL. Right. And so therefore we communicated that to President Aristide that he could not depend on us to protect him against these thugs, these criminals, and these rogues?

Mr. NORIEGA. That is essentially correct, yes. We told him through public statements that we were not going to do that.

Mr. RANGEL. And as a result of this, President Aristide thought that it was in his best interests and the best interests of the Haitians for him to leave?

Mr. NORIEGA. Yes, sir.

Mr. RANGEL. And we facilitated that leaving?

Mr. NORIEGA. Yes, sir, we did.

Mr. RANGEL. And we did take him out of Haiti?

Mr. NORIEGA. At his request.

Mr. RANGEL. Yes. And he requested, because he was fearful for his life and other Haitians that would die as a result of the information we gave him, right?

Mr. NORIEGA. I think it wasn't necessarily just the information we gave him, but I think——

Mr. RANGEL. Well, it encouraged him to leave, I would think.

Mr. NORIEGA. Yes. If you read his resignation letter, that is the reason.

Mr. RANGEL. Well, I want to know, if someone leaves a country that is elected, because he is fearful for his life, is that not a coup d'etat?

Mr. NORIEGA. I don't think so, sir.

Mr. RANGEL. Well, that is what is explained in the dictionary. How would you describe a coup d'etat?

Here is a man that is informed by the United States Government that we cannot protect him, and the rebels and thugs and rogues are going to come and they are going to kill him and his family and Haitians would die. Do you want to leave? He says, "Yes." You make him leave.

Why is that not a coup d'etat?

Mr. NORIEGA. We did not make him leave, sir.

Mr. RANGEL. I didn't say you made him leave. He asked to leave.

Mr. NORIEGA. At the very end you said, and "you make him leave."

Mr. RANGEL. You helped him to leave, I meant to say. Forgive me.

Mr. NORIEGA. At his request.

Mr. RANGEL. At his request. He begged you to help him to leave to get out of there so he would not get killed, and his family, because he feared that these rebel forces that we informed him would kill him and other Haitians, and he left. Now, why is that not a coup d'etat?

Mr. NORIEGA. It isn't what I would regard as a traditional coup d'etat.

Mr. RANGEL. Tell me the difference. When the man is running for his life, here comes the military, they are armed, they are going to kill them. We know it, we tell him that.

He says, please get me out of here. We get him out of there. Why is that not a coup d'etat?

Mr. NORIEGA. He resigned, sir.

Mr. RANGEL. Now, did we ask him to resign?

Mr. NORIEGA. No, we didn't. We told him that if he needed to leave——

[Chairman Ballenger asked that Assistant Secretary Noriega provide an expanded response to the question posed by Congressman Rangel. Mr. Noriega's response follows:]

No, we didn't. We told him that if he needed to leave, we could facilitate his departure.

Mr. RANGEL. Be very careful, Mr. Noriega, because it is reported. Did we ask him to resign? Was that a condition of helping him to leave the country?

Mr. NORIEGA. We told him that for us to be able to facilitate his departure——

[Chairman Ballenger asked that Assistant Secretary Noriega provide an expanded response to the question posed by Congressman Rangel. Mr. Noriega's response follows:]

We told him that for us to be able to facilitate his departure that he had to decide what was best for Haiti. If he decided to resign, we would work with him on a destination. I do not consider that a condition for helping him to leave. Aristide and his security advisors made their own assessment of his position.

Mr. RANGEL. Yes, of course. That is easy.

Mr. NORIEGA. We did not want to have a situation where we were going to have to——

[Chairman Ballenger asked that Assistant Secretary Noriega provide an expanded response to the question posed by Congressman Rangel. Mr. Noriega's response follows:]

We did not want a situation where we were going to have to deal with the consequences of a political vacuum. If Aristide had left Haiti with his status as president unresolved, the street violence would have continued. Aristide understood this—he said so in his resignation letter—I agree to leave if my resignation can prevent a bloodbath.

Mr. RANGEL. You didn't want to have a situation, so you told him that unless he resigned, we would not be able to facilitate his departure.

Mr. NORIEGA. Because we wanted to have some sort of a sustainable political——

[Chairman Ballenger asked that Assistant Secretary Noriega provide an expanded response to the question posed by Congressman Rangel. Mr. Noriega's response follows:]

Because we wanted to have some sort of a sustainable political framework after Aristide's departure if he decided to leave, it was understood that he would resign and show us his letter of resignation. Haiti's constitution provides for a succession if the Office of the President becomes vacant for any reason. If Aristide had not resigned, the office would not be vacant even if he had left the country. His successor could not have taken office, and there would have been a power vacuum that armed insurgents could have exploited. Again, Aristide understood this—this is why he submitted a resignation before leaving.

Mr. RANGEL. I didn't ask the reasons, Mr. Noriega. I am just asking you this.

Mr. BALLENGER. If I may say something, Charlie, you ought to give him a chance to answer at least one question before you throw another one at him.

Mr. RANGEL. But this is such a simple one here.

As a condition of assisting this man, saving his life, that of his family, one of the conditions of helping him was that he resign; is that not true?

Mr. NORIEGA. We did not want to have a situation where——

[Chairman Ballenger asked that Assistant Secretary Noriega provide an expanded response to the question posed by Congressman Rangel. Mr. Noriega's response follows:]

We did not want to have a situation where political chaos would ensue if Aristide left the country without resigning. Aristide had to make this decision himself—he could have stayed and the violence would have continued. If he decided to leave without tendering a resignation, political turmoil and violence would also have continued. I believed that if we helped Aristide leave the country without seeing his letter of resignation that we might be contributing to the uncertainty and turmoil in the country and, ironically, that he might accuse us of taking him against his will. Ambassador Foley and I have discussed this, and we agree that, in light of the fact that Mrs. Aristide is an American citizen, and in order to attempt to avoid a bloodbath, we would have been inclined to help Mr. Aristide depart Haiti even if he refused to show us his letter of resignation.

Mr. RANGEL. Oh, Mr. Chairman.

Ms. WATERS. Make him answer.

Mr. NORIEGA. Well, if you listen to the answer, it might satisfy you.

Mr. RANGEL. Now my time is going to expire. That is not fair.

If he had not signed that letter of resignation, would you have helped him to leave the country?

Mr. NORIEGA. Probably, yes, in the final analysis.

Mr. RANGEL. But you told him—at that time, he was told that he had to resign in order to leave the country.

Mr. NORIEGA. I think in the humanitarian interests, particularly since his wife is an American citizen, we would have been prepared to take him——

Mr. RANGEL. But you told him that he had to resign if he wanted to leave the country.

Mr. NORIEGA. We told him, because we wanted to have a sustainable solution where we could avoid bloodshed, where we could be——

[Chairman Ballenger asked that Assistant Secretary Noriega provide an expanded response to the question posed by Congressman Rangel. Mr. Noriega's response follows:]

We told him that we wanted to have a sustainable solution where we could avoid bloodshed, where we could be assured that violence would not continue. We did not tell him he had to resign, but it was understood that he had decided to leave and to resign. Both decisions were his to make and he made them.

Mr. RANGEL. And twice he was asked for that resignation, and he would not have left unless he signed it; is that correct?

Mr. NORIEGA. We wanted to be able to have a basis for a sustainable political solution.

Mr. RANGEL. But you told him that unless he signed it, he could not leave the country.

Mr. NORIEGA. We wanted to have a sustainable political solution, and the only way to be able to achieve that——

[Chairman Ballenger asked that Assistant Secretary Noriega provide an expanded response to the question posed by Congressman Rangel. Mr. Noriega's response follows:]

We wanted to have a sustainable political solution, and the only way to be able to achieve that, if Aristide chose to leave the country, was that his formal resignation be part of that solution.

Mr. RANGEL. And without that resignation, it would have been a coup d'etat by anyone's standard.

Mr. BALLENGER. The gentleman's time has expired.

Mr. NORIEGA. We have a letter of resignation, sir.

Mr. RANGEL. You sure did, and I would have signed one too.

Mr. BALLENGER. Ms. Waters.

Ms. WATERS. Thank you very much, Mr. Chairman. I thank you for allowing those of us who are not Members of the Committee to be here today. I want you to know that several of you, including you, Mr. Chairman, have said that it is a fabrication that he was forced out, that there was no coup d'etat, he was not kidnapped.

I talked to President Aristide this morning. He called me, and he maintained that he was forced out, he was literally kidnapped, he did not go of his own will, so I want to put that on the record.

Secondly, I want to put on the record that I have been to Haiti three times since January 1, and I have met with the opposition, that is, Mr. Apaid, Jr., and some of those from the committee of 184 and talked to many people about what was going on.

In addition to that, I was in Haiti a week ago this past Saturday where you came and led the delegation of the international community, where Mr. Aristide signed off on the CARICOM proposal. So I want to put that on the record.

But I am very interested in some things that you have said, and I do want yes or no answers. Don't take up my time.

I want to know, you have said that you have no responsibility to protect a Head of State. Are you going to protect the new Chief Justice that was just sworn in, who is now the Head of State of Haiti, or not?

Mr. NORIEGA. We believe that he is part of this——

[Chairman Ballenger asked that Assistant Secretary Noriega provide an expanded response to the question posed by Congresswoman Waters. Mr. Noriega's response follows:]

We believe that he is part of the interim government that will govern Haiti during the political transition period, that is, before free and fair elections are held to put a new permanent government in place. We have to make sure that the political transition is effective and democratic, so yes, we will protect him.

Aristide was protected by a private security firm, paid for by the Haitian government. He had security protection throughout all of the events preceding his resignation. His security detail went to the airport with him, and boarded the plane as well.

President Alexandre does not have the advantage of a private security firm, which the interim government cannot afford, and the Haitian National Police are incapable at this point. As the police force and Haiti's interim government become stronger, Haiti's domestic security forces will become responsible for protecting high-level officials.

Ms. WATERS. Are you going to protect him or not, yes, or no.

Mr. NORIEGA. Yes, we are, because he is part of a sustainable political solution.

Ms. WATERS. Did you refuse to protect Mr. Aristide, who was then the Head of State? So you have a different standard for these two; is that correct?

That is all I want to know, yes or no.

Mr. NORIEGA. These are very different men and very different political solutions.

Ms. WATERS. So, yes, for the chief justice; no, for Mr. Aristide. So you don't have a policy that is consistent about having no responsibility to protect Head of State.

Mr. NORIEGA. That is not what I said the policy was, ma'am. You are misstating what the policy was.

[Chairman Ballenger asked that Assistant Secretary Noriega provide an expanded response to the question posed by Congresswoman Waters. Mr. Noriega's response follows:]

That is not what I said the policy was, ma'am. You are misstating what the policy was. Interim President Alexandre is a vital part of the transition to a democratic Haiti through free and fair elections. For the transition to be successful, he has to be protected from harm. Issues concerning protection for Aristide before his resignation were different. He had his own private security detail, paid for by the Haitian government. President Alexandre does not have such protection, because the interim government can't afford to pay for it and Haiti's domestic security forces are too weak now. As a matter of policy, we protect President Alexandre because the future of democracy in Haiti depends on it, and we can arrange this protection under the umbrella of stability that the Multinational Interim Force provides. Before his resignation, Aristide had his own personal protection, not to mention the pro-Aristide armed gangs standing between him and the insurgents. We did not need to give Aristide protection.

Ms. WATERS. Let's go on to the next question.

Mr. Noriega, people are assuming that you knew——

Mr. NORIEGA. You are misstating what the policy is.

Ms. WATERS [continuing]. That the so-called "rebels," who they were. I just want some yes or no answers.

Did you know about the history of Louis-Jodel Chamblain? Did you know that he was the right hand of Emmanuel Constant, who is now up in New York; and did you know that he had murdered Mr. Antoine Izmery, along with thousands of other Haitians? Did you know that before they reentered Haiti in this last coup d'etat that took place? Did you know about him? Had you ever heard about him and his history?

Mr. NORIEGA. Yes, I have.

Ms. WATERS. Have you ever met him?

Mr. NORIEGA. No.

Ms. WATERS. Did you know about Mr. Guy Philippe? Did you know that he was a convicted drug dealer and that he attempted a coup on President Aristide in 2002, and that he is responsible for killing 26 members of Lavalas. Had you heard about him before he entered Gonaives?

Mr. NORIEGA. I had heard of him, but not——

[Chairman Ballenger asked that Assistant Secretary Noriega provide an expanded response to the question posed by Congresswoman Waters. Mr. Noriega's response follows:]

I had heard of him, but not of any specific allegations about the activities you mention. We knew that Philippe was in the Dominican Republic. We also knew that in 2003 armed groups were attacking government facilities in the central plateau region, but we had no information connecting Philippe to these attacks.

Ms. WATERS. You knew about his history as a convicted drug dealer?

Mr. NORIEGA. I did not know the details of that.

Ms. WATERS. Did you know that he had been a killer, that he was accused of killing?

Mr. NORIEGA. I do not know any details that——

[Chairman Ballenger asked that Assistant Secretary Noriega provide an expanded response to the question posed by Congresswoman Waters. Mr. Noriega's response follows:]

I do not know any details that would link Philippe to accusations of involvement in killings. Of course, I know from the media that he was one of several leaders of so-called rebel gangs that were involved in political violence, including killing. I also am aware of accusations of his involvement in other forms of criminality.

Ms. WATERS. Did you know that he was in exile?

Mr. NORIEGA. I do not know the details.

Ms. WATERS. Do you know that he was in exile?

Mr. NORIEGA. I knew that he was in exile, yes.

Ms. WATERS. Did you know that he had returned and he was up in Gonaives and Cap Haitien?

Mr. NORIEGA. I knew that he returned; I saw it on television.

Ms. WATERS. Did you know about Mr. Jean Tatoune and did you know that he was a member of FRAPH, and did you know about him before he came back into the country?

Mr. NORIEGA. No, I have never heard of him.

Ms. WATERS. Had you heard that he was involved in the massacre at Raboteau?

Mr. NORIEGA. I had heard of that incident.

Ms. WATERS. Had you met Mr. Guy Philippe before he returned to Haiti?

Mr. NORIEGA. No, I have never met him.

Ms. WATERS. Did you ever met Mr. Emmanuel Constant?

Mr. NORIEGA. No, I have not.

Ms. WATERS. Did you know that he was the head of FRAPH?

Mr. NORIEGA. I have heard that.

Ms. WATERS. Did you know that Mr. Chamblain was his right hand?

Mr. NORIEGA. I have heard that from you folks.

Ms. WATERS. Did you know that Mr. Constant was hired and worked for the CIA?

Mr. NORIEGA. No, I don't know that.

Ms. WATERS. It was in the public domain. It was in the papers. You never knew it? You never heard it?

You are not sworn in, but you are on record. Did you know that Mr. Constant worked for the CIA?

Mr. NORIEGA. Ma'am, I am telling you, we don't generally comment on these things, but I do not know that.

Ms. WATERS. You do not generally—you are qualifying your statement.

Mr. NORIEGA. I am telling you that——

Ms. WATERS. What you are telling me is, you don't want to tell me that you know.

Mr. NORIEGA. I am trying to tell you, but you won't give me an opportunity.

[Chairman Ballenger asked that Assistant Secretary Noriega provide an expanded response to the question posed by Congresswoman Waters. Mr. Noriega's response follows:]

I am trying to tell you, but you won't give me an opportunity. I am telling you that I have no knowledge that Constant in fact worked for the CIA. I believe that when he first came to the U.S., he claimed that he had worked for the CIA, but that is all I know.

Ms. WATERS. Okay. I think I know enough.

Now, you knew that these thugs had returned and that they had taken over Gonaives and Cap Haitien. Did you at any time publicly denounce the thugs that you knew were thugs before they came in and invaded Haiti? Did you ever denounce them?

Mr. NORIEGA. We said that these people should have no business in the political process and they should lay down their arms.

Ms. WATERS. Did you ever attempt to make them lay down their arms or to tell them that they were in exile, they were crooks and criminals and that they should not be in that country?

Mr. NORIEGA. They shouldn't be in Haiti. We have told them they should lay down their arms and go home. These violent folks have no——

[Chairman Ballenger asked that Assistant Secretary Noriega provide an expanded response to the question posed by Congresswoman Waters. Mr. Noriega's response follows:]

They shouldn't be in Haiti. We have told them they should lay down their arms and go home. One of our guiding principles for engagement in Haiti is that power will not be turned over to those who have participated in political violence, including irregular armed groups. Another principle is that Haitian citizens will be held accountable for past crimes through the system of justice, not through revenge.

Ms. WATERS. But you did nothing to enforce it?

Mr. NORIEGA. We are doing that now, ma'am.

Ms. WATERS. Yes, after the fact. After the fact, the same crooks and criminals and thugs and killers that you knew were in the country, that you did nothing to intervene with, you are now, after the fact, saying they should leave; is that right?

Mr. WELLER. Mr. Chairman, regular order.

Mr. NORIEGA. Ma'am, I said——

Mr. BALLENGER. The gentlewoman's time has passed.

Pardon me, Mr. Secretary, but I am relieving you of having to answer that question.

Mr. NORIEGA. That is all right. No problem.

Mr. BALLENGER. Ms. Jackson Lee.

Ms. JACKSON LEE. First of all, let me thank the Chairman and particularly the Ranking Member for the effort they have made to have this hearing, which happens to be particularly timely, but all of the Members who worked so hard that are on this particular Committee that really generated this meeting, all of the standing Members that are there—Congressmen Payne and Meek, Barbara Lee and Ms. Watson and others who are on the Committee—I thank you very much, and I thank you for the courtesies of allowing us to be here.

Mr. Noriega, this is not a personal inquiry, it is not personal against you. I can tell you that there is a great deal of emotion because many of us have taken personally the bleeding in the streets, the mutilating and the murdering that has been occurring. And, of course, we take personally words such as a "rule by tyranny," and we take personally the seemingly unceasing attack on an ex-priest that through a great deal of his life has spent making efforts to the extent of possibly a loss of life to preserve democracy.

To this very distinguished gentleman that is in the room let me, first of all, acknowledge you and offer to you my deepest understanding, because those of us who lived through the era here in the United, States as we still fight against racism and hostilities and discrimination, are reminded of those who marched across the Edmond Pettis Bridge and the dogs and hoses that came about, and the fact that some of those who were marching were unfortunately terribly injured.

If you would, accept our sympathies.

To Mr. Noriega, let me pose this series of questions to you: Have you ever had a sense of fear of your life or the fear of your life and that of your family members? Do you have any history of that or any way that you could understand that by personal experience?

Mr. NORIEGA. Yes, yes, absolutely.

Ms. JACKSON LEE. So you have been in fear of your life?

Mr. NORIEGA. Yes.

Ms. JACKSON LEE. Might you share with us?

Mr. NORIEGA. No.

Ms. JACKSON LEE. You have been in fear of your life when and where?

Mr. NORIEGA. That is none of your business, ma'am.

Ms. JACKSON LEE. Well, let me say this. Since you are going to be hostile, let me say this.

Mr. NORIEGA. No, no. It is a silly question.

Ms. JACKSON LEE. My business is to find out whether the Administration lied and whether or not you kidnapped and coerced Mr. Aristide. So that is my business.

Mr. NORIEGA. Please ask me those questions, and I will answer them.

Ms. JACKSON LEE. I would imagine—excuse me. I am talking, not you. Since you started off being rude, then let me be rude. In any event, let me just say this.

My understanding of Mr. Aristide's position on that eve where he was, if you will, thrown out of his own country, is that he was told by American officials, maybe with the involvement of the CIA, that his life was in jeopardy and that the security would be removed.

My question to you is whether or not you have any firsthand knowledge of that activity.

My second point is—and you don't need to comment on this—I am reminded of the attack on Chairman Karzai's, or President Karzai's life in Afghanistan, reminded of the fact that we did not ask him to leave his country, but we provided the necessary security so that, thank God, his life was spared. He didn't have to make that decision.

Do you have any firsthand knowledge of saying to President Aristide that your security would be immediately removed?

Mr. NORIEGA. It is not true. As a matter of fact, there is an organization that, as a private contractor, has provided security for——

[Chairman Ballenger asked that Assistant Secretary Noriega provide an expanded response to the question posed by Congresswoman Jackson-Lee. Mr. Noriega's response follows:]

It is not true. As a matter of fact, there is an organization that, as a private contractor, has provided security for Aristide, paid for by the Government of Haiti. This organization provided for Aristide's security throughout all of the events that led to his resignation. A U.S. government security team consulted with his security detail on the prevailing security conditions. We approved of that contact because we were concerned about the security of U.S. citizens, including Mrs. Aristide and the Americans who served in his private security detail. However, I am not aware of the details of these exchanges. After those conversations, Aristide contacted the Embassy, through his private security firm, to ask what the U.S. Ambassador thought would be best for Haiti. Our answer was that he, Aristide, had to make that judgment. Aristide's private security personnel stayed with him after he made the decision to resign, accompanied him to the airport, and boarded the aircraft with him for the trip to the Central African Republic.

Ms. JACKSON LEE. Do you have any knowledge of saying to him that his security would be removed at that time.

Mr. NORIEGA. I am trying to answer the question. It is not true.

Ms. JACKSON LEE. If that is not true, then I assume that you would welcome, as I have asked both the leaders of this House for a full congressional investigation that would investigate the Administration as to whether or not that is true. Would you welcome that investigation?

Mr. NORIEGA. The Congress has an obligation to oversee——

Ms. JACKSON LEE. You would welcome that investigation, yes or no.

Mr. NORIEGA. The Congress has an obligation to oversee the Executive Branch.

Ms. JACKSON LEE. Is that yes or no? Is that yes or no? Is that yes or no.

Mr. NORIEGA. We would cooperate with any——

Ms. JACKSON LEE. And you would welcome that investigation, yes or no?

Mr. NORIEGA. We will welcome—we will cooperate with any inquiry that the Congress deems appropriate.

Ms. JACKSON LEE. Thank you very much.

Let me proceed with my questions on another important aspect that I am concerned about.

Is the United States a member of the U.N. Security Council?

Mr. NORIEGA. Yes.

Ms. JACKSON LEE. So as I understand it, by way of a report on February 25, 2004, the U.N. News Service, the United Nations Security Council today deplored the Haitian opposition's rejection of proposals from two regional organizations that could form the basis for a peaceful compromise. And so you were—the United States was a part of that offering of a compromise——

Mr. WELLER. Mr. Chairman, regular order.

Ms. JACKSON LEE. Thank you very much, Mr. Chairman. Let me just conclude, Mr. Chairman, by saying this.

Mr. WELLER. Mr. Chairman, regular order.

Ms. JACKSON LEE. CARICOM has been totally disrespected by this Administration.

Mr. WELLER. Regular order, Mr. Chairman.

Ms. JACKSON LEE. And you have violated the relationship with the Caribbean——

Mr. WELLER. Regular order, Mr. Chairman.

Ms. JACKSON LEE. And we will never be able to mend it, because there is no way of providing the support that the United States has.

Mr. WELLER. Mr. Chairman, regular order.

Ms. JACKSON LEE. All I can say, Mr. Chairman, is that we have failed to be the kind of friend to Haiti that we should have been.

Mr. BALLENGER. Everybody else had to stop, so I am trying to be fair to everybody.

Ms. Corrine Brown is next.

Ms. CORRINE BROWN OF FLORIDA. First, let me say that I hope you received my letter of apology at our last meeting. I did not mean anything personally to you, but I stand by what I said about this Administration's policy, pertaining to the Haitian people, is racist, and there is no way around it.

In our discussion, there was a lot of discussion about elections, and of course, everybody knows that I take any discussion about elections personally, because I experienced, I guess, the American-style coup d'etat.

I heard you say something about not a traditional coup d'etat in Haiti; well, we had not a traditional coup d'etat in Florida; in my district alone, 227,000 votes were thrown out. And I personally went to Haiti and monitored the election, and I can tell you it was just as fair as the one that we had in Florida.

Now, my concern—and my concern was there about the Haitians that have been turned back, how we have dual policies, we do not let not one Haitian come into this country, we send them back into the middle of this war that is going on, and we turn on the television and we see people being slaughtered. So my concern still is for the Haitian people. We have our military there, and I am grateful that they are there, but they are standing by while people are being slaughtered in the streets.

What are our plans for the Haitian people? In talking to other leaders in the Caribbean countries, they are—they indicated that the United States of America blocked us going in, intervening. We stopped the other members of the international community from going in and helping to stabilize this country.

Can you tell me what you know about that to be true, and what are we going to do to help the hard-working Haitian people?

Now, I know it is a difference between them and Iraq, because in Iraq they have oil, and in Haiti they have nothing but a history—and we just left Black History Month—they do have a history of helping the United States.

Now, I want to know, what are we going to do to help those people, my brothers and sisters, those children?

Mr. NORIEGA. Yes, ma'am. Thank you very much. I did receive your letter, and I have never for a moment doubted that your concern and engagement and interest and passion about the subject was anything less than sincere and motivated by your interest in the well-being of the Haitian people.

The United States did not block other countries from intervening. There was some allusion that maybe we did this vis-a-vis France. The suggestion was that, somehow, Secretary Powell was being deceptive about that; and of course, that is not true. We did not block them——

[Chairman Ballenger asked that Assistant Secretary Noriega provide an expanded response to the question posed by Congresswoman Corinne Brown. Mr. Noriega's response follows:]

Yes, ma'am. Thank you very much. I did receive your letter, and I have never for a moment doubted that your concern and engagement and interest and passion about the subject was anything less than sincere and motivated by your interest in the well-being of the Haitian people.

The United States did not block other countries from intervening. There was some allusion that maybe we did this vis-a-vis France. We did not block them or any other country from intervening on a bilateral basis, but no country chose to intervene before Aristide's resignation. This was for the same reasons I described for the U.S. decision not to intervene. No country wanted to place troops and lives at risk by putting them into the middle of an unresolved, armed conflict. Your question suggests that perhaps we stopped the international community from going in to stabilize Haiti. I think this may be a reference to the UN Security Council Resolution that some Caribbean Community member states applied for on February 26. If so, I would respectfully point out to you that the Security Council voted 15–0 not to involve the UN at that point. In deciding not to intervene, the Security Council gave the same reasons I have stated for not involving the U.S.—it did not want to put a UN stabilization force in between two warring factions.

To answer your question about what we are doing to help the Haitian people, we are doing a lot and will do much more. The U.S. has provided over $3 million in emergency aid since mid-February, on top of the $55 million in regular assistance budgeted for fiscal year 2004. We supported, and of course will continue to support, re-engagement of the International Financial Institutions. Since last July, when the Haitian government cleared its arrears to the Inter-American Development Bank (IDB), it has approved loans totaling $398 million. The IDB has distributed $47 million of this amount, all but $30 million of the rest are project loans that will pay out over 5–10 years, thereby making a substantial contribution to Haiti's long-term development. On a bilateral basis, the Administration expects an intensive engagement in Haiti's reconstruction over the next several years to help restore the capacity to govern, develop a professional and independent police force, promote economic development, and support free and fair elections.

Ms. CORRINE BROWN OF FLORIDA. Sir, it was not just France; we talked to several different countries. I fear to call their names, because, you know, if we are not in lockstep with this Administration, they take you out. So I am not going to call anybody's name, any country's name, not me.

Mr. NORIEGA. I understand the discretion that you are showing by not naming particular countries, but I can say that any country that wanted to send police or troops was free to do so. Of course, the United States would not be in a position to prevent any one of the 150 countries in the world from contributing to Haiti.

Ms. CORRINE BROWN OF FLORIDA. My understanding, after talking to these various leaders, is that the United States of America, under the Bush Administration, blocked the international community from going in and stabilizing this country. I mean, they were in the process of trying to do something.

My understanding on Sunday, and we went in on Saturday night, in the heat of the night, in the middle of the night and took out Aristide.

Mr. NORIEGA. Regarding the reference to blocking assistance, I think I would be aware of any of that, and I do not have any—there is no——

Ms. CORRINE BROWN OF FLORIDA. Did we tell other countries? Now, be careful. Did we tell other countries that we did not want them to intervene?

Mr. NORIEGA. No, we did not do that. We did not do that. And as far as—one final thing to the personal security thing that I think Congresswoman Jackson——

Ms. CORRINE BROWN OF FLORIDA. You are going to have to answer her question on her time.

Mr. NORIEGA. I am sorry. I thought——

Ms. CORRINE BROWN OF FLORIDA. I want to protect Aristide, but I want to know about the Haitian people. They are being shot down as we speak here today. What are we doing?

Mr. NORIEGA. We will gradually build up this presence, bring in other countries that will provide security, get the Haitian National Police stood up again, let them do their work in a professional way, bring some resources in, some technical assistance, get them to start doing that.

We will also have to look at the economic side, look at ways to create jobs and investment.

Ms. CORRINE BROWN OF FLORIDA. Thank you, Mr. Chairman.

Mr. BALLENGER. Ms. Christensen.

Ms. CORRINE BROWN OF FLORIDA. Thank you, Mr. Chairman.

Mr. BALLENGER. Well, thank you.

Mrs. CHRISTENSEN. Thank you, Mr. Chairman.

I have been in and out, so I am not sure what questions have been asked and answered. But let me start with this.

For at least the past couple of years, Members of the Congressional Black Caucus have been working to have the $145 or $150 million in development loans released to Haiti, and at every turn, at every turn, it was pointed out to us that it was our country who was blocking the release of those funds.

Would you not say that the inability or denying Haiti access as the basis of development assistance to help develop their infrastructure contributed to this? Would you not say that we were complicit in the downfall of that government?

Mr. NORIEGA. Ma'am, the decision to link the delivery of that international financial assistance to a political settlement was made in late 2000. In September 2002, based on OAS Resolution 822, that I helped shepherd through the OAS Permanent Council, we delinked that. So, quite frankly, this Administration undid something that the previous Administration did by allowing that aid to start to flow. The IDB lending began.

And I will ask Adolfo Franco to address that.

Mr. FRANCO. Yes, Congresswoman. In the first instance, loans from the Inter-American Development Bank had to be made consistent with the rules of that bank, and as you know, Haiti was in arrears with that bank, and until the arrears were cleared and Haiti was able to secure a bridge loan, consistent with the bank's own rules, the United States could not do—it was not possible to move forward on those loans.

However, I would tell you this. We are the largest bilateral donor in Haiti. We provided $16 million more than the Congress requested for Haiti last year.

Mrs. CHRISTENSEN. Our contributions have been diminishing. In addition to that, we had many, many meetings with representatives of the IDB in Haiti and here, and we know that different approaches to dealing with that have been used in other countries, and Haiti was never afforded the opportunity that other countries similarly situated had.

Mr. FRANCO. As you know, Congresswoman, Haiti was able to secure a bridge loan to clear its arrears, and I believe President Iglesias was in Haiti in July.

Mrs. CHRISTENSEN. By that time, so much time had passed.

Ms. WATERS. Only $3 million of that money has been given to Haiti. They say they cannot meet the conditions, even after they made them do the bridge loan.

Mr. FRANCO. These are the Inter-American Development Bank's conditions. These are not the conditions of the United States Government. These are the conditions set forth by the bank's own rules.

Mrs. CHRISTENSEN. We were pretty much assured that if we could get our country to agree, the IDB would be willing to restructure that loan in any possible way that had been used in other countries. They outlined several ways for us to do it, but we could not get our country to agree to it.

Mr. FRANCO. I have been personally in contact with the bank officials, both bank officials and the U.S. executive representative of the bank, and that is not true.

What was difficult for Haiti, because of its arrears and because of its difficult situation was to clear that issue before the loans could move forward. Once that was cleared, the loans did move forward.

In terms of the disbursement mechanisms, Congresswoman Waters, those are the bank's disbursement mechanisms. I do not believe anybody until today has suggested that we manipulated the bank's rules, the first time I have heard it. I have never heard that from my independent official at the bank or any executive director at the bank.

Mrs. CHRISTENSEN. Well, let me just ask one other question, because what we have—our discussions differ from what we are hearing here today; and forgive me if this question has been asked.

The U.S. was part of the development of the CARICOM proposal and endorsed that proposal?

Mr. NORIEGA. Yes, ma'am.

Mrs. CHRISTENSEN. What was the process whereby the U.S. Government decided to abandon that and to take unilateral action that resulted in President Aristide's leaving?

Mr. NORIEGA. Each country made a decision for itself on what to do after the CARICOM plan was not implemented. It was not implemented because the opposition refused to accept and participate in it.

Mrs. CHRISTENSEN. Was CARICOM involved in your decision?

Mr. NORIEGA. They were aware of our decision. They all made decisions for themselves not to intervene.

Mrs. CHRISTENSEN. But there was essentially an agreement, was there not, by virtue of that proposal being essentially signed off on by CARICOM——

Mr. NORIEGA. We did want to work together.

Mrs. CHRISTENSEN. Did you break that agreement, and why?

Mr. NORIEGA. You are exactly right. We did want to work together. There was a consensus to try to work together, but countries had to make a decision on whether they would commit their own troops.

Mr. BALLENGER. Okay.

Congressman Porter Goss.

Mr. GOSS. Thank you very much, Mr. Chairman. I apologize for having to leave, so I may have some questions that are repetitive.

But first of all, I would like to thank Mr. Noriega and the other gentlemen at the table. I want to thank you for the very fine work you have done in a very difficult situation.

I know you are very familiar with the situation in Haiti; you have been working on it for years, trying to relieve the plight of a country that is full of people that are burdened with medical problems, food problems and, of course, leadership problems in their struggle to get to democracy. That is well-known. It is not just my opinion, it is certainly the opinion, apparently, of all of the other countries that have been involved with trying to help Haiti as well.

The efforts that you have made, I think, have led to results that are probably the best that we can have. The amount of misinformation surrounding what is going on is extremely disturbing and, I am afraid, may actually be leading to inciting some further violence and some further bad happenings and actually, threatening the lives of some of our Armed Forces there. So I would hope that any discussion that we have, in public particularly, would be handled in such a thoughtful, polite way, that it would be constructive to a solution of the problem, rather than to inciting and emoting passions that are clearly out of place at this time.

My question is, first of all, is there any truth in the fact that Mr. Aristide was kidnapped?

Mr. NORIEGA. No, sir. And you are correct to point out that the statements that he was and the mentioning of the names of U.S. Foreign Service Officers who were directly involved in helping that man on television, and accusing them of helping kidnap and strong-arm him, put the lives of those individual people on the ground in Haiti in jeopardy, and it is extraordinarily irresponsible.

Mr. GOSS. Thank you. I agree with you totally.

Secondly, with regard to the question of Mr. Aristide's freedom to make his own choice, could you comment on whether the government forced him to leave or whether he was given an opportunity to make a decision?

Mr. NORIEGA. He had an opportunity to make a decision, and I appreciate the opportunity to expand on the answer. There was some reference earlier that the United States said we would pull his security.

As a matter of fact, when this violence was beginning in earnest, we got word that his private security company which was providing his security wanted to augment their presence by adding additional people. I made a point of telling people that would be involved in the licensing of that request, if you get that, expedite it.

We, by all means, want to have the man's personal security taken care of. We were not, however, in the final analysis, willing to put American servicemen on the ground to be part of a political process that would do no more than keep him in power in an unchecked way outside the context of a political agreement where we might actually be able to have a sustainable political process in place.

Mr. GOSS. I congratulate you for arranging, under difficult circumstances, for the safe departure of Mr. Aristide.

Was there any involvement by the CIA in his departure that you are aware of?

Mr. NORIEGA. I am not aware of any involvement.

Mr. GOSS. I understand that you have not had the opportunity to answer fully some of the questions that have been put to you. Are there any of the questions that have been put to you that you would like to further expand on?

Mr. NORIEGA. A couple of points.

Mr. GOSS. Please, sir.

Mr. NORIEGA. On the disintegration of the Haitian institutions, which we supposedly encouraged, we actually had $1 billion worth of assistance going in there over the last 10 years, and it was squandered because these institutions were undermined.

Take the specific example of HNP, the Haitian National Police. They were undermined by underfunding by the Haitian government, by politicization almost immediately, by the use of them to carry out political murders. And finally Congress made the decision to cut off assistance to the HNP because of narcotics corruption.

It was not a decision of the Executive Branch to do that, and I believe it was done during the previous Administration. But Congress decided that it could no longer invest in that institution, and it is very important, because the gangs that Aristide used to govern the situation——

Ms. WATERS. Regular order, Mr. Chairman. Regular order, Mr. Chairman.

Mr. GOSS. Thank you very much.

Mr. NORIEGA. I am sorry.

Mr. BALLENGER. Jan Schakowsky.

Ms. SCHAKOWSKY. Thank you, Mr. Chairman. I appreciate your allowing those of us who care about Haiti, but are not on this Committee, to ask some questions.

Let me just first say it is obvious, Mr. Noriega, that you think that the very distinguished Congressional Black Caucus, Members of Congress who, in my view, have the most expertise and the most interest in Haiti, not only for President Aristide, but for the people of Haiti, who almost to a person disagree with you, are all wrong. And it seems to me that that would justify a full and objective investigation of exactly what happened.

We need to understand, since there is such disagreement, every dollar that was spent by the United States in Haiti over the last while leading up to this, how the USAID dollars were spent or the CIA dollars were spent; and we ought to examine carefully the intelligence.

You know, many Members in this Congress relied in the past on intelligence that happened to be all wrong, and we need to look at that carefully as well, the intelligence that you based your decisions on.

I am very interested also in what happened that night. I was in conversation with Mrs. Aristide in Haiti at about 6:30 p.m., and there was absolutely no hint whatsoever that this was going to be the night when they were leaving. So I was wondering if there is a State Department memorandum or a written record or a plan that involved the United States that we could have a copy of now, if there were any communications that were written that we could look at that would help to explain exactly what happened.

Mr. NORIEGA. Ma'am and Mr. Chairman, the Committee, through its oversight responsibilities and powers, can request information from the Administration and we will accommodate it in the normal way.

Mr. BALLENGER. That is what I was hoping, that people would submit questions, and I am sure you will be glad to answer them.

Ms. SCHAKOWSKY. I will submit additional questions.

What time was the first conversation with President Aristide, is one question I have about this? And was the letter of resignation composed by, not just signed by, actually composed by President Aristide?

Mr. NORIEGA. I do not know who composed the letter, but it was not composed by us. I assume that he wrote it. It had his flare.

But the first conversation with him, I believe, was after 9 p.m. We had received word through an emissary that he wanted to pose some questions to us and that he——

Ms. SCHAKOWSKY. Are you saying, for the record here, that the first contact was from Mr. Aristide to the Embassy or to U.S. representatives to discuss his leaving?

Mr. NORIEGA. To discuss his departure. We had contacts with his emissaries throughout all of this period of time.

Ms. SCHAKOWSKY. About leaving?

Mr. NORIEGA. No, no, no. It was about staying, as a matter of fact.

Ms. SCHAKOWSKY. Exactly. That was my sense at 6:30 p.m.

Mr. NORIEGA. That is right.

Ms. SCHAKOWSKY. Are you saying, though, that he made the first overture? This is important to get on the record.

Mr. NORIEGA. The first comments that clearly suggest that he was considering leaving came from an emissary of his, who posed some questions to us, to Ambassador Foley. The questions were——

[Chairman Ballenger asked that Assistant Secretary Noriega provide an expanded response to the question posed by Congresswoman Schakowsky. Mr. Noriega's response follows:]

The first comments that clearly suggested that Aristide was considering leaving came from an emissary, who posed some questions to us, to Ambassador Foley. The questions were—did the U.S. think it was in Haiti's best interest for Aristide to stay or to go; would we protect his wealth and property; what would happen to his supporters and key Cabinet ministers; and did he have a choice of destination. These questions came to us through Aristide's private security personnel. So yes, Aristide did make the first overture.

Ms. SCHAKOWSKY. I have heard those, but you are saying that at no time before that was there any suggestion from the U.S. Government in any way that he should resign and leave, and that we would—we would help him leave?

Mr. NORIEGA. I am not aware of every conversation that took place with a so-called U.S. Government official.

Ms. SCHAKOWSKY. When was the plane ordered?

Mr. NORIEGA. I think it was probably after 1 a.m. It would have been after he indicated that he was interested.

Ms. SCHAKOWSKY. When he was on the plane, were they told that they could not even raise the window shades?

Mr. NORIEGA. I am not aware that that is the case. I have heard that allegation, but I have heard other allegations that are absolutely inaccurate.

Ms. SCHAKOWSKY. Was he told on the way to the Central African Republic where he was going? In advance of what we heard was about 20 minutes before they landed, did he know?

Mr. NORIEGA. I do not think so. I think he was told right before the arrival.

Ms. SCHAKOWSKY. Why would that be?

Mr. NORIEGA. I can answer the question if you——

Mr. BALLENGER. Go ahead.

Mr. NORIEGA. There were members of his security detail who were armed. This is a very unusual "kidnapping" where you let the man's bodyguards carry arms. Frankly, we were concerned that because they had weapons on the plane, that they might react, because he was not going to his desired location, but we were taking him somewhere near there, because the desired location had turned him down. They didn't want to accept him. I am sorry.

Mr. BALLENGER. Congressman Kirk.

Mr. KIRK. Mr. Secretary, good to see you. When did French Foreign Minister Dominique de Villepin withdraw support for President Aristide?

Mr. NORIEGA. It must have been about 4 or 5 days before his departure. We did not follow suit as he clearly was out in front of us on that.

Mr. KIRK. As I remember, the French Government was very public about—after having been staunch supporters of President Aristide, of saying that they felt that some sort of transition was necessary for law and order and democratic growth in Haiti?

Mr. NORIEGA. I think they asked him to consider what was best for the Haitian people.

Mr. KIRK. My understanding of the Secretary's working relationship with the Foreign Minister of Development is—in many ways has been reborn after some disagreements over Iraq.

Can you give me an assessment of how the French and United States Governments now see this problem?

Mr. NORIEGA. They see it as a shared problem, that the international community shares responsibility to try to help the Haitian people at this point. We are working together with them, putting some force on the ground to help the Haitian people by tranquilizing the situation, providing a secure and stable environment so this political succession to a new government can continue.

Mr. KIRK. Is there any significant difference between the French and United States position on Haiti?

Mr. NORIEGA. Not really, sir.

Mr. KIRK. Let me take you back to September 18, 1994. President Clinton had asked President Carter and then private citizen Colin Powell to go to Port-au-Prince and meet with General Cedras. It is my understanding that that was a very tense meeting. I was in a previous capacity; I was a lieutenant junior grade in the Navy Command Center at the time, and I remember full well the duty captain giving some very direct orders to private citizen Colin Powell.

President Clinton had ordered the invasion of Haiti to put President Aristide back into power. The 82nd Airborne Division had been launched out of Camp Lejeune, and when we told Colin Powell that United States forces were en route, we ordered him to leave the Haitian military headquarters there.

In a very dramatic moment, Colin Powell said he was not leaving, that he was going to stay there because he felt that he could negotiate a peaceful withdrawal of the coup d'etat leaders and bring President Aristide back to power peacefully. He describes actually being in the truck with General Cedras on the way to see the then-nominal President with hand grenades rolling on the floor as he thought he could bring a deal back.

I can tell you that it was with some personal bravery on Colin Powell's part, because the order to take out the Haitian military command had already been given by President Clinton. And in that military rule that some idiot never gets the word, we were furiously calling units telling them not to fire, because Colin Powell was still on the premises.

To his great credit and personal bravery, he brought about a peaceful settlement, and General Cedras left, and Americans entered Haiti and reinstalled President Aristide into power without a shot being fired, I think due to the personal bravery of Jimmy Carter and Colin Powell.

Mr. NORIEGA. And Sam Nunn.

Mr. KIRK. Sorry, and Senator Sam Nunn, correct. So I want the record to reflect the personal braveries.

I think it is a bit ironic to criticize Colin Powell, when he, probably more than anyone else, stared at General Cedras face-to-face, backed him down; and what was an invasion ordered by President Clinton then became a peaceful deployment of the international community to restore order there.

Mr. NORIEGA. Yes, Congressman, and I think that is why it is a source of great disappointment that 10 years later, the great investment of treasure and lives having been put on the line for President Aristide came to naught, and we saw a leader who was not able to lead effectively or honestly or justly and, unfortunately, sowed the seeds of his own demise in this circumstance.

Mr. KIRK. It might be that we need to—without defending the career of any Haitian politician, we need to defend the constitution of Haiti.

Mr. BALLENGER. Congressman, we cut everybody else off. I would like to ask unanimous consent that Mr. Meek and Mr. Conyers be the last to ask questions so we can get to the next panel.

So without further ado, Mr. Meek.

Without objection.

Mr. MEEK. Thank you, Mr. Chairman.

President Paquiot, I want to welcome you to the U.S. Congress. I am glad that you are here to share your testimony with me, and my family and I prayed for your speedy recovery, even when the incident took place.

Secretary Noriega, I must say that with as many Haitians that are trying to receive temporary protective status or even safe refuge in the United States, that you would bring the President here to speak before this Committee to drive your point home is really—in my opinion, really sad.

Mr. NORIEGA. I did not do that, sir. He is a witness at the next panel.

Mr. MEEK. He got here somehow, okay?

Mr. BALLENGER. He was my witness.

Mr. MEEK. Well, Mr. Chairman, I apologize to Mr. Noriega.

Mr. NORIEGA. That is all right.

Mr. MEEK. But the bottom line is that we have Haitians—and Secretary Dewey, I want to say the reason why it is down to three now is because the Coast Guard—am I correct that they are in the bay in Port-au-Prince right now? How close is the Coast Guard as it relates to being off the coast of Haiti, our U.S. Coast Guard?

Mr. DEWEY. Our Coast Guard maintains a presence off the coast.

Mr. MEEK. So you can see it from the coast; is that correct?

Mr. DEWEY. I am not sure you can see it from the coast.

Mr. MEEK. Well, television accounts, large shots, you can see our Coast Guard cutters there.

How many people have been repatriated?

Mr. DEWEY. Approximately 900.

Mr. MEEK. Approximately 900. I think when the President made the statement, Mr. Chairman, that Haitians should stay in Haiti, I think he really meant it, because if he did not put the force on the ground, he definitely put the force in the water. When we are there repatriating, Secretary Dewey, are they repatriated in port in Port-au-Prince?

Mr. DEWEY. In the vicinity of Port-au-Prince, Congressman, Killick Coast Guard Base.

Mr. MEEK. How does that happen? They just get off and they walk on to the street and go home, I guess?

Mr. DEWEY. That is essentially correct.

Mr. MEEK. Okay. The reason why, Mr. Chairman, that you do not have Haitians taking to the sea is because they actually have a bull's-eye on their backs when they get off at Port-au-Prince. So if they are trying to escape persecution, they will definitely lose their lives.

One other thing I want to add. As it relates to temporary protective status, I think it is very important that this Administration understands—for the bloated bodies that are in the street in Haiti, I do not know how many Haitians have to lose their lives.

Let's just talk about under normal circumstances, when Haitians are interdicted at sea or even when they make it to the port and shores of Miami. Our Homeland Security objects to their being released on probation or what have you, so I think this Administration has spoken to how it feels about Haitians.

Mr. Noriega, let me ask you, as it relates to the future of the Haitian people—we have met before, in the past, not in this hearing, but in other hearings. I am a Member of the Committee on Armed Services and Homeland Security Committee. I will tell you that I take great pride in our armed services and also for their safety. I do not want to say that you personally want to put their safety in jeopardy, but I must say the moves of the, Administration setting the tone that is in Haiti right now, I think would make things very difficult for a safe haven for our armed services.

Now, let me tell you this. In no way do I, nor should any other Member of this Congress, feel that they are putting the lives of our troops in jeopardy because we question the Executive Branch. I just want to let you know that.

I take personal offense when I hear that if Members are saying things—and I do not call names, and I do not think we should call names of people on the ground, but I would say this. For Members of the Congress not to be able to speak freely about how they feel, about the positions that the Executive Branch is taking, let alone the rebel forces who went through Guy Philippe, whom you seem to be very vaguely familiar with—this is him on the front page of *The New York Times*, parading through the streets of Port-au-Prince, thanks to the United States of America.

Here he is here, once again, *The Washington Post*, right here in our capital city, on the front cover. Does it look like he is not in charge? I want to tell you right now, he is very much in charge.

Let me ask you about the Prime Minister. Where is the Prime Minister now of Haiti?

Mr. NORIEGA. I am not sure.

Mr. MEEK. Can he leave his office?

Mr. NORIEGA. I am not sure.

Mr. MEEK. Is he protected?

Mr. NORIEGA. Yes.

Mr. MEEK. Mr. Guy Philippe said he was going to arrest him?

Mr. NORIEGA. I heard something of that nature.

Mr. MEEK. Did he have a meeting yesterday at 4 p.m. and he said any police chief who didn't show up that they would have to answer personally to him?

Mr. NORIEGA. I didn't hear that, but I don't doubt your word on this.

Mr. MEEK. Mr. Chairman, I just want to say that I think it is important not only that this Committee continues to move forth and get some of these questions answered, but this Committee definitely take the time out to go Haiti to find out exactly what is going on and also aboard our Coast Guard cutters to make sure there are translators that are there. Our meeting at the U.N. with the Secretary General, he was concerned about our refugee policy as it relates to giving people real interviews, not just some interviews. And that is the reason why, Mr. Secretary, you don't see a mass migration away.

And that is the reason why we still continue to see executions in Haiti. Mr. Noriega, I look forward to working with you to provide the very safety we need in Haiti

Mr. CUMMINGS. Mr. Chairman.

Mr. BALLENGER. Mr. Cummings.

Mr. CUMMINGS. Thank you very much, Mr. Chairman. I really appreciate your courtesy. Mr. Noriega—

Mr. BALLENGER. Can I ask a question? Can I say that you are the last individual?

Mr. MENENDEZ. Can we call Mr. Conyers' name out?

Mr. BALLENGER. Is Mr. Conyers not here?

Mr. CUMMINGS. I just have a few questions. Mr. Noriega, you know, I had an opportunity to talk to Secretary Powell on Saturday. And during those discussions, I was of the clear impression that President Aristide was in good hands. Secretary Powell was very clear that apparently there were 400 troops surrounding him. And that there were—there was a private security agency and that there was just absolutely no question about the fact that he was safe. I know this question may have arisen before because I am curious since I was involved in this personally, you know, can you tell me what happened that suddenly Sunday morning, he apparently—things changed or did they?

Mr. NORIEGA. It is interesting to me, too. We believe that his personal security was more or less tended to.

Mr. CUMMINGS. What did you say?

Mr. NORIEGA. We believe that his personal security was tended to. I think he was in good hands. There was perimeter security around the palace. And there was close-in security by a professional security firm that has been with him for many years, maybe 5 or 6. And we were concerned in general that was there an acute threat to him. There was some question as to how reliable some of the people in the palace guard were, but we had an impression that the some of the people around him were able to deal with any problems of that kind. But the impression was that there was not an immediate, acute threat to him. That was my impression.

And I was rather surprised that he decided to leave. And up until the last minute, up until the time he got on the plane, he could have changed his mind, and I frankly expected him to change his mind. That is why we didn't ask for a plane until the very, very last minute—relatively in the last minute in the process, because we wanted to have a real sense whether he was really interested in leaving or not.

Mr. CUMMINGS. So I take it that you were surprised when he said that he was taken away pretty much against his will?

Mr. NORIEGA. I was very surprised. Well, actually when I thought about it, it was not too much of a surprise that he would do that. I guess I was shocked at the chutzpah, because there are so many witnesses to all of this, including his personal guards who now have said publicly he wasn't kidnapped. And I was disappointed that that allegation was repeated so widely. But as far as we were concerned, we were at his request, facilitating his safe departure from the country.

Mr. CUMMINGS. One of the things that Secretary Powell also talked about was the difficulty that might come about. And by the way, Secretary General of the U.N. also said the same thing that there might be some difficulty in reestablishing a democracy here, you know, getting it moving again because you have got the rebel forces who are trying to take apart—you know, be a part of the process. You have Aristide supporters who want to be part of the process. And it seems as if things appear—you know, trying to pull these forces, there are other forces coming together to be part of the process. How do you see that working out?

Mr. NORIEGA. It is going to be difficult and we need to let the Haitian people make these decisions for themselves. There is a process for doing that. And little by little, I think we can establish some kind of political order and strengthen the institution of the government.

Mr. BALLENGER. Mr. Secretary and all you fellows, those that didn't have to answer all the questions, you have done a wonderful job. I apologize for the length of time and without further ado, you are free to go and we will call the next panel.

Mr. MENENDEZ. I assume that questions for this panel as well as the next, written questions are still open because we have a series of detailed questions that we want answers to.

Mr. BALLENGER. We would like to be able to get the full answers that you never got to give.

Mr. NORIEGA. I had my shots.

Ms. WATERS. Mr. Chairman, is there some way that you can encourage the answers to be given in a timely fashion? Some of us are still waiting to have our letters responded to that we sent to the State Department.

Mr. BALLENGER. He is more sympathetic to me than you, so I will ask him to do that.

Ms. WATERS. I will tell him, get our answers returned that we give to you.

Mr. NORIEGA. You deserve answers.

Ms. WATERS. And we are still waiting for some. I have sent you some letters that have not been answered. So please get it back to us, okay? Thank you, Mr. Chairman. I don't mind asking.

Mr. BALLENGER. We have a bunch of people that have been waiting a long time. And I am scared they are going to call on a vote, so if we can get the tables changed. And I know we have a couple members on this next panel that are very short on time and I am surprised they are still here. You have my apologies. I tried to cut it short.

Mr. MENENDEZ. Mr. Chairman, could I recommend that we have a rolling, as we have done in the Full Committee, that some Members go vote now and others come back so we can listen to these witnesses in recognition of the time?

Mr. BALLENGER. That is a great idea. Mr. Paquiot, we are going to keep going and we have two more people—he has to catch a plane.

Mr. MENENDEZ. Could I ask you what the order of the witnesses will be?

Mr. BALLENGER. The way we have it figured, Mr. Paquiot, Mr. Maguire and then Mr. Sachs. And the names I did not call, let me apologize to you, but those gentlemen had warned us ahead of time that they had limited time.

Mr. BALLENGER. And Mr. Sachs, good luck. Mr. Paquiot.

STATEMENT OF PIERRE-MARIE PAQUIOT, PRESIDENT, STATE UNIVERSITY OF HAITI

Mr. PAQUIOT. Mr. Chairman, and Members of the Subcommittee, I wish to thank you for the opportunity to testify before you this afternoon in order to share with you some of the bitter experiences of the Haitian people in general and my suffering in particular. Also, I appreciate the opportunity to engage with you in discussions on Haiti's future. Mr. Chairman, with your permission, I would like to submit the statement for the record.

Mr. BALLENGER. Without objection, yes, sir.

Mr. PAQUIOT. First of all I would like to say I am not the voice of any kind of political party in Haiti. I am not representing any kind of opposition. I am just a citizen concerned by the situation going on right now in Haiti and I would like to share with you some of my thoughts.

Haiti entered the 21st century with a grim reality. Poverty is the norm. Our people have inherited a vicious cycle that they are progressively less able to escape. Violence prevailed society and economy development eludes us. Tensions between the leaders of the various opposition political parties in Family Lavalas are the results of the May, 2000 local and parliamentary elections. The ensuing violence escalated to a point that all the gangs have been attacking opposition leaders and others who dare challenge the system. Journalists were subject to abuse in some senses and paid the ultimate price of death by practicing their profession. It is from this that I share my story.

The State University of Haiti is made up of 15 schools with approximately 800 faculty members and about 15,000 students. The Haitian Constitution of 1987 grants independent status to the State University of Haiti, although 100 persons come from the State and the autonomy of the university has been the subject of contention between the institutive body and the former President of Haiti, Mr. Aristide. And indeed, President Aristide's attempts to control the university over the past few years were met with strong and sustained opposition from the university. When President Aristide took office in February, 2001, I met with him to examine the problems facing the university. And as a matter of fact, I have to tell you that I was a very strong supporter of President Aristide. And in fact, I was fired from the university during the coup d'etat because of President Aristide. I submitted to the President a document which contained a set of recommendations for addressing the most crucial problems facing the nation. To this day, Mr. Aristide neither acknowledged nor acted on any of the recommendations. Ultimately, the problems between President Aristide and the university peaked on May 18, 2001, which is a flag day in Haiti, and which is also celebrated in Haiti as university day.

It was on this day that I, the President of the university delivered a speech to the Nation reminding the political parties, President Aristide's political party and also the opposition, the importance of our national motto, l'Union Fait La Force, which means liberty, equality and brotherhood.

Apparently, Mr. Aristide did not approve of my speech in which he was reminded of my offer to make the university facilities available as a neutral ground for his party and the various political party leaders to discuss the contested local and parliamentary election of May, 2000, the suggestion to which they had both initially agreed to. And soon after the speech, all breaks of conflict broke out in various schools inside the university. I don't have much time, so I will skip some details to go forward. And I am going on December 5. On December 5, 2003, a small group of students who are demonstrating against President Aristide—as they have the right to do it as any citizen, inside the school of human sciences, while President Aristide's armed thugs attempted to enter the campus to subdue the protest.

When I heard this was taking place, I immediately ended a meeting I was having with the Minister of Education of Mr. Aristide and went to the School of Human Science in order to examine first-hand the extent of damages to the university property and see how best to facilitate the safe exit of students from the campus without being harmed by Aristide's forces.

While I was inside talking with the students, a group of thugs armed with guns, clubs and rocks invaded the campus shooting, further destroying property and physically assaulting people, forcing those they brutalized and say [speaking in native language], which means "long live Aristide." I was beaten unmercifully and suffered two broken knees. I am not here to lament on my situation. The point is I want to share with you the situation that is going on in Haiti so that we can do something.

I don't have any hard feeling about President Aristide. As a matter of fact, I am very sad for President Aristide because he was very popular in Haiti and now he is in exile and somehow he is responsible for what happened to him. From there, I spent weeks in hiding. And given the extent of the injuries I suffered, it was doubtful whether I could ever walk again.

Mr. Chairman, I constantly consider myself lucky because I can sit before you today to give you eye witness testimony. Many of my fellow citizens will never see another day, whether they were against Aristide or for Aristide, that is not the point. Lives have been prematurely destroyed and ended during the struggle for freedom and freedom from fear. I can testify today in Washington, DC, thanks to God and to the many friends and caring individuals who contributed my safe departure from Haiti to get medical care here in the United States. Officials of the International Foundation for Electoral Assistance worked very hard in collaboration with partners like the Haitian Resources Development Foundation, the Public Diplomacy Office, and the consular section of the United States Embassy in Port-au-Prince to ensure the timely and safe exit from Haiti for me and my family.

Since my arrival to the United States of America on January 9, 2004, I have received tremendous support from the New Orleans medical and legal community and from the Haiti democracy project. The events of December 5, 2003 triggered the ultimate ground swell of opposition to President Aristide. People at least at the university level and all people from all walks of life realized then that the repression sponsored by Mr. Aristide or his government had no limit and had no respect for any institution.

It became extremely clear that Mr. Aristide was the principal source of problem and he did not have the legitimacy to be part of the long-term solution to heal Haiti. After many years of political turmoil due to the disputed election results, failed policies, mismanagement and human rights violations, Haiti and her friends in the international community currently face a very crucial challenge in developing an approach based on local leaders, national priorities to address the many development and political problems the countries has suffered. So I will——

Mr. BALLENGER. Mr. Paquiot, if you don't mind.

Mr. PAQUIOT. I will stop here, you know. What we need now in Haiti is the strong support of the international community. President Aristide belongs to the past. We must look forward so that nothing like that will ever again happen in Haiti.

Mr. BALLENGER. I don't know whether Mr. Sachs or Mr. Maguire. Mr. Maguire, I think you were the first one and you were recommended a long time ago. I am not going to the House Floor to vote so we can continue.

STATEMENT OF ROBERT MAGUIRE, PH.D., DIRECTOR OF PROGRAMS IN INTERNATIONAL AFFAIRS, TRINITY COLLEGE

Mr. MAGUIRE. Thank you, Mr. Chairman. I am very grateful for this opportunity to share my knowledge on Haiti with you. I have been working on Haiti 25 years, 20 of them as a civil servant in the same organization as Adolfo Franco. And what I see in Haiti occurring now is what I would call deja vu all over again. And I think this implies that if we are really going to understand Haiti, we need to look at not what is just going on, but we have to look backward. Secretary Powell said last week said he was disappointed with President Aristide and I think we all have been. There is much to be disappointed about.

And I would say we also need to be disappointed elsewhere. We need to be disappointed with the opposition to Mr. Aristide, their continuing intransigence, their failure to engage and even when they had Mr. Aristide in a corner two Saturdays ago, their refusal to engage with the CARICOM proposal does not merit them to be called a Democratic opposition. They are an opposition. They have still yet to earn the label "democratic."

They have been determined to broker their way into power. And what we see today in Haiti is not a struggle over issues, ideas or principles, it is a matter of a struggle over power. I think Secretary Powell's disappointment should also be extended to those whose policies and practices were enacted on his watch, policies and practices toward Haiti. I have outlined those in a paper here which I will be glad to submit to you published in November called, "United States Policy Toward Haiti, Engagement or Estrangement."

I traced in here in much greater detail than I can now how our policies have evolved in the last 5 years or so to be those that are meant to isolate the Haitian government, to withhold resources from it and to punish it. I would speak from experience, Mr. Chairman. I don't know if you recall this, but at one point I brought to you in March, 2001, Mr. Neptune, who was, at the time, the President of the Senate, Mr. Leslie Voltaire, who was one of the ministers and Mr. Bazin, another minister. I had invited them to come to Trinity college for a symposium so they could have their voices heard in Washington.

Initially, however, I had invited the Prime Minister and First Lady. I was told by intermediaries from our government, that this would not be possible that I was trying to embarrass the administration. And I felt this was a shame because we needed to have all voices on the table. We need to listen. We do not engage the government of Haiti. We talked at them and criticized them. There was this parallel presumptive policy I believe working over the past several years working to strengthen the opposition and embolden it and suggest through signals sent from Washington that that opposition zero option of not engaging with the Aristide government had the support from Washington.

I don't say this just myself. Our former Ambassador to Haiti, Honorable Dean Curran said it in his address to the Haitian-American Chamber of Commerce of July of last year when he was leaving. I would like to quote what Ambassador Curran said. He said:

> "There is incoherence in Haiti that has troubled me, the incoherence of the way Washington's views are interpreted here. Those of you who know me who will realize that since I have arrived here as President Clinton's Ambassador and then President Bush's, I have always talked straight about U.S. policy and what might and might not be new policy directions. But there were many in Washington and Haiti who preferred not to listen to me, the President's representative, but to their own friends in Washington."

The sirens of extremism on one hand or apologists on the other, they don't hold official positions. I call them the "Chimeres" of Washington. We had our Ambassador saying that, complaining and being concerned that there were signals coming from Washington that prohibited and emboldened the opposition and prohibited them from being part of a political solution. I think we need to look deeply into that because we have had a policy in my view that seemingly has been driven by a deeply rooted and strongly held aversion to one man, Jean-Bertrand Aristide and has seemed determined to put Haiti at risk, either to emasculate Mr. Aristide politically or to force him from office.

Mr. Aristide has many, many faults. I am not trying to defend him, but I think our policies pushed Mr. Aristide and his government more and more into a corner with predictable results. With fewer and fewer resources, the government was left managing scarcity. And in the Haitian political reality, managing scarcity means managing power and managing power means managing the street gangs. This is a long-held practice in Haiti. And I would say we are seeing the same practice being enacted today.

I would characterize what happened over the past 3 years as the gradual strangulation of the Haitian government with, ironically, Mr. Aristide providing the rope. But we do really not really engage him. We did not try to reinforce anything that he had done positive. And something in the last panel, there was a lot of discussion about Mr. Aristide's involvement in drug trafficking. I think we should note for the record that Mr. Aristide in 2003 turned over to the U.S. DEA Haiti's two leading drug traffickers, Jacques Ketan and another man named Jasmay Edijuan, and a number of smaller drug traffickers. Would he have done that if he was as complacent in drug trafficking as came out and was accused in the first panel? I don't think so.

But in any case, the departure of Mr. Aristide has been achieved and the phrase that comes to mind is that of victory. Those who wanted his departure both in Haiti and beyond it has seen Haiti descend into lawlessness, with gunmen and revenge and the settling of scores, the kind of dechoukaj that has government officials running to the airport now under United States protection fleeing the country, and the destruction of Haiti's infrastructure, the virtual vulcanization of the country by gangs.

And I think we need to look at the issue of narco-trafficking which, again, Haiti is essentially right now a narco-trafficking free state. There is no order out there in the countryside because of what has been going on. What can we do? I think we need to forge a bipartisan approach toward Haiti. And I think what would help us forge that approach is to first examine the issue of the Washington "Chimires" who are sending mixed messages to Haiti. And I noticed in *The Washington Post* the other day that *The Washington Post* was suggesting in its editorial that one organization that needs to be examined very carefully in this equation is the International Republican Institute and its role with working with the Haitian opposition. I suggest you need to look at that very carefully. I would also suggest——

Mr. BALLENGER. Could you sum it up, please?

Mr. MAGUIRE. We need to support in Haiti a policy of political inclusion. All political actors in Haiti have been working toward exclusion. It is the struggle for power. We need to get all the political actors under the tent so all can have responsibility in the process. This will not happen by having the Lavalas people chased out of the country now by armed thugs, and it will not happen by having an electoral process in Haiti where it is always winner take all. We need to look for a solution in Haiti that can be a proportional representation so that a small political party with 10 percent of the votes gets 10 percent of the seats and 10 percent of the responsibility to engage in the process. I will stop there.

[The prepared statement of Mr. Maguire follows:]

PREPARED STATEMENT OF ROBERT MAGUIRE, PH.D., DIRECTOR OF PROGRAMS IN INTERNATIONAL AFFAIRS, TRINITY COLLEGE

Thank you, Mr. Chairman, for inviting me to speak before you and other members of the subcommittee and the U.S. House of Representatives today. I am happy to have this opportunity to share my insights and analysis on what is going on in Haiti. I have followed Haiti and Haiti-US policy issues for 25 years. Over that time I have come to know the country both from the 'bottom-up' through work at the Inter-American Foundation, a U.S. government agency, where I held responsibility for its grassroots development programs in Haiti, and from the 'top down' through both work at the U.S. Department of State in the Bureau of Western Hemisphere Affairs and scholarly activities at Johns Hopkins, Georgetown, and Brown Universities. I continue my involvement with Haiti as the Director of the Trinity College Haiti Program in Washington, DC. This program has been supported by the Ford and the Rockefeller Foundations.

DEJA VU ALL OVER AGAIN

Since this is a time of year when many of us begin to turn our attention to baseball, allow me to open my remarks by citing a phrase made famous by one of the sport's most colorful characters, Yogi Berra, who coined the expression "deja vu all over again." What we are seeing today in Haiti is something akin to that expression. And, as the expression implies, to understand the present we need to look backward.

Today, in the streets of Port-au-Prince and in other cities and towns of Haiti, we have been seeing the kind of murder and mayhem that characterized the country between 1991 and 1994, following a violent coup d'etat carried out by Haiti's army, leading to three years of brutal de facto military rule. Gunmen in fatigues roam the streets, menacing citizens and waving their automatic weapons arrogantly. Bodies mysteriously turn up at intersections in city streets, some of them face down with hands bound and bullet holes in their backs. Rampaging mobs of civilians and erstwhile soldiers and members of paramilitary death squads attack public and private property, looting, burning and destroying in a practice that Haitians call dechoukaj, or uprooting.

Elected and appointed government officials, in fear of their lives, are either going into hiding within Haiti or fleeing the country. In press reports released earlier today, it is stated that U.S. Marines have become ambulant bodyguards for Haitian officials rushing to the airport to save themselves. Also, we have begun to receive reports of meetings between the armed thugs dressed up in military fatigues and members of the unarmed opposition, and of tense confrontations between US military officials and the thugs. And, finally, we have begun to receive reports that cracks are already forming in the facade of unity among the armed and unarmed opponents of the recently uprooted, elected President, Jean-Bertrand Aristide, as Haiti's next struggle for power begins in earnest.

Yes, Mr. Chairman, this is certainly a case of "deja vu all over again."

MULTIPLE DISAPPOINTMENTS

Last week, Secretary of State Colin L. Powell stated that he had been "disappointed" with Haiti's now-deposed president, Jean-Bertrand Aristide. Secretary Powell is correct in this statement, as there is no doubt that Mr. Aristide provided much to be disappointed about. But I wonder if Mr. Powell is also disappointed in Haiti's self-proclaimed democratic opposition, a group of political and economic leaders who have also given us much to criticize and regret. The single-minded intransigence of this largely ad hoc group toward achieving its one, unifying objective—the removal of Mr. Aristide from office—has motivated it to behave rather undemocratically. Its leaders have failed to engage in true democratic process as measured by elections and by negotiated solutions to political problems. Instead, they have acted with a veto from an empty chair from the negotiating table, repeatedly undermining or thwarting internationally-led attempts to find a solution to Haiti's political crisis. Also, and particularly over the past two months, they have practiced that deeply rooted Haitian political practice of giving a 'wink and a nod' to violence in the street if you believe it furthers your political objectives.

I wonder, as well, if Mr. Powell was disappointed, or perhaps even outraged, by the failure of the unarmed opposition to respond to the latest international urgings, two weekends ago, when both he, via telephone, and his Assistant Secretary for Western Hemisphere, Mr. Roger Noriega, in person, pushed for this group to finally agree to take its seat at the negotiating table—when the odds appeared highly favorable for it to achieve an objective of political inclusion. The CARICOM plan, a solid recipe for achieving a negotiated, non-violent solution to Haiti's long lasting and disastrous political crisis, supported not only by the United States, but by all the hemisphere's democratic governments, was simply rejected out-of-hand by this so-called democratic group.

This failure of US influence—perhaps we can say of US diplomacy—is doubly shocking since the personalities who comprise this opposition have been widely perceived as allies—even sycophants—of Washington. Among these personalities are individuals who have participated in an array of political strategy meetings organized by the International Republican Institute using US government funds, and who have repeatedly visited Washington over the past three years. And, at least one of the highest profile leaders of this faction, Mr. Andre Apaid, is a US citizen.

As this veteran Haiti-watcher scans this political landscape, I get a strong sense of Haitian *deja vu all over again*, as self-styled and unelected political leaders seek the ways and means to broker their way into power. In their mind's eye, again taking a page from deeply rooted Haitian political practice, their means justify their ends. And what are those ends? Allow me to state, Mr. Chairman, that what we have been seeing in Haiti is not a political struggle of competing issues, ideas, and principals. What we have been seeing in Haiti is nothing more than a struggle among the political class and its allies, and the incumbent government to seize, and/or to hold on to, power. Let us hope that the dust of confrontation and violence settles in Haiti and that moderate, reasonable voices, with viable ideas, will emerge from among those struggling for power and some true democratic credentials will begin to be earned. Let us hope, also, that new, more democratic voices, less tainted by participation in the tragic political confrontations of the past three years, will come forth to relieve the country of its largely failed leadership on both sides of the current political equation.

THE CONDUCT OF U.S. POLICY TOWARD HAITI

In terms of disappointment, Mr. Chairman and members of the sub-committee, I also wonder whether this sense of Mr. Powell has extended to those who have been largely responsible for the conduct of U.S. policy toward Haiti since January 2001. As I have outlined in Trinity College Haiti Program Briefing Paper Number 8, *US Policy Toward Haiti: Engagement or Estrangement*, published last November, over the past ten years, US policy toward Haiti has evolved from one where our government was constructively engaged with the government of Haiti in an attempt to nurture democratic institutions and democratic practice in this country trying to find its way out of 200 years of bad and mostly authoritarian governance, to a policy that worked to isolate the Haitian government, withhold resources from it, punish it, and push it into a corner.

Concurrently, as we constantly chastised that government, our efforts focused more and more exclusively on working with Haiti's opposition groups. In following this path, we sacrificed carefully constructed leverage and influence with Haitian elected political actors, many of whom are already pre-disposed to be distrustful of the United States as a dominant force in Haitian political reality that has not always made choices that have worked toward the benefit of Haiti's people.

If I may, Mr. Chairman, I would like to submit Briefing Paper Number 8 as a part of my written testimony since it elaborates this analysis in much greater detail than I have an opportunity to do in this testimony today.

Not all in Washington abandoned that leverage and influence we worked to achieve over many years. You may recall, Mr. Chairman, that in March 2001, I escorted to your office several high Haitian government officials who had traveled to Washington only a month after the inauguration of Mr. Aristide to his second term in office to participate in a symposium on Haiti at Trinity College. Among them were Mr. Yvon Neptune, who at that time was the President of Haiti's Senate, and Mr. Leslie Voltaire, the then—and current—Minister for Haitians Living Overseas. Also a part of the Haitian government delegation that visited you were two ministers who, even though members of the opposition, had accepted Mr. Aristide's invitation to join his government's cabinet. One of these ministers was Mr. Marc Louis Bazin, Mr. Aristide's principal opponent in the 1990 election who, subsequently, briefly served as the Prime Minister of the 1991–1994 de facto military regime. What better example could we have had of the potential for political reconciliation in Haiti than Mr. Aristide and Mr. Bazin working together. Sadly, because Mr. Bazin had rejected participation in the bitterly recidivistic opposition to Mr. Aristide (at that time called the "Democratic Convergence"), his credentials as a member of the opposition working within the Lavalas government were not accepted by Aristide's opponents in Haiti and in Washington.

Much to your credit, Mr. Chairman, you were open to meeting these Haitian government officials and engaging them in constructive conversation. And they were anxious to engage you. You even made an extra effort by taking time from your busy schedule to travel up North Capital Street to Trinity's campus the next day to listen to them speak at the symposium.

Sadly, Executive Branch officials reacted quite differently to this opportunity for engagement and dialogue. Not only did ranking officials in Washington choose not to engage these Haitian government officials, but, in the run-up to the symposium, they urged me not to invite them to Washington, adding that this would embarrass the new American administration. This, Mr. Chairman, is my own personal story of a golden opportunity the Bush Administration lost to engage, to maintain/strengthen influence and leverage in Haiti, and to assist Haiti emerge from its dark political past. Surely, this is not the only time that administration officials refused an opportunity like this.

Rather than taking advantage of this and similar opportunities, it seems to me that our government was not only busy isolating Haiti's elected government, but, through various intermediaries and political operatives in Washington, it was allowing signals to travel to Port-au-Prince that emboldened the opposition and its "zero option" policy of intransigence by suggesting that the opposition had Washington's support.

THE CHIMERES OF WASHINGTON, D.C.

This is not my assessment alone. This concern that presumptive policy signals were being sent to Port-au-Prince from Washington, and that those signals were highly damaging to efforts to resolve what was, back then, a relatively reparable political crisis, was shared by none other than the U.S. Ambassador to Haiti. In his farewell address in Port-au-Prince last summer to HAMCHAM, the Haitian-American Chamber of Commerce, the career diplomat who headed our embassy in Haiti, the Honorable Brian Dean Curran, reflected on Haiti's long-standing political crisis remarking:

> "There is an incoherence (in Haiti) that has troubled me: the incoherence of the way Washington's views are interpreted here. Those of you who know me will realize that since I arrived here as President Clinton's Ambassador and then President Bush's, I have always talked straight about US policy and what might and might not be new policy directions. But there were many in Haiti who preferred not to listen to me, the president's representative, but to their own friends in Washington, sirens of extremism or revanchism on the one hand or apologists on the other. They don't hold official positions. I call then the *chimeres* of Washington."

And who, pray tell, might these irregular actors be? I would suggest, Mr. Chairman, that the committee takes steps to get to the bottom of this. It might begin by heeding the supposition of the *Washington Post* that the International Republican Institute has played an important role in the 'wink and nod' messages from Washington sent to the opposition. In its February 19th edition, the Post editorialized: "In particular, it (the administration) has declined to exercise its considerable leverage on the civilian opposition parties, some of which have been supported by such U.S. groups as the International Republican Institute and which have rejected any political solution short of Mr. Aristide's immediate resignation."

In sum, Mr. Chairman, it seems to me that our policy—and practices—toward Haiti in recent years have been driven, unfortunately, by a deeply rooted animosity to one man—Jean-Bertrand Aristide—that has been held among a relatively small but powerful group of actors in Washington. Policies rigorously enacted under the auspices of this zealous group in order either to emasculate Mr. Aristide politically or to force him out of office, as we are seeing right now, have put the citizens and country of Haiti at grave risk, and have created potential spill over effects both in the Caribbean and on to our shores.

To achieve the narrow political goal of getting Mr.Aristide, the *chimeres* of Washington have, in essence, enacted policies that have devastated Haiti. What better example can one identify of the irresponsibility of being willing to throw out the bathwater in order to get at the baby.

ACTS OF DESPERATION

As I reflect on the result of these policies of isolation, non-engagement, constant criticism and punitive action I get the sense of the gradual strangulation of an elected government. As the noose around its neck tightened, it was pushed increasingly toward ill-advised and desperate acts. The suspension of international assistance was a particularly key element of strangulation. The government of Mr. Aristide, like all governments in this tragically poor and resource-starved country, was deeply dependent on external assistance in order to enact government programs. During his inaugural address of February 7, 2001, Mr. Aristide took a quite unusual—perhaps even unprecedented—step for a Haitian President when he outlined a series of social welfare, infrastructure development and investment goals of his government, suggesting that his term in office be judged according to his ability to meet these goals. These plans were derived from the Lavalas Family party's "White Paper" for Haiti, an unusual attempt—for Haitian political parties—to set forth a platform that directed itself toward the country's multitude of social, economic and environmental problems.

Sadly, following the virtual complete suspension of bilateral and multilateral aid to his government as a result of the May 2000 election's eight flawed senatorial vote counts and the Haitian government's bewildering failure to address this issue, few resources were available to the government to work toward these goals. As Mr. Aristide and his government were pushed more and more into a corner, predictable results emerged. With fewer and fewer resources to manage, the government was left to manage scarcity and, became increasingly desperate and corrupt. And, in Haiti's political reality, managing scarcity means managing power, with equally predictable results. Mr. Aristide, presiding over a resource starved government under constant assault from political opponents both in and beyond Haiti, took to the streets, aligning his government with impoverished urban youth—the now infamous *chimeres* of Haiti—who, by way of organized gangs, served as a means of managing the maintenance of power.

Interviews with urban gang leaders over the past several months on various National Public Radio (NPR) broadcasts have been quite revealing in this regard and have underscored the enormous tragedy of both the government's strangulation and its descent into the streets. Those interviewed have repeatedly suggested that they would have preferred to have a legitimate government job as opposed to becoming a member or leader of a street gang. Sadly, with no jobs available, the life of a *chimere* presented itself as a viable option.

Mr. Chairman, when I was a boy growing up in the New Jersey suburbs in an area that had just recently been farmland, I occasionally encountered a rabbit that had found its way into my back yard that was enclosed with a chain link fence. Sometimes, I attempted to catch the rabbit, gradually backing it into a corner of the fence as what I perceived as the best strategy to capture it. I never did manage to catch one of those elusive critters, but I recall vividly how the rabbits that I managed to back into the corner of the fence became increasingly desperate as their maneuvering space shrank. In fact, I recall vividly on one occasion how a panicked rabbit that I had edged into the corner acted with such desperation that bashed itself against the fence, injuring itself in its attempts to elude my grasp. Aghast at the blood streaming from the animal, I quickly backed away. This was the last time I tried cornering a rabbit in order to capture it. It was not my goal to force self-inflicted damage.

I relate this story, Mr. Chairman, because I think of it when I reflect on what has happened in Haiti over the past several years. As the government of Haiti was increasingly backed into that corner, it acted more and more like that panicked rabbit of my youth, injuring itself in desperation. Ultimately, as its maneuvering space shrank, the government, in its increasing desperation to escape the trap, inflicted many wounds on itself. What a tragedy of huge proportions.

A PYRRHIC VICTORY

The departure of Mr. Aristide, at least for now, has been achieved. Those who have sought it for quite some time are certainly rejoicing their political victory. But their victory is proving to be a Pyrrhic one as Haiti descends deeper on the slippery slope of lawlessness. Revenge killing and settling scores—in Port-au-Prince and elsewhere in the country—have become the new *ordre du jour*. Prisons throughout the country have been emptied. Secondary cities, towns and villages across the land have become the domain of gang leaders establishing fiefdoms in what is now a balkanized country. And, with the descent into lawlessness comes the probable scenario of Haiti's emergence as a kind of narco-trafficking free state, as the countryside's runways and ports fall within the domain of the local warlords, many of whom already have a history of involvement in drug trafficking.

The victory is Pyrrhic also, Mr. Chairman, because it was achieved through the slow strangulation of Haiti's capacity to respond to the humanitarian, social and environmental challenges and crises before it. And, in recent weeks, we have seen in particular a rash of significant damage to the country's already weak humanitarian and development infrastructure, as roads and ports have been severely damaged and destroyed, and public and private buildings looted and burned.

Perhaps the most Pyrrhic element of this victory, however, has been its achievement at the expense of the Haitian population's faith in democracy. This is illustrated most vividly by the enthusiastic welcome being given by some to the return of the gunmen. While there should be no doubt that this welcome has been fueled by a realistic sense of self-preservation by those who do not have the guns, by the gratitude of those released from Haiti's jails and their families, and by former military and paramilitary figures who have been waiting patiently for such an opening to occur, this welcome is also fueled by another factor. Haiti's citizens are deeply disappointed, indeed, disgusted, with the comportment of all of the country's political leaders who, over the past decade, have been so intent on their own, personal struggles to maintain or attain power that they have sacrificed their country. To coin a phrase, they have been fiddling while Rome has been burning.

This disenchantment with democracy is an enormously tragic and dangerous development. Haitians have harbored 'dreams of democracy' since the 1986 ouster of the Duvalier dictatorship. Their dreams have repeatedly been turned into nightmares. It is in everyone's interest in this room that we work together to deflect that disenchantment and restore faith in the resolution of disputes through participation, engagement, the peaceful mediation of differences, rule of law, and the rejection of all forms of political intimidation, violence and recidivism.

BREAKING THE CYCLE OF DEJA VU

I will leave to others the debate and the necessary investigation over the circumstances of Mr. Aristide's abrupt departure from Haiti last Sunday. Surely, the removal—regardless of how it occurred—of a democratically-elected leader prior to the completion of his term—is a set-back to Haiti's democratic process and a threat to other nations in the hemisphere; indeed around the world. Regardless of whether or not Mr. Aristide is restored to the presidency to complete his term of office ending on February 7, 2006, however, there are several steps we can take, actions we can support, and principles that can guide us that will contribute toward a sustained resolution of Haiti's seemingly unending internal and external political warfare.

First, from a Washington and US perspective, we must forge a bi-partisan approach toward Haiti. Of course, this being Washington and ours being a democracy, we will agree to disagree over certain specifics. But, even amid our disagreements, we must be prepared to examine our role in Haiti's affairs in a more even-handed manner that does not chose sides, stem from deeply rooted personal animosities, or seek to profit from Haiti's misfortunes.

In this regard, it is of great necessity that the *chimeres* of Washington be removed from any real or perceived role in the future of U.S. policy toward Haiti. We must put an end to 'wink and nod' messages coming out of Washington. These messages—and actions that reinforced them—have caused considerable damage not only to Haiti, but also to the credibility of Washington's leadership on Haiti and around the world. I would urge you, Mr. Chairman and members of the subcommittee, to examine the roles of these *chimeres*, who, as the US Ambassador suggested, were aiding and abetting Haiti's tragedies. Specifically, I would urge you to clarify the validity of various allegations that have been leveled at the International Republican Institute for its role in exacerbating and reinforcing an atmosphere of political intransigence and violence in Haiti. I would urge you, also, to explore alleged links among Haiti's resurgent gunmen once based in the Dominican Republic and drug trafficking, weapons smuggling, and money laundering.

Second, I would urge us support policies and practices that will reinforce the notion of political inclusion in Haiti. Let us work—successfully this time—not to play favorites, but rather work to get all the legitimate political actors under the political tent. It is of vital importance that Haiti's once and future political actors all participate in the governance of their country and accept the responsibilities that come along with it. To this end, the framework offered by the CARICOM plan is an excellent place to start. Acts of *dechoukaj* aimed at members of the Aristide government and the Lavalas party, and the urgent flight from the country of these political actors is not.

Third, and directly related to the need to have all legitimate political actors gain inclusion in governance, we must support steps to put an end to Haiti's tried and true political practices of 'winner takes all' and 'loser undermines the winner.' In this regard, Haiti's electoral laws that prescribe a winner takes all approach toward each and every elective office should be re-examined. In my view, Mr. Chairman, this approach, particularly in a country that has had one dominant party competing with many smaller ones, has only exacerbated polarization and confrontation. Some form of proportional representation, perhaps in Haiti's Chamber of Deputies, would help to ensure broader political participation. A party that captures, say, 10 percent of the votes nationwide, could be awarded 10 percent of the seats in that parliamentary body. This would both bring that element into the process and force upon it the responsibilities of governance.

Fourth, there is an immediate need to move against the armed thugs and convicts who have been freed from prison, and to re-establish some semblance of rule of law. In this regard, Haiti's civilian-led police need immediate strengthening and support, and its judicial system requires intense and long term support. The thugs must not find their way into the police force. Putting this genie back into the bottle will be a difficult, but necessary element not only to allow the country to move forward, but to provide a needed push toward ending impunity. The return of the army and of the FRAPH gunmen and criminals is in the best interests of only those particular individuals, not of the Haiti, its citizens, and the international community.

Fifth, we need to be prepared to stick with Haiti over the long haul. Staying the course will mean that our attention to Haiti can not be merely intense and short term, as it was in 1994/95, and then leaving the country to its own devices, while enacting partisan-driven policies in Washington that harmed gains that had been made. If nation-building is an expression that gives some of you heartburn, think of perhaps another approach—call it "nation-nurturing"—where we provide active and sustained support to the non-governmental—and government—bodies in Haiti that will develop the country and its required institutions. In other words, we do not have to build Haiti, but we should have a long term commitment to all Haitians to help them rebuild their own country.

CONCLUDING REMARKS

Mr. Chairman, the tragic developments in Haiti, that are still unfolding, are to some considerable extent the result of failed US policies and practices that have sacrificed the well-being of Haiti to achieve a narrow political goal—the removal of one man from elected office. These policies and practices have not served Secretary Powell; they have not served President Bush; they have not served the United States Congress, they have not served the American people, and they have surely not served the long-suffering people of Haiti.

Again, I thank you for this opportunity to share my thoughts and analysis with you, and I stand ready to work with all of you to help improving the way the government of the United States relates to and works with its Caribbean neighbor.

Thank you.

Mr. BALLENGER. I recognize Congressman Rangel. You are a constituent of Congressman Rangel's, I think, Mr. Sachs, are you not?

Mr. RANGEL. Thank you, Mr. Chairman for giving me the honor to introduce to you a friend, a constituent, an international scholar, a professor at Harvard that is now at the great university of Columbia in my district, and that is Dr. Jeffrey Sachs, the Director of the Earth Institute of Columbia University. We are sorry for the delay, but I am pleased that you managed to stay. Thank you Dr. Sachs and Mr. Chairman.

Mr. BALLENGER. Mr. Sachs. All yours.

STATEMENT OF JEFFREY D. SACHS, DIRECTOR, THE EARTH INSTITUTE AT COLUMBIA UNIVERSITY

Mr. SACHS. Thank you very much, Chairman. You asked a few minutes ago why we would stay through such a long hearing. There are two reasons: One is I would go anywhere where Congressman Rangel is and I would follow him around the world because he is the most remarkable person, and I am so honored that he is my representative in the Congress. But there is a second reason, which is that I think I speak for many Americans that are deeply frightened today. We are frightened partly for Haiti, but we are truly frightened for America because we don't know what is happening in this country.

What we hear doesn't add up. It reminds me when I am asked to believe the Administration of Groucho Marx's old line, "what do you believe me, or your own eyes." Doesn't meet the smell test when I hear Mr. Noriega. And what I have heard directly, and I am experienced probably as much as any person on this planet in international development and in countries like Haiti and in Haiti, what I hear about what is happening does not make sense, Mr. Chairman. And so I come here to appeal to you, to Congressman Menendez and to the rest of the panel to exercise Democratic oversight over the Executive Branch with urgency now.

I heard a lot of speeches. A lot of your colleagues seem to know all the answers, but there are a lot of urgent questions you must find answers to. And I don't believe that you are working hard enough in the Congress yet to find out the answers to something that is at a threat to American democracy.

Now I and others have been in touch closely with the people around President Aristide, his wife. We have been in contact repeatedly. I have talked to his attorney. What you have been told and what we have been told is flatly denied by President Aristide and his wife. And I believe that rather than hearing congressmen like Congressman Weller or like others say we believe, I think it would be good to find out rather than just to believe. Where is Mr. Aristide? How safe is he right now? I know as of this morning, they fear for their safety. I know that as of this morning, they do not believe they can communicate freely with the outside world.

Are you sure? I heard Mr. Noriega just say right now the U.S. has no responsibility. This was a most shocking answer to me as an American citizen after airlifting a President out of his country and depositing him in the Central African Republic to be told by the Assistant Secretary of State, it is not our responsibility is simply amazing. What is his current status? We heard so many contradictions today. Mr. Aristide's departure was never a U.S. demand. That was in the testimony but I heard Mr. Noriega flatly contradicted himself. It was a demand. It had political reasons he said, but yes, it was a demand. And I heard it directly as well from Mr. Aristide's attorney that his client was not allowed on the airplane without giving the letter of resignation to Mr. Moreno in the Embassy in Haiti.

Do you just believe it or do you exercise oversight to find out, Mr. Chairman, because we need to know these things. Because in one case, it is a resignation and in another case, it is a coup. We need to understand these facts. What was said to Mr. Aristide about his security? Congressman Cummings said that Secretary Powell assured President Aristide—was assured of and assured Mr. Aristide of his security as of Saturday afternoon. Mr. Aristide's attorney has said that his client was told that the U.S. would not protect his personal security or family security.

Mr. Noriega said early in the testimony, Mr. Chairman, said early in the testimony that yes, we weren't going to protect him. Said later in the testimony that no, he was not at any personal risk, he was very surprised that he decided to leave under those circumstances. What are you going to believe, me or your own eyes? What about the withdrawal of U.S. support for CARICOM. Curious, isn't it? The Caribbean leaders are absolutely aghast of what we have done. One of them had the gumption to say so on the record knowing that we can turn our governments it seems and has a history of doing so. But he said at no time was CARICOM action plan predicated on the unconstitutional removal of President Aristide from office.

The removal of President Aristide in these circumstances sets a dangerous precedent for democratically-elected governments. What about U.S. links to the rebels? Please don't take these denials at face value, Mr. Chairman, because history constantly shows the CIA fingerprints after the fact. Let's find out what Guy Philippe was doing when we talked to him, what Jodel Chamblain is doing there as the head of the rebels. Let's ask not to hear that our Defense Department doesn't know how M–16s from the Dominican Republic got in their hands. Maybe they were "sold." Maybe they were given. Let's find out. It is absolutely alarming.

Then what was the support from congressionally voted funds to the International Republican Institute going to an opposition that blocked the CARICOM agreement? We are supporting the opposition. Is that right? We are giving millions of dollars to the opposition that Mr. Noriega went down to negotiate with them and got a negative answer? Are you curious? I am curious as an American and I am appealing to the Chairman of this Subcommittee to be curious as well. It doesn't make sense. What do you believe, Mr. Noriega or your own eyes? What about all of the love and care for

Haiti that we heard today? Now here's an area of some expertise of mine——

Mr. BALLENGER. Could you summarize?

Mr. SACHS. I will summarize. I will summarize of why I am frightened and why millions of Americans are frightened and why we are looking to you for leadership. Now I came back from Haiti in early 2001 and spoke to the leadership of the Inter-American Development Bank, the International Monetary Fund, the World Bank, and the Organization for American States. And they all told me that the Bush Administration had put a complete freeze on all multi-lateral assistance. I know something about that business certainly as much as anyone in this room. And I know what it means for the United States to put a freeze on this aid. And then when I hear people concerned about the children of Haiti where nearly 100 children die before their fifth birthday out of every thousand that are born where we froze all aid for 3 years.

Mr. BALLENGER. Is this a summary?

Mr. SACHS. As Dr. Maguire said, we have strangled that country. I would like some answers as an American citizen. I am grateful for the chance to tell you how frightened we are for our own democracy, Mr. Chairman. We do not know what our country is doing and we appeal to you and your Committee to get real answers to these questions. Thank you very much.

Mr. BALLENGER. If I may interrupt for a second in the fact that I wondered myself about the safety of the President. And so the Steele Foundation is an organization that has been providing—taken care of his safety for years that are paid for by the Haitian government. And I called the president of the Steele Foundation and last night he told me for sure that there is no doubt in my mind that they were completely protected by our men. And then he said this morning he called me back and said I just wanted to check it out, and I will tell you now I will swear on a stack of Bibles that we had armed guards there at his request and we did whatever he told us to do.

Mr. SACHS. Mr. Chairman, may I make a suggestion to you and our colleagues. Please call President Aristide in the Central African Republic. Please call President Aristide to find out for yourself whether you are correct in that assessment because they feel at risk of their lives.

Mr. MENENDEZ. Mr. Chairman, I would like to call, since you have said they are willing to swear on a stack of Bibles, I wouldn't mind having them before the Committee to do so.

Mr. BALLENGER. Ambassador Tim Carney, career foreign service officer at the Department of State, served as Ambassador to Haiti during the Clinton Administration and we welcome you aboard, and sorry for the long wait you had to go through.

STATEMENT OF THE HONORABLE TIMOTHY M. CARNEY, FORMER U.S. AMBASSADOR TO HAITI

Mr. CARNEY. I am delighted to be here. I am delighted to see before me some Members whom I welcomed into my residence in Port-au-Prince and who welcomed me into their offices here in Washington and repeatedly, I might add.

What do we have in Haiti? Well, we now have an opportunity for the international community to support a political process there, not a personality. It is essential that we provide resources for Haitians to determine their future. Our first priority, sir, must be to ensure security while former and still respected Haitian national police elements reconstitute themselves. In this context of security and a political process, I will associate myself with Mr. Payne in underscoring that the most vital mandate for the interim international force and for the follow-on security entity is disarmament. You put your finger on that, absolutely. In parallel with providing security, we all must facilitate the political process that Haitian parties themselves are embarked on in the framework of their Constitution. I believe that at the outset, three interrelated crises must receive Haitian attention and get the aid and advice of the international community. Those three crises are the rule of law, the economy and the environment.

And specifically, Haiti needs institution building, especially those institutions that ensure law and order, police, magistrates and the courts. Second, Haiti has to have adequate laws and procedures for economic stability and to foster development. Those must be in place. They need, for example, to be able to have people establish titles to their own property so they can put them up for collateral for improvement. Foreign investors whose capital is important to create jobs, must have the security of their investments in Haiti's economy.

And third, the crumbling environment there needs urgent attention. Clean water is a particularly urgent need. That aquifer under Haiti is already starting to salinate and of course got to stop cutting down trees to make charcoal. Must have propane in their homes so Haitians can cook. The most important reality for we in the international community is an understanding that Haitian success in bringing their nation into this 21st century with the stake in the prosperity of our hemisphere is not a job for days or months, it is one that is going to take years of imagination, discipline and hard work.

My last thought, sir, is to congratulate France, Canada and the United States for help bringing about the circumstances that can realize these goals, the U.N. and its agencies, the international financial institutions and most of all the hard work of Haitians are the way forward. Thank you, sir.

Mr. BALLENGER. Thank you. Now Ambassador Marville. You have extensive experience in Haiti and have served as an election observer in 1997 and 1998. Ambassador Marville was named Secretary General of the Organization of American States to head up the Electoral Observation Mission for the legislative and municipal and local government elections held in 2000. Recently participated as a member of CARICOM mission to Haiti led by Prime Minister James Mitchell of St. Vincent, and the Grenadines to review the situation in Haiti. And I thank you for being here and would thank you for staying as long as you have, sir.

STATEMENT OF THE HONORABLE ORLANDO MARVILLE, FORMER HEAD OF THE ELECTION OBSERVATION MISSION OF THE ORGANIZATION OF AMERICAN STATES (2000)

Mr. MARVILLE. Thank you, Mr. Chairman, and through you, the rest of the Committee. I stayed actually longer than you may have imagined because I traveled all the way here this morning. I was informed that I would have to testify before you sometime late last night and what I have is handwritten. Interestingly, much of what I want to say has been covered, but I will go through some of it anyway. And I think the most fundamental point I want to make, I want to make at the beginning.

Haiti is not only Haiti of now, it is also Haiti of the past. I think we have to understand some things. What I have to say is probably of no comfort to anyone. The truth is nonpartisan. And unlike Haiti, it cannot be used as a political football. When I went to Haiti, I went to Haiti with all the feelings of a man of the Caribbean with African ancestry who had great respect for a rag-tag army that back in the early 1800s defeated what was supposed to be the invincible army of Napoleon for its own independence.

The U.S.A. was already independent. But the U.S. independence had no effect on the rest of the hemisphere. Haiti, on the other hand, I must assure you, the revolt of the captives in Haiti resulted in revolts in Barbados, Jamaica, Guyana, throughout the Caribbean. Additionally, the British were then forced to manumit slaves by 1834. For the rest of the northern segment of the Americas, there was absolute silence and shunning for 100 years the slave holding powers of Europe and North America isolated Haiti. This is the international community worked up to today. And I think we have to understand what has been happening, what needs to happen.

I wanted to go through the process of elections, which we consider flawed not because of the shoestring democracy process that occurred, but because of a tradition that had developed in Haiti where the winner has to have everything. As a result of that, we wrote a letter, a private confidence letter to the president of the Republic and to the president of the electoral commission indicating that, in fact, there had been a fraudulent attempt to change the numbers rather than going back and pleading with them to have the second round. Somebody within the electoral commission leaked the letter to the press and everything went down. I was called immediately before the letter was leaked by the president of the Republic.

We had a lengthy conversation. I indicated that he had to bite the bullet and he had to tell Mr. Aristide. He said, you know, a man who has been robbed of 4 years of power, is difficult to talk to. I said if you bite the bullet, I myself will be one of the first people to go out and seek investments from the Caribbean and elsewhere, which I considered an absolute necessity. The rest is history. A lot of it is sad. It is sad what I remember for instance that at 6 a.m., I was in a polling booth in Petionville, Haiti. And people were lined up as if there were food rations or something.

When the voting began, they pressed against the door and the police were not able to keep absolute control. But in the midst of this a very pregnant woman appeared and the crowd made way for her. And then I went through it. Anyway, getting back to the point, sir, we have had since then situations which have been not very pleasant. First of all, we had a very small electoral observation team. The fact that it was small was because a lot of the funding that could have been provided from here was blocked by a single Member of the Senate.

Additionally, when we came to update the Congress, we were able to meet, I think two or three Members of the Democratic party, but only the persons who provided information to the Republicans. It seemed all the time that there was a question of who is in, who is out and that is the political football. I know I don't have a lot of time, so I will jump to the present because there are some things that are absolutely necessary and a few points. The present offers perhaps the final window of opportunity for the international community and Haiti's brothers in CARICOM.

I notice my colleague, Ambassador Carney, permitted CARICOM to come good, as they say. Haiti must not be made once more a political football. There is also no quick fix. Haiti needs food, medicine, physicians, clean water and any number of efforts to bring what is one of the hardest working and most talented populations in the hemisphere to return to acceptable human levels. Thereafter, not only will there be a great need for social infrastructure improvement, but serious assistance must be offered in creating an apolitical police force and an adequate justice system as well as preparing for elections, which I believe may require 2 or more years before they can be successfully conducted. Some of the monies suspended before should be used immediately for these purposes.

Finally, with respect to the question of proper elections, the time period I suggest is based first on my own experience where it is extremely important to have a proper and permanent electoral council. It is extremely important to have all parties on board on this issue. We cannot have the legal opposition saying no. We can't have Lavalas saying no. The time taking to do a census in Haiti would be considerable because it is a country where parts of it are practically inaccessible and it takes time to get there. Additionally, we need to be sure of proper paraphernalia, metal ballot boxes and proper ballots, et cetera and also sufficient monies to support electoral observation. Even after that, Mr. Chairman, we are going to need a period of considerable assistance to allow the country to get on its feet. And this is not something that can be done.

Mr. BALLENGER. Could you summarize?

Mr. MARVILLE. I am at the end practically. In a year or 2, it requires the international community, by which I mean the North American countries, Europe, Japan, Latin America and together, they must work with CARICOM, which I think, in some ways, sympathizes with, understands, misunderstands maybe, but is an important aspect of this whole process.

Mr. BALLENGER. Thank you, sir. Just a few questions. Ambassador Carney, I have been to Haiti many times and I planted with C.A.R.E. International—I planted 3 million trees. That was 20 years ago and I will bet you there is not a tree left. We put a hospital in Leogane, and I understand it still exists there. A little old lady came to visit me and she was not only the mayor of her town in northern Haiti, but she was also a teacher. And she said could you get us anything to help us out with? And I said what do you need? And she said I need pencils and paper. It kind of shocked me. Well, what I did is I got 800,000 sheets of 8½ by 11 paper and 50,000 pencils because of my business connections, and we shipped it.

And about a week or 10 days after I shipped it, the Salesian order of the Catholic church called me up to say that we are terribly sorry to tell you, sir, but they burned her school down. Would you mind if we gave her maybe a thousand pencils and 10,000 sheets of paper and kept the rest of it for the church? And I said no, sir. That is one of the reasons that I seem very frustrated in trying to do something positive about Haiti.

But one of the things that really kind of bugs me is with the armed guards and the arms that have been there, what would you recommend to control the gangs and how to disarm them? When we sent our 20,000 troops in there and they refused to disarm, and I think our troops cut loose with a couple of guns and killed maybe five or six of them, and all of a sudden, they gave the guns over, but it appears that the drug trade is reinforced, resupplied guns. Do you have any suggestions as to a method of somehow disarming the mobs that they have?

Mr. CARNEY. Let me first accept my colleagues' criticism and unreservedly add CARICOM to those who deserve congratulations. Disarming, it has got to be done by appeals. But there is no doubt in my mind that there is going to come a day when there is going to have to be action that hopefully will not involve large-scale shooting. But I think if we are going to do this right, we are going to have to be willing to lock and load if the situation requires it.

Now in that context, I believe we should definitely have Haitian police with us. And my understanding is that right now as we are sitting here there is an effort going forward to call up those Haitian national policemen who were either fired from the year 2000 on or who quit in disgust who have a reputation that can return with respect and professionalism to their duties.

Mr. BALLENGER. I hope—and I understand that of course some of the police that stayed on, I guess were corrupted by the program and so forth, and I don't know how you separated the situation, but I understand your point. That is really the only base you have to work with I think as far as law enforcement and law and order for the country itself.

Mr. CARNEY. I know the Haitian Coast Guard has remained of good reputation, but we are talking fewer than 100 men in that element.

Mr. BALLENGER. Bob.

Mr. MENENDEZ. Thank you, Mr. Chairman. Thank all of the panelists for their endurance and their participation, and I particularly want to thank Dr. Maguire and Dr. Sachs, who we asked to be with us. And I just want to make a brief comment before I ask a question or two, and that is, it seems that this hearing, the whole course of the majority is to discredit President Aristide, and I don't particularly have the greatest affinity for President Aristide, but that is not the issue. The issue is what is our policy as it relates to supporting democratically-elected governments? What is our policy in terms of standing up, including for those who we may not care for because we don't agree with their policies, but who were democratically-elected, who this government recognized as the duly democratically-elected entity.

It goes far beyond Haiti. It goes to the message that there is unrest in significant parts of this hemisphere. And if I were in some countries like we have already seen, like Bolivia, Ecuador and other places, I would say I understand how to get to my goal.

Let me create confrontation, maybe violent confrontation and then ultimately a political solution where we say to the newly-democratic entities step aside because when we send a message that we don't intend to get involved unless there is a political solution, and ultimately that says to those who do not want a political solution because they want a conclusion, not a political solution, but a conclusion that brings them to power, then I think we have gone down an incredibly dangerous path in this hemisphere. And that is what I think today's hearing is largely about. Very important to what is happening in Haiti, but this broad ability to wipe it away so easily by seeking to discredit one individual is I believe disingenuous.

Dr. Maguire, let me ask you, if I go ahead and I say to those who are seeking violent overthrow that I won't do anything in terms of either of my country or those of the international community until there is a political solution, what do you think that that says to entities, whether it be in Haiti or other groups in this hemisphere for that fact or any part of the world?

Mr. MAGUIRE. I think it tells them they can act with impunity and get away with it. And this is one of the tragedies of the scenario that is unfolding right now where we have personalities with known criminal records, known human rights violators, people who orchestrated coup attempts in 2001, the attack on the palace that was orchestrated by Mr. Guy Philippe. He tells them that rule of law doesn't matter. He tells them that impunity is at large again in Haiti. And you know, one of the things that frightens me considerably is that we are seeing now through the press reports, through the newspaper that Mr. Meek held up, we are seeing Mr. Philippe kind of greeted as some kind of a folk hero. But let us step back from that, and let us say that Mr. Philippe and his comrades over the past 3 weeks have emptied every prison in Haiti, including the penitentiary and those people surrounding them and giving them a joyful welcome are certainly happy. They and their families are happy that these people are out of jail and this includes people who were tried and found guilty for the Raboteau massacre under a wonderful judicial process that showed that the Haitian government could do it. It was lauded everywhere in the hemisphere and these people are back on the streets.

Mr. MENENDEZ. One final question, wouldn't some of the statements I heard from the Assistant Secretary about all of the alleged narcotic trafficking that it has been pointed out that President Aristide did hand over to the United States major narcotic dealers, what do we say then about Afghanistan where we are supporting a government in which the there is more opium grown today in Afghanistan than when we took over and we are actually looking the other way on these warlords and what are they growing in Afghanistan, and yet we are strongly supporting President Karzai, who I believe we should be supporting. But isn't there a duality of position or a——

Mr. MAGUIRE. There is an incredible contradiction. I see the contradictions throughout. I see them today where certain people have indicated a concern about human rights violations that occurred in 1995, the murder of Madam Duoshay Bertrand. I hear people talking about the concern of the murder of Lingo Bringall. But I don't hear people talking about the concern of the murder of other people who don't happen to be affiliated with the opposition.

Mr. BALLENGER. Before Mr. Weller, let me first tell everybody Mr. Paquiot missed his plane to stay here and testify, so I would just like to thank you, sir, for the sacrifice you made there.

Now, Mr. Weller.

Mr. WELLER. Thank you, Mr. Chairman. And I also, as a member of this panel, want to thank those who are on the second panel for your patience and being here this evening.

Mr. Paquiot in particular, thank you for sticking around. I recognize it is a sacrifice for you to be here as well as to miss the flight, stay an extra day, when I assume you want to be home with your family at this time.

Mr. Paquiot, I really welcome your participation in this panel today. All too often in many of these hearings, we have experts from outside of countries such as Haiti telling us what should be done in your country, and you are a distinguished leader as president of a prestigious university, and your personal sacrifice as a victim of Aristide's thugs is heart-breaking. My heart goes out to you as well as my prayers for you and your family, as well as your country and the people of your country, because every American wants things to be better in Haiti for you and your people.

You are part of the solution, and looking to the future as one of the respected leaders of Haiti, what would you recommend? What do you foresee as the necessary steps to strengthen democracy in Haiti, to make democracy work for the people of Haiti? What would you recommend? I really appreciate your participation today.

Mr. PAQUIOT. I thank you for the opportunity you give me to answer your question. I think we tend to focus too much on personality, like Aristide, for instance. We have a lot of people like that in the country. We had a lot of—the history of Haiti, we had a lot of people who thought they were Messiahs, they were above everybody. I heard lots of people here at the table talking about what should be done in Haiti.

We have to address the very problem that we Haitians face. And as a matter of fact, you know, I do not think that Haiti should be like an issue in American policy, because I have been hearing a lot of things this afternoon. The problem is not that. The problem is the Haitian people who have been suffering for 200 years. Even when Haiti was independent, it was not recognized as an independent country, even by the United States. I think the United States recognized Haiti for an independent country maybe 60 years after Haiti was independent. So you have to understand a country that was based, you know, on slavery, and it is quite "normal" that you have those kinds of situations, because you must build things on the economy, reinforcing the economy. It is a long-term process.

You must have institutions. That is the kind of thing that you do not have in Haiti. When you do not have institutions, strong institutions, in a country, you tend to believe in personalities. And since Duvalier left, we went through a whole process of disillusionment.

So I think that most of the things that should be done have already been said at this table. I heard people talk about that.

We have basic problems in Haiti like problems with electricity, like problems with water, problems that you would not think that a country in this century would have to face. So I think those are the kinds of things that should be addressed and not necessarily put the emphasis on somebody. And that is why me, and along with a lot of Haitians who have been very disappointed by Mr. Aristide, I thought it was going to do a lot of things. As a matter of fact, at the university we do not even discuss about the issue of whether it was or not, you know, being well-elected, because we thought that he should have been given the chance to do something, and as a matter of fact, he failed in that.

So I think what we should do, what the international community should do, is to address the real problem of the Haitian people, that we need strong institutions, education, and things like that. This will be a long process. So as far as I am concerned, I think that is the kind of thing that we will have to do in Haiti if we want that something like that will never happen again in this country.

Mr. WELLER. Thank you, Professor.

Quickly, using the remainder of my time, Ambassador Marville, thank you for the leadership that Barbados has played, particularly in CARICOM and in the Caribbean region. What role do you think that CARICOM should play in helping Haiti in the immediate future? What role do you see for CARICOM?

Mr. MARVILLE. CARICOM has any number of skills with respect to elections. I come from a country which has had a tradition of Parliament that dates back to 1639. Back in 19—I do not know when, immediately after the fall of Duvalier, when Namphy became a general, our then Prime Minister offered Namphy whatever assistance he wanted in trying to put an elected government in place. Namphy listened and then went off, and nothing happened.

CARICOM can do a lot of these things. There are several factors at play here. We have populations in two or three countries which already speak clearly, who, for instance, served as police and soldiers along with the U.S. forces in 1994, and they have been very effective because they could reach people at the local level. We are not from Haiti, but our connections with Haiti are real.

This is one of the things. I would suggest that whatever the international community thinks it wants to do, CARICOM is a necessary ally in that process.

Mr. WELLER. Thank you very much. Thank you for your time.

Mr. BALLENGER. Mr. Delahunt.

Mr. DELAHUNT. Yes, thank you.

I think your recommendations are excellent. I think now that this Administration has accepted the concept of nation-building, and I know, Ambassador, you have been involved in that process recently, that underscores what I think I am hearing. There has to be a permanent commitment, there has to be patience, and there has to be appropriate resources.

My remarks at the beginning, and I think you corroborated an observation that I made, when this Congress did not provide the funding for those election monitors to the OAS, it was a point in history that will be reviewed and examined as a turning point. Because I met you, Ambassador, I was one of those Democrats that you referred to, large D Democrats. We were there. We observed the election. There was a euphoria, until, of course, the interpretation was provided that a plurality was sufficient as opposed to a majority to avoid a runoff. But the reality has been, consistently for the past 10 years, we have turned our back on Haiti, and we have not made that necessary commitment.

I would like to just bring one other—I think it was you, Mr. Maguire, and maybe others—and let me direct this question to my friend Ambassador Carney. The International Republican Institute, I have had very serious concerns with the activities of that group for some time now, not just in Haiti, but elsewhere. I have witnessed their role in a variety of countries, and I think it is time we reexamined all of the so-called democracy-building programs.

Are you aware, Ambassador, that—and maybe I am incorrect in this statement—that the IRI is operating out of the Dominican Republic? Are you familiar with that?

Mr. CARNEY. No, sir. You will recall that I retired in early 2000——

Mr. DELAHUNT. You were fortunate then.

Mr. CARNEY [continuing]. And am not up to speed on that at all.

Mr. DELAHUNT. Either Mr. Sachs or Mr. Maguire or anybody else.

Mr. MAGUIRE. I can tell you that I am fully aware that the IRI has had meetings in Miami with the democratic opposition. In fact, the date is etched in my mind because it was the day of the aborted coup attempt in Venezuela. I think that was April 12, 2002, if I am not mistaken. And at this time I just happened to be in Miami for a meeting that had been scheduled long before that of Haitian diaspora organizations by the National Coalition of Haitian Rights.

Mr. DELAHUNT. Let me interrupt you for a moment. Are you familiar with an individual by the name of Stanley Lucas?

Mr. MAGUIRE. I know Mr. Lucas. He is the IRI point person on Haiti, and I was quite seized when, in Haiti in 2001 in January, I saw in a video run on State television, a clip of Mr. Lucas drinking champagne with Prosper Avril and the other generals after a coup had been thrown. And I thought, well, you know, if I were running the IRI, I certainly would not want a person with this kind of a history and background running its programs in Haiti for me. I also understand that Mr. Lucas has been asked by AID, as AID has funded the IRI for these various meetings, that he——

Mr. DELAHUNT. The funding is no longer coming from the National Endowment for Democracy; is that what you are saying?

Mr. MAGUIRE. Well, what I understand is that AID was kind of directed to fund the IRI.

Mr. DELAHUNT. Was kind of directed?

Mr. MAGUIRE. Yes.

Mr. DELAHUNT. Kind of directed. What do you mean by kind of directed, Mr. Maguire?

Mr. MAGUIRE. Well, in my conversations in Haiti with various people who know this much better than I do, AID was pretty much mandated to support the IRI.

Mr. DELAHUNT. By Congress?

Mr. MAGUIRE. I do not believe so.

Mr. DELAHUNT. Well, I think, Mr. Sachs, you make a very good point, and I would recommend to the Chair that we take the time over the course of the next 6 months or a year to really—you know, we create commissions around here rather frequently. I really think it is important for us to review the roles of the institutes, the NDI, the NED.

Mr. Chairman, you know that we have had great success, at least in a transitory way, bringing people of different perspectives together to discuss democracy. I just fear that what we are doing here is we are creating advocacy groups that are not working in the best interests of the United States in nurturing democratic institutions.

Mr. BALLENGER. Mr. Payne.

Mr. PAYNE. Thank you very much. I could not agree more. I think that the concept of NDI and IRI and the rest are good. I think, though, it is rare that an institution has really taken on a political binge like IRI. But I was there at the original election of President Aristide when IRI had a report that was colorful. It was all done; it was given on the night of the election, IRI's report on the election. It had to be printed somewhere in the United States, and it had to be printed before the election, because that was the election evening. I was there, Mr. Goss was there, we were all observers.

The IRI has taken this Haiti question and made it a political issue, and it is unfair, because I think that the concept of IRI and the DRI, National Democratic Institute are good, but I think that in Haiti and in Venezuela, the IRI has overstepped its boundaries. As a matter of fact, the National Endowment for Democracy has asked IRI to take a look at their new leadership who, as you know, many of the IRI people ended up in the Bush Administration, as they should. They are good card-carrying Republicans. And there is a new group of IRI people who I do not think understand democracy-building rather than taking part in politics.

So there is no question that IRI has had a political—as a matter of fact, NDI was still working, and the IRI was asked to leave.

Once again, the CIA who had been in Haiti, as you know, forever had Bazin winning the election and were embarrassed and shocked that this guy Aristide won 70 percent of the election. Bazin, great guy; beautiful French pictures in his house, very talented World Banker. Aristide is running around out there having the people understand that he is trying to change their way of life. And so how the CIA could have misread the fact that this is a popular movement and the first election, to me it just shows how flawed our intelligence agency happens to be. It made no sense at all.

Just sort of in conclusion, the whole question of the impact that Haiti has had on the United States, I think the Ambassador mentioned its importance. Haiti fought in the Battle of Savannah. We had a celebration in the State Legislature in New Jersey because they fought with the Colonies to take the British out of our independence, the Battle of Savannah in particular. It was Haiti who, when we defeated the French, caused the French to sell the Louisiana Territories, which had to then open up the West so Lewis and Clark could move on into the West, because France was broke because they lost so much. And Haiti contributed as much as the original Thirteen Colonies to France as the whole Thirteen Colonies gave to Britain, and, therefore, France lost that and became in need of funds and sold the Louisiana Territory.

Why do I say that? Because we have been involved; Haiti has been an advocate for the United States, and, as a matter of fact, the United States would not recognize Haiti because they did not want to have a black diplomat when we had slavery.

We could go on and on with Haiti. Even as I conclude, the planting of trees that I really commend the Chairman for doing, the reason that the erosion has happened so much was because in World War II, our War Department asked Haiti to cut down its natural habitat and try to grow rubber trees because we were cut off from the Pacific region. There was a Haitian person who was—who knew that they would not grow, but they continued to do it. Erosion set in, it has never been turned back, and now this whole question of that flawed policy, of Haiti attempting to help the United States in World War II, somehow helped to create the problems that we are seeing there.

So there is an involvement of Haiti. As a matter of fact, Simon Bolivar, who went and freed Latin America, lived in Haiti and studied there.

Let me just conclude by saying it is unfortunate that we had this policy. It is wrong that we have not recognized this Republic. I hope that in the future we will have a decent policy as relates to this country. They deserve better.

Since my time has not expired, Mr. Carney, let me ask you a quick question, since the orange light is still on. I know you work with the opposition, and I am glad you agree that disarmament and the DDRR programs should go on. But can you tell me why the opposition that you work with, with the business community, why they refused the CARICOM proposal?

Mr. CARNEY. I can tell you what they told me. I am not sure I can tell you the whole story.

The argument, and as a group of us initially put it to the opposition, was to accept the CARICOM proposal in a statement that made no mention of Mr. Aristide at all. They found that impossible. They said that in order to keep credibility with their base, and that organization is rooted in civil society, something new in Haiti, in my experience, that they simply could not refuse to mention President Aristide at all. An argument was then that they not make it a precondition that he leave his office; rather, it be stated as a goal. And the contention was even that would simply undermine them to the point that the only results would be Guy Philippe's welcome in Port-au-Prince as the liberator, which would effectively marginalize them politically for Haiti's future.

Mr. BALLENGER. Mr. Meeks.

Mr. MEEKS. Thank you, Mr. Chairman. I neglected to say last time, thank you for conducting this hearing.

Let me ask first, Mr. Paquiot, simply, do you believe that Haitians should receive asylum here in America? Do you believe that Haitians should receive asylum as a result of the violence, et cetera, that is going on in Haiti right now?

Mr. PAQUIOT. Well, I think that the dual policy consisting of having a policy for Cubans and one for Haitians is not fair, because, for instance, when a Cuban leaves Cuba right now, it is not for economic reasons, it is because they have their friends, their family in Miami, and they are, you know, comparing the lifestyle.

Mr. MEEKS. So you believe our policy should change?

Mr. PAQUIOT. I believe we should have the same standard for everybody.

Mr. MEEKS. Now, Ambassador Carney, let me ask you, in helping with the opposition, et cetera, I am told, and you can correct me if I am wrong, that your project brings some of the opposition members to the United States and works with them in that way. And I wanted to follow up just basically on the question that Mr. Payne had initiated. So how long was your involvement? Did the negotiations take place as to whether or not they should or should not accept the CARICOM agreement? Can you just tell me was there any true engagement, and was there anything that could have happened that we could have had really at the negotiating table, and whether or not, you know, the United States said anything to you or to anybody at the front and said, hey, get these guys at the negotiating table so that we can try to have a diplomatic solution?

Mr. CARNEY. The event was essentially a long phone conversation that took place last Tuesday, I believe it was, Tuesday a week ago. It was not done at the behest of the U.S. Administration or of CARICOM; it was rather an initiative by three or four of us who either lived in Haiti or have followed Haiti continuously for the last, in some cases, 14 or 15 years. The interlocutors in Port-au-Prince basically had already given a temporizing response to the Department of State. There had been more time asked for before a definitive response came through, and it was in those interstices that we put a call through and tried to make some points that this kind of a political process with firm international guarantees might be the way forward.

Mr. MEEKS. Did they know that these expatriates and thugs and criminals would soon be coming back in, and there would be violence that would take place very shortly?

Mr. CARNEY. If I recall, at the time the armed opposition led by the men whose identities we have had adequately described were quite close to Port-au-Prince; 25 miles comes to mind, subject to correction.

Mr. MEEKS. Okay. Now, let me ask then, based upon the fact that I think that we all agree who these individuals are, I was wondering whether the Board of Haitian Democracy and whether the opposition would agree and would push for the United Nations and/or some international court to come in so that those individuals who have been released from prison or who have been involved in the prior atrocities in Haiti, that they now go back before this body of justice so that, one, they could be reincarcerated, and two, that they not be allowed to participate in any shape, form, or fashion, whether it is in negotiations, or holding an office or anything, to deal with part of any negotiation in dealing with the democracy or trying to establish a democracy again in Haiti.

Mr. CARNEY. I believe that idea has merit and ought to be put into the political process in Port-au-Prince.

Mr. MEEKS. So I am just wondering, would the Board come out with some kind of a definitive statement in that regard that you would submit to our State Department as well as to the Secretary-General of the United Nations saying that you would urge such a tribunal to be put in place?

Mr. CARNEY. I will put it to the Board and argue its merits, but I cannot speak for what the Board might do. I am just a member of the Board, not the Chairman.

Mr. BALLENGER. Ms. Lee.

Ms. LEE. Thank you, Mr. Chairman. Let me thank you again and our Ranking Member for these hearings, and I also thank our panelists for being here. I believe what we are hearing today and what many of us know to be the case in terms of United States policy toward Haiti, and especially in the last 3 years, does warrant a fuller congressional investigation by the appropriate Committees, perhaps this Committee, with the Intelligence Committees, with Judiciary and all Committees that have some jurisdiction over our role as it relates to Haiti.

I wanted to ask any of the panelists to give me some feedback. Congressman Conyers and I are introducing a resolution to establish an independent commission to investigate these matters, and I would like to hear from you what you think should be part of this commission and the investigation, what questions should be asked as we pursue this.

Let me just start by asking Dr. Sachs to respond, and then any of the panelists could feel free to give me your ideas on that.

Mr. SACHS. Thank you very much.

First, I would like to say that we are just 3 days into what looks like a coup, with the U.S. heavy involvement. So I think it is a matter of real time, not just a matter of 6 months or a year or 2 years, but for this Committee to use its oversight powers right now to understand what has happened in the last 5 or 6 days, to reach President Aristide, to ensure his safety, to demand that the State Department ensure his safety and his ability to speak freely to you and to the whole—to Members of Congress that need to understand what has happened, because you will not have a political solution in the next few days or the next few weeks unless we understand what actually has happened.

And the more I hear U.S. Government officials saying that we have to look forward, not back, that is a recipe for disaster when we are 3 days into a removal from office of a President on a U.S.-chartered plane, taken to the Central African Republic, where the man is not even in contact safely with the rest of the world.

So it is a little bit premature to start doing big theory before you secure his physical safety and his ability to speak with you and with the rest of the Congress, so that we understand, because there is one interpretation which has a lot of, unfortunately, evidence behind it, which was that this was a U.S.-led effort to remove him from office against his will, and at the threat of imminent death to his family.

Now, if that is the case, that is a quite remarkable conclusion. We do not know yet whether that is the case, but the evidence seems to point in that direction in many different ways. And it was not flatly contradicted today, by the way, because what Secretary Noriega said was that, yes, indeed, he was told that he had to resign to get on that airplane. He said that. And that, of course, is what President Aristide has told those that he has reached by phone and told his attorney and others.

So we are in real time right now, with an extraordinarily dangerous situation, a President carried away on a U.S.-chartered plane, and we do not know where and what his physical status is, and he does not want to be there, I know. He wants to be in a safe place, not in the Central African Republic. And this Committee has a responsibility, with all due respect, in its oversight, in my opinion, to help ensure that that is the case.

Now, if we find the worst, and I think we may actually find the worst, that has lots of implications about how to restore democracy. And CARICOM leaders will have lots of views about that, because as we have talked to them in recent days, they believe that there is a grave threat to democracy as the way events have transpired against their clear needs in the region, and Prime Minister Patterson was absolutely explicit about this.

So I want to urge that this is not a time, in my view, for theory quite yet. This is a time for quick action, with the Committee taking a lead responsibility to ensure that the State Department gives you answers about what was the U.S. role in the forcible removal from office of a President in our hemisphere.

Mr. MAGUIRE. If I may add some comments, it is a trite phrase now, but I think we need to connect some dots here. I think we need to ask why was Guy Philippe not arrested in the Dominican Republic when the Government of Haiti asked for him to be arrested, and who was protecting him there? I think we need to ask what kind of links there have been of the flow of drugs from Haiti to the Dominican Republic, and how that has played into the financing of various activities. And I think we have to ask why the United States Ambassador had to intervene to keep a Haitian notorious for drug trafficking from attending an IRI fundraiser in early 2003.

Ms. LEE. Thank you, Mr. Chairman.

Mr. BALLENGER. Mr. Rangel.

Mr. RANGEL. Mr. Speaker, once again, thank you and the rest of the Committee for calling these hearings.

Let me take advantage of the Ambassadors that are here and ask them, what does coup d'etat mean as it relates to the American understanding of the—international understanding of that French term, coup d'etat, Ambassador Carney? I am going to ask Ambassador Marville as well, but since both of you are professional diplomats, what does it mean to you?

Mr. CARNEY. A blow against the State, if you will, the forcible seizure of power, and there are any number of ways to perpetrate one. There was a book, in fact, done in the mid-1960s by Edward Luttwak.

Mr. RANGEL. That is good for me.

Ambassador Marville.

Mr. MARVILLE. I concur with that. It is a forcible takeover of power, but that is an old definition. I think one is moving toward a definition of a takeover by force, a subtle takeover, a soft coup, hard coup, and so on.

Mr. RANGEL. Now, does anyone doubt that President Aristide was in fear for his life before he exited Haiti, and that the American Embassy and all of the good forces there facilitated his removal, and that he left because he was afraid that armed rebel forces might kill him? Is there any doubt about that story that we tell?

Mr. CARNEY. I am sure those were elements in it, but I do not know the whole story.

Mr. RANGEL. I know, but no one challenges that. Is there any question in your mind?

Mr. MARVILLE. Yes, there will be a question, but I do not have any answers. I do not know what the details are.

Mr. RANGEL. What question could there be? Do you doubt that he left because he thought he was going to be killed?

Mr. MARVILLE. No, I do not doubt that.

Mr. RANGEL. Do you doubt that he left because we told him that he should leave? You were here when Noriega testified?

Mr. MARVILLE. That is not what I am saying. What I am saying is that I do not know the precise details of the whole exercise, and there is a lot of doubt over what happened, and that is——

Mr. RANGEL. Let's take an academic thing. From what we know from what Secretary Noriega said, that he was warned that his life was in danger and he left, we agreed, because his life was in danger. What does not make this a coup d'etat as Ambassadors understand it? Rebels, force, fear, flee.

Now, if it is a coup d'etat, can legitimate governments in the international community recognize somebody who came into power as a result of the seizure of a government through force? Can it be done in Barbados? Can it be done in the United States? Can we recognize the person who seized the government through arms illegally?

Mr. MARVILLE. Unfortunately, sir, this has always been done.

Mr. RANGEL. By whom?

Mr. MARVILLE. By communities in general. There is a——

Mr. RANGEL. Well, name me somebody. Who took over a government by force when the President was elected, and the United States or the Government of Barbados said, welcome, we never did like the guy that was elected anyway; was that ever done by your government?

Mr. MARVILLE. No. I am saying, sir——

Mr. RANGEL. No, no. Was it ever done by the United States or by your government, or any civilized government?

Mr. MARVILLE. No, it has not been done by our government. It is not part of our tradition.

Mr. RANGEL. Okay. That is all I am talking about, tradition. Do you know of any situation where this has been done, where the thugs, which Noriega called them thugs and crooks, and all the people came over, chased out the President; have they ever been recognized as a legitimate government that you know of, Ambassador?

Mr. CARNEY. I cannot think of one, but I somehow suspect there is.

Mr. RANGEL. If indeed this is the circumstances we are dealing with, would it not be correct that our position should be the restoration of the legal government in Haiti?

Mr. SACHS. Yes, sir, absolutely. And if we determine——

Mr. RANGEL. What choice do we have?

Mr. SACHS. If we determine that those are the facts, as they seem to be, that is absolutely what the CARICOM——

Mr. RANGEL. I want to hear from the Ambassadors, the Ambassadors. What choices do we have except to say our position is the rule of law, not for Haiti, but for all civilized countries, especially in the Caribbean?

Ms. WATERS. Especially.

Mr. MARVILLE. Sir, you have pointed to a danger that we recognize. However, I was giving you an answer that is part of diplomacy. Unfortunately, governments in general have accepted coup d'etat as a de facto reality, even if they have——

Mr. RANGEL. Let me get closer to home. Who is your Prime Minister? Was he elected?

Mr. MARVILLE. Yes, of course.

Mr. RANGEL. Do we have opposition?

Mr. MARVILLE. Yes.

Mr. RANGEL. Suppose we do not like your Prime Minister, but we like your opposition; suppose people came from outside of Barbados, supported your opposition, and then after they got there, we deal with the opposition. Is that tradition?

Mr. MARVILLE. Since you asked the question, I would suggest that anybody who tried that with Barbados would be dumber than dumb.

Mr. RANGEL. Well, I hope that you support the CARICOM who believed that the restoration of the rule of law is important to CARICOM, just as it is important to Haiti. I want to thank the Ambassadors for understanding this better than I do.

Mr. BALLENGER. Ms. Waters.

Mr. CARNEY. Let me answer what I believe is at the heart of the disagreement between the two sides of this hearing, and that is there is a large—largely shared belief that Mr. Aristide had so attenuated his legitimacy and so compromised his own devotion to democracy as to render a U.S. view of his restorability dubious.

Mr. BALLENGER. That is a good answer.

Ms. Waters, it is your ballgame.

Ms. WATERS. Yes. Mr. Chairman and Members, first I want to thank you again for allowing us to be here, but to entertain any conversation that talks about our respect and support for democracy around the world calls into question the fact that we give Egypt billions of dollars. I do not think that is a democracy. On and on and on. I mean, I could just call the roll on it. So there are some contradictions here.

But I want to say to the panel, this business of the opposition, in this discussion when we talk about the opposition, we are talking about Mr. Andre Apaid, Jr., and the so-called Group of 184. How many people here know that Mr. Andre Apaid is an American citizen with an American passport? How many people know that the United States has never responded to the question: What the heck is an American citizen doing creating a coup d'etat in somebody else's country? Was that ever discussed in CARICOM?

Mr. MARVILLE. No.

Ms. WATERS. Have you ever heard it discussed by Mr. Noriega, anybody?

Well, how many people know that Mr. Apaid owns about 15 or 16 factories in Haiti? How many people know that? Can I hear you?

Mr. SACHS. Oh, yes.

Ms. WATERS. You know that?

How many people know that President Aristide, in the work that he was doing, was fighting for and insisting on an increase in wages for these poor workers in these factories? How many people know that? Can I hear you?

Mr. MARVILLE. Yes.

Mr. MAGUIRE. Yes.

Mr. SACHS. Confirmed.

Ms. WATERS. How many people know that Mr. Apaid has been accused of not paying his taxes, and that Mr. Aristide was insisting that he pay his taxes? Does anyone know that?

Mr. SACHS. Yes.

Ms. WATERS. You heard that before?

Mr. SACHS. Heard that.

Mr. MAGUIRE. Yes.

Ms. WATERS. How many people know that Mr. Aristide was not only fighting for increased wages in the factories, fighting for the business class to pay their taxes so that they could have some money for infrastructure; how many people knew that he was fighting against this indentured servitude of young girls who work in the homes of the privileged, who work from sunup to sundown taking care of babies, scrubbing floors in exchange for food and a place to sleep? Anybody understand anything about that?

Mr. CARNEY. Yes. I am familiar with that concept.

Mr. MAGUIRE. Mr. Aristide was an advocate of doing something about restavek, which is what you are talking about, this practice, but particularly strong before he was actually elected to office.

Ms. WATERS. Okay. So this priest from Cite Soleil, referred to as a priest of the slums, was fighting for increased wages, fighting to make the rich pay their taxes, and against these children being used basically as slaves and servants in these homes.

How many people know that the figure that the Chairman and others referred to today of $850 million did not go to the Aristide government?

Mr. MAGUIRE. In fact, I believe the United States cut off most bilateral aid probably by around 1998 or so; however, we continued to fund the Haitian Coast Guard, which is bilateral aid.

Ms. WATERS. All right. How many people understand that there is a difference between bilateral aid that goes directly to the government and the funding of nongovernment organizations? How many people understand that?

Mr. MAGUIRE. Understood.

Mr. SACHS. Congresswoman.

Ms. WATERS. Yes, please, respond quickly.

Mr. SACHS. Yes, very, very quickly. When I spoke with President Aristide in 2001, he laid out a very sensible, responsible economic vision and wanted to work with the Inter-American Development Bank, the International Monetary Fund, and the World Bank, and, thus, I was particularly shocked to come back to Washington to find a U.S.-imposed freeze on all of those institutions.

Ms. WATERS. How many people know that if you do not have that kind of aid, you have no money for the infrastructure, you have no money to clean up the water, no money for the police, no money for the fire? And while Mr. Aristide has been blamed for not doing anything about poverty, do you understand how he was strangled by the lack of aid, bilateral or otherwise? How many people understand that?

Mr. SACHS. Let me speak as a macroeconomist to say that it is even worse than that, because they drained him of foreign exchange reserves. As he continued to service the debts to the international institutions, the exchange rate collapsed, the inflation rose, and the economy collapsed, and that was the deliberate result of the strangulation of aid.

Ms. WATERS. Well, I hope we can get rid of some of the lies and misconceptions about all of this money that has gone to the government, when, in fact, it has not, and I do not want to hear that said anymore. So I just wanted to get that on the record.

Mr. WELLER. The gentlewoman's time has expired.

Ms. WATERS. Thank you so very much.

Mr. BALLENGER. Ms. Jackson Lee is recognized for 5 minutes.

Ms. JACKSON LEE. Let me again express my appreciation to the Chairman and Ranking Member for their courtesies.

Mr. Paquiot, again, thank you, and let me just make a statement. All of us want to have Haiti go forward. I only wish that we had done our job previously and provided the appropriate aid through our monetary organizations and USAID so we would not be here today.

Let me pose a quick question to Ambassador Carney to understand the funding of your organization. Is it mostly what we would call the economic elite?

Mr. CARNEY. To the extent the organization has any funding at all, it is donations——

Ms. JACKSON LEE. Generally supported by people of better economic means.

Let me just ask this other question.

Mr. CARNEY. I do not know, to be specific.

Ms. JACKSON LEE. Well, would you say that numbers of individuals involved with the organization were not happy with President Aristide?

Mr. CARNEY. A large number are not happy with him, that is correct.

Ms. JACKSON LEE. What I would say is that we have had—I think it is recognized that the United States has Green Party and Independents, Republicans and Democrats, many of whom disagree, and I might imagine that they disagree with the present Administration. I think as the longest-standing democracy, we would stand up in arms, and I use that figuratively, to oppose a group that would engage in a coup d'etat because they were opposed to the leadership of our Nation. I just want to put that on the record; I am not posing a question to you right now.

Let me go to Mr. Sachs and Mr. Maguire because I would like to—even as you are academics, you have a very strong grounding in Haitian politics, diplomacy, and also the needs of the Haitian people. I think we should put that on the record. My line of questioning to the earlier witness, the Assistant Secretary, that led him to, I think, offer a gaffe in telling a Member of Congress what was or was not the business of Congress—and I will look forward to his apology for that; I am sorry that we did not have a second round. I was not intending to intimidate him, but to ask a serious question.

I say that because my line of questioning was, if you were in fear of your life, would it not be much easier to accept anything if you believe that someone was going to leave you abandoned with no security, no protection, and, therefore, your only option is to get up and get out? Mr. Sachs, does that sound reasonable? You are in fear for your life, you are relying upon a certain protective element, and that seems to be being removed from you immediately, such as what was happening to President Aristide on Saturday night and early Sunday morning.

Mr. SACHS. The best evidence is the USDCM actually told Mr. Aristide and his wife that you are all going to be killed unless you get on the airplane.

Ms. JACKSON LEE. Would you translate that to a degree of coercion that you had to leave immediately and that your family was in jeopardy?

Mr. SACHS. I think it was utterly coercive.

Ms. JACKSON LEE. Let me just say that I applaud the work of my colleagues. I have asked both the Leader and the Speaker to convene immediate congressional hearings of the Intelligence Committee, other relevant Committees, this one is certainly relevant, for the time certain that I think you are speaking of. Do you think that is what we need to move on as quickly as possible, that we would have immediate investigatory hearings in this body right now, subpoena records or ask for records to determine what happened in the last 48 hours?

Mr. SACHS. I think—I hope you go into evening session to do that this evening, because in real time, this country is at profound risk. A President's whereabouts are not known, his physical safety is not known, and his story is being suppressed, I fear.

Ms. JACKSON LEE. Do you think it is appropriate because we are a democracy that we should determine whether the CIA was actively involved in both a coup d'etat and a deposing of a democratically-elected President?

Mr. SACHS. I most certainly do, especially because it looks like the CIA had its fingerprints all over the 1991 coup, and as Santayana said, if you do not learn from the past, you are doomed to repeat it. And we may be in the middle of repeating it right now, because when the Congressional Black Caucus 13 years ago asked for an investigation, it was just laughed off, and we are back again, with all of the fingerprints once again there. So, yes, this is urgent. This is not just theoretical.

Ms. JACKSON LEE. Let me get another question to you, because you are so knowledgeable. The good Ambassador Marville said it would have been dumber than dumb to go against Barbados. Unfortunately, Haiti is a victim, a small victim, a victim without a military that the duly-elected democratic military President yielded, if you will, and made a decision to be as peaceful as he could.

Have we not damaged—based on Grenada and other interaction with CARICOM—have we not drastically damaged the relationship between the United States and CARICOM, which offered a peace settlement of which the President of Haiti agreed to and the United States gave no, if you will, both military support or political support to that, even though they were a member of the United Nations Security Council that voted to go with CARICOM's offer of peace and resolution and diplomatic solution? Did we not or have we not drastically violated our relationship with CARICOM and that cohesion in between the Western Hemisphere?

Mr. WELLER [presiding]. The gentlewoman's time has expired.

Ms. JACKSON LEE. Would the gentleman be able to answer, Mr. Chairman?

Mr. WELLER. The gentlewoman's time has expired.

Mr. MENENDEZ. Mr. Speaker, the gentlewoman's time having expired does not mean that we do not allow witnesses to answer. So I would urge the witness to be able to answer.

Mr. WELLER. With all due respect to my good friend from New Jersey, this is the rule we have been following. We have cut off witnesses before, including the Assistant Secretary of State.

Mr. MENENDEZ. Mr. Chairman, we have let them make introductory answers.

Mr. WELLER. The gentlewoman from the Virgin Islands is recognized for 5 minutes.

Mr. MENENDEZ. Is the gentleman not permitted to answer? At this stage you are going to be abrupt? I would let the gentleman have—I ask unanimous consent to let the gentleman have 1 minute to give an answer.

Mr. WELLER. The gentlewoman's time has expired. We have cut off other witnesses.

Mr. MENENDEZ. I ask unanimous consent for 1 minute to let the gentleman answer.

Mr. WELLER. The gentleman has 1 minute.

Mr. SACHS. I will just take 15 seconds. The CARICOM leadership is aghast at what happened and believes that democracy in the whole region has been jeopardized and is continuing to be jeopardized until the situation is properly restored on a constitutional basis.

Mr. WELLER. Thank you.

Ms. JACKSON LEE. Thank you.

Mr. WELLER. The gentlewoman from the Virgin Islands is recognized for 5 minutes.

Mrs. CHRISTENSEN. Thank you. I, like Congressman Meeks, was remiss in not thanking the Committee for allowing those of us who are not on the Committee to participate in what has been a very important hearing.

I just want to follow up on the last question from my colleague, Ms. Jackson Lee, because I had asked the question of Secretary

Noriega regarding our country's unilateral decision to move ahead, having been in agreement with CARICOM. I was just informed that CARICOM held a press conference not more than 2 hours ago, and the essence of what their statement was is that CARICOM does not accept the removal of Aristide; demands the immediate return of the democratic Government of Haiti; that they demand an impartial, transparent investigation by the U.N. into the circumstances surrounding his removal; and that they will have no dealings with the so-called Government of Haiti.

So if you would like to just expand on the question about the deterioration in whatever was left of the relationship between our country and our closest neighbors, our third border, I will let you go ahead.

Mr. SACHS. I think CARICOM leaders are very frightened about a President in their region being carried off by a U.S. airplane in the middle of the night under threat of death, being told that if he does not get on the plane with a handed resignation, his family will be killed, and then taken to the Central African Republic without knowing where he is going. That has made some of the leaders nervous.

Mrs. CHRISTENSEN. Thank you.

Mr. SACHS. It should scare the wits out of them.

Mr. MAGUIRE. Could I just add one thing here?

Mrs. CHRISTENSEN. Sure.

Mr. MAGUIRE. I am not surprised that people in Jamaica would be nervous. If we go back just a decade or 2, we did have occasions in Jamaica where the opposition boycotted the elections, as the opposition in Haiti did in November 2000. So there has got to be kind of a reverberation of deja vu again, I will use that term, among Haiti's neighbors. And I do think that we need to listen carefully to Haiti's neighbors. As I have said, you know, when Haiti sneezes, Florida catches a cold, but the neighbors catch the flu.

Mrs. CHRISTENSEN. Right. And we are one of those neighbors.

I do not have any further questions. I did not make an opening statement, and I would just like to close by saying to Mr. Paquiot that, you know, I regret hearing about and seeing your grave misfortune and injuries, but especially so because our country abandoned Haiti, as you have heard so clearly, and allowed this to happen. And so you are really a victim at the very least of our omission or failure to act, but at the worst our contributing towards, as we are uncovering this afternoon, our support of the opposition.

It is interesting that we in the CBC have been criticized for focusing all of our attention on President Aristide the person, and if caring about our brother is something to criticize, well, I surely accept it. But the panel has reminded me, and I think it has made it very clear, that it is not us who brought the focus of our foreign policy toward Haiti or the crisis that we are now in, it is not us that brought that focus to Aristide, it is the U.S. Government, our leadership, who hated this man so much that they not only allowed the country to be destabilized by it, but they really fueled that destabilization and allowed the 8 million or so people of Haiti, who really believed in us, believed that we would help bring democracy and trusted us to do that, to suffer unnecessarily just to get rid of him. So I just wanted to make that statement.

Ms. JACKSON LEE. Will the gentlewoman yield?

Mrs. CHRISTENSEN. Sure, I will yield.

Ms. JACKSON LEE. First I would like to—I do not know if it is appropriate; I am not a Member of the Committee. Am I allowed to ask unanimous consent to submit letters into the record?

Mr. WELLER. Yes, without objection.

Ms. JACKSON LEE. I thank the gentlewoman for yielding, and I just have one brief question to——

Mr. WELLER. If the gentlewoman would yield, another Member of the Committee can submit it into the record for you at your request.

Mrs. CHRISTENSEN. I just—you wanted to ask a question?

Ms. JACKSON LEE. Yes.

Mr. MENENDEZ. Would the gentlewoman yield to me?

Mrs. CHRISTENSEN. Sure.

Mr. MENENDEZ. I ask unanimous consent to include in the record letters written by Ms. Jackson Lee to Leader Pelosi and Speaker Hastert.

Mr. WELLER. Without objection.

Ms. JACKSON LEE. Are you still yielding?

Mrs. CHRISTENSEN. Go ahead.

Ms. JACKSON LEE. I just have a quick question, Mr. Sachs, on the asylum question. Does it not appear to you from your study to be a dual standard that we have already said this is a tumultuous condition in Haiti, and that we are not allowing or do not seem to be allowing Haitians to apply for asylum here in the United States?

Mr. SACHS. It is quite shocking and obviously very locally driven politically and very painful to watch.

Ms. JACKSON LEE. I thank you.

Mrs. CHRISTENSEN. I want to just use my last second to thank you all for staying, for your patience, and for your commitment to bringing some truth and clarity to this issue.

Mr. MENENDEZ. Mr. Chairman, if I may, I just want to take the opportunity to thank Chairman Ballenger for the courtesies that he extended in this hearing, particularly to nonmembers of the Committee. We appreciate that. Obviously, there is a great deal of interest in this issue, and we appreciate the manner in which he conducted the hearing and the manner in which he gave opportunities to Members to make statements, ask questions, and we look forward to continuing opportunities to continue to pursue this issue in the days ahead. I just want to take this opportunity to thank the Chair.

Mr. BALLENGER [presiding]. I would like to thank you guys for toughing it out the way you did, and, Mr. Paquiot, especially you, because of the physical condition that you are in and also to miss a plane. I am sure you all missed appointments that you had planned on.

Mr. Maguire, I had notification last week that you were going to be on short notice and that you were going to have to leave, and I thank you kindly for sticking around, and I am sure Mr. Sachs had the same problem.

Ms. WATERS. Would you thank Mr. Paquiot on behalf of all of us?

Mr. BALLENGER. Yes. Mr. Paquiot, everybody thanks you for sacrificing your time and yourself for being able to participate in this.

Mr. WELLER. Mr. Chairman and the Ranking Member, thank you for your comments. On behalf of those of us who have participated today, we particularly appreciate everyone who participated on our panel and for your patience. And to our two international visitors, thank you for the time that you have given to be here today.

I ask unanimous consent for all Members to have 5 legislative days to revise and extend their remarks and submit written questions for the two panels for a response.

Without objection, the Committee stands adjourned.

Mr. BALLENGER. Thank you, sir.

[Whereupon, at 7:25 p.m., the Subcommittee was adjourned.]

APPENDIX

MATERIAL SUBMITTED FOR THE HEARING RECORD

PREPARED STATEMENT OF THE HONORABLE CHARLES B. RANGEL, A REPRESENTATIVE IN CONGRESS FROM THE STATE OF NEW YORK

I want to thank Chairman Ballenger and Ranking Democratic member Menendez for holding this hearing on Haiti.

The crisis in Haiti is of great importance for this country and the international community. The situation in Haiti is of deep concern to many members of Congress, particularly members of the Congressional Black Caucus who worked so hard to restore Jean Bertrand Aristide to the Presidency to which he was elected by the people of Haiti.

Members of the Congressional Black Caucus, including myself, met with Secretary of State Colin Powell, National Security Advisor Condoleeza Rice, and President Bush at the White House last week prior to the removal of Haitian President Aristide from power.

We thought we were in agreement with the Administration on the importance of pursuing a negotiated agreement between President Aristide and the Opposition that would have achieved power-sharing and the completion of Aristide's presidential term. This weekend, upon Aristide's removal, we met with UN Secretary General Kofi Annan at the United Nations to request the engagement of the UN in the Haitian crisis.

Thank you for this opportunity to speak to the members of this sub-committee and panel directly to offer my thoughts on the situation in Haiti.

In reading the press, it is always interesting to see how easily right wing conservatives disparage the rule of law when it suits their purpose.

Those who question the legitimacy of my call for an investigation into the facts and circumstances of the role of the US Government in effecting the forcible removal from office of the constitutionally elected President of Haiti accuse me of just wanting to be negative and critical of the President.

I have been accused of using improper and inflammatory language. The truth is that what I am doing, through the use of appropriate and accurate language, is seeking to hold the Government of the United Sates accountable for its actions in Haiti over this past weekend.

Isn't this exactly what President Bush and his Administration claim to be doing in Iraq and elsewhere, promoting democracy and the rule of law?

Let's examine the facts and the language I have applied to them.

I have asserted that the Government of the United States perpetrated a coup d'etat in Haiti on Saturday night and Sunday morning when the Deputy Chief of Mission went to the home of President Aristide with security forces and informed him that his enemies were at the gates and the United States was not prepared to defend him.

As a result, he had two choices: either sign the letter of resignation conveniently prepared for his signature and accept an escorted departure from Haiti or refuse to sign the letter of resignation and face certain death in a matter of hours.

What is a coup d'etat? It is defined in the Oxford Dictionary as "a violent or illegal seizure of power."

In Haiti on Saturday night/Sunday morning the United States Government used the threat of violence against the constitutionally elected President of Haiti and his family to obtain his resignation and departure from Haiti before the end of his constitutionally determined term of office. That action, I maintain, meets the definition of a coup d'etat.

What is a resignation? The Oxford dictionary says it is the act of voluntarily leaving or quitting a position.

Is, as in Haiti on Saturday night/Sunday morning the United States Government obtained a signed letter of resignation under the threat of imminent violence and death as a consequence if the President did not sign, that a valid resignation, or was it obtained involuntarily by force and thus invalid?

I have been accused of using irresponsible and inflammatory language in describing President Aristide's forcible removal from office a "kidnapping." An examination of the meaning of the word again justifies its use. What is "kidnapping?"

The Black's Law Dictionary, 4th Edition, says that "at common law, kidnapping is the forcible abduction or stealing and carrying away of a person from his own country to another." On Saturday night/Sunday morning the United States Government engineered the forcible removal of the lawfully elected President of Haiti from his own country and arranged that he be carried away to another. President Aristide was indeed kidnapped and apparently by the Government of the United States.

I maintain that I have described the role of the United States in the removal of Jean Bertrand Aristide from the Presidency of Haiti in violation of the constitution of Haiti and his forced exile accurately.

Prepared Statement of the Honorable Gregory W. Meeks, a Representative in Congress from the State of New York

Early Sunday morning, Haitian President Jean-Bertrand Aristide was found to resign his office and went into exile. Thus, a tragic page has been turned in another sad chapter of the painful history of the world's first Black independent nation. Americans should take no joy in what has occurred. They should be very concerned about what lies ahead, bearing in mind that whatever happens to Haiti from this point indirectly happens to America.

More than 1,000 Haitians have sought refuge in the United States, only to be returned to their deeply troubled nation. More refugees are sure to come as the widespread looting, street violence, and killings already under way during the past week intensifies in the wake of Aristide's departure.

President Bush has sent in a contingent of U.S. Marines. Other nations are contributing troops to an international peacekeeping force authorized by the United Nations Security Council.

Hopefully, these steps will quell the violence and anarchy. Hopefully, they will expedite the restoration of order and put into place a government acceptable to all Haitians. President Bush is staking a lot on hope. Unfortunately, hope is a poor substitute for policy—especially good policy.

Which is why Americans should not take comfort in what has transpired, nor pride in the role of their own government. The Bush administration is deeply complacent in the ouster of a democratically elected president of an independent country. The long term interests of the American people as opposed to the immediate interests of the Bush Administration demand that todays congressional hearing on Haiti find answers to three questions: Why did developments in Haiti take the course they have? What are the implications of yet another U.S.-backed coup? Where will things go from here?

While it cannot be said that Aristide played no role in the demise of his presidency, it is also true that withholding badly needed U.S. and international aid made it doubly difficult for the Aristide government to fulfill its responsibilities to the Haitian people. Over the past several weeks, as gangs of armed thugs, former torturers and death squad leaders, coup plotters, drug dealers, and convicted murderers—to paraphrase Colin Powell's words, mounted an armed rebellion against the duly elected government, the Administration rejected Aristide's call for international assistance. The Administration only supported the Caribbean Community's (CARICOM) plan of action for resolving the crisis in response to intense pressure from the Congressional Black Caucus—a plan to which Aristide agreed but the opposition rejected.

The Administration's posture assured the opposition that it would not have to reach a compromise. They could simply hold out and let the thugs do their dirty work. In effect, the Administration promised to send in the marines if and only if Aristide resigned. Lacking sufficient internal forces to restore law and order, Aristide—facing the specter of revenge killings, more looting, and massive waves of refugees fleeing to the United States was given no choice. The Administration claims the resignation was consistent with Haiti's constitution. That may be formally true, but in essence we are witnessing the 33rd coup d'etat in Haiti's history—most of them engineered by the United States.

The Administration suggests that the crisis was solely Aristide's fault. It also accuses the ousted Haitian president of electoral fraud. I have been among those who criticized Aristide for autocratic governance, for failure to develop democratic institutions, and for insufficient steps to improve the material conditions of the Haitian people.

But, in a democracy, elections should be the principal means by which leaders are replaced. Instead, President Bush has strengthen undemocratic and anti-democratic methods, while further weakening Haiti's already fragile democratic institutions. Moreover, what exactly is the agenda of the opposition and of the armed rebels that our government tacitly supports? What costs will the American people incur? What will happened when the marines leave? What message are we sending to other countries in the hemisphere experiencing internal political difficulties? Will these nations be more or less inclined to tolerate dissent?

What Haiti needs most is the rule of law and an orderly constitutional process. It urgently needs large scale humanitarian assistance in the form of food, clothing, medical care, and shelter. It also needs stability, sustained help in creating a coherent civil society, and a long term economic development commitment from the United States, the UN, CARICOM, the Organization of American States, and the international community. CARICOM is to be commended for its balanced approach to resolving this crisis. Let us hope the UN maintains a peacekeeping presence and when the time comes contributes election monitors.

The Administration has once again demonstrated that it is fully capable of ousting a head of state that it does not like. It has shown itself to be far less capable when it comes to reconstruction and nation-building. Yet, it is precisely on these questions that once again the credibility of the United States hinges.

PREPARED STATEMENT OF THE HONORABLE MAXINE WATERS, A REPRESENTATIVE IN CONGRESS FROM THE STATE OF CALIFORNIA

I have been to Haiti three times during the last two months, most recently, about ten days ago. It was clear to me that a *coup d'etat* was in progress, and I communicated my concerns to Secretary of State Colin Powell on a regular basis. As recently as a week ago, Secretary Powell had repeatedly stated that the United States would not call for the resignation of President Jean-Bertrand Aristide, the democratically-elected President of Haiti, or support any attempts to remove him from office. Yet, obviously, by this past weekend, the Bush Administration abandoned that position, reversed course, and pressured President Aristide to leave.

What happened? Why would we not commit U.S. forces to stabilize the democratically-elected government of Haiti when we had no reluctance to commit those same forces once President Aristide was removed? Were the Haitian people less worthy of protection from violence and unrest when President Aristide was still in power? Were their circumstances any less dire? It appears that our government was perfectly content to let the Haitian people suffer the burdens of this violence and civil unrest until President Aristide's departure was achieved.

Perhaps this sheds some light on why Ambassador Roger Noriega, the Assistant Secretary for Western Hemisphere Affairs and the former chief of staff for Senator Jesse Helms, was permitted to pursue a policy of undermining President Aristide's government for so many years. Ambassador Noriega has a long history of being aligned with the anti-Aristide business owners in Haiti and undermining the democratically-elected governments of Haiti. Ambassador Noriega has been working closely with the opposition in Haiti. The Ambassador's statements throughout the political crisis that led to President Aristide's removal have been extremely one-sided.

For several years, the United States blocked $145.9 million in development loans to Haiti by the Inter-American Development Bank. These loans were supposed to fund health, basic education, rural road development, potable water and sanitation programs, but the United States government prevented the money from ever going to Haiti until the Congressional Black Caucus intervened last year. Denying Haiti access to basic development assistance undermined the ability of the elected government of Haiti to serve the needs of its people and further impoverished a poor population.

The United States government also helped to organize and train the political opposition in Haiti. The International Republican Institute (IRI) has been providing the opposition training for political party development, communications strategies, public opinion polling, web site development and public outreach. IRI has a blatantly partisan approach. It trains opposition groups but flatly refuses to work with Lavalas party members or other supporters of President Aristide. IRI's Haiti Program is funded by American taxpayers through the U.S. Agency for International Development (USAID). IRI is currently operating under a two-year grant from USAID obtained in late 2002.

While I was in Haiti, I met with leaders of the opposition, including Andre Apaid, the leader of the Group of 184. Unfortunately, Andre Apaid is not the democratic leader that the Administration would have us believe. Andre Apaid was a Duvalier-supporter, who allegedly holds an American passport and operates sweatshops in Haiti. Andre Apaid refused to accept the CARICOM proposal as the basis for negotiations to resolve the political crisis. He repeatedly rejected President Aristide's offer to negotiate, and he refused to participate in any negotiations whatsoever.

The opposition has accused President Aristide of drug trafficking and corruption. Yet when asked for documentation, they have not been able to produce anything more than rumors, innuendos and allegations. No one has ever identified any money allegedly stolen by President Aristide.

President Aristide has given the United States special authority to assist with drug interdiction efforts by allowing the United States to interdict drugs in Haitian waters. The government of Haiti does not have the resources needed to wage a tough and consistent war against drugs, and the President of Haiti begged the United States for assistance to eliminate drug trafficking.

Many of the thugs that took over Haiti in the last few weeks are former members of the Haitian military or members of the feared death squad known as the Front for the Advancement and Progress of Haiti (FRAPH). FRAPH members were responsible for numerous human rights violations during the three years following the *coup d'etat* in 1991. Guy Philippe, who yesterday declared himself the new chief of Haiti's military, is a former police chief and military officer, who was accused of a previous *coup* attempt in 2002. Louis Jodel Chamblain, was a leader of FRAPH and was convicted in abstentia for his role in a 1994 massacre. He has also been accused of drug trafficking.

When President Aristide disbanded the Haitian military following his return to Haiti in 1994, the former military officers were never disarmed. Many simply went over the border into the Dominican Republic, taking their M–1 and M–14 weapons with them.

I am especially concerned by the possibility that the U.S. government may have armed and trained the former military officers and death squad leaders who carried out last Sunday's *coup*. In 2002, the United States supplied M–16's to the Dominican Republic, supposedly for use along the Haitian border, and stationed 900 U.S. troops alongside Dominican guards at the border. Many of the thugs that have taken over Haiti are now armed with M–16's. The U.S. government must investigate how these thugs were armed and explain how the M–16's got into their hands.

The United States has also maintained a ban on weapons sales to Haiti. This has left the Haitian police force ill-equipped to maintain law and order in the face of groups of armed thugs, former military officers and death squad members. The people of the city of St. Marc placed boxes, rocks and cars in the roads to protect themselves from the approaching paramilitary groups. The Administration should explain why this ban on weapons sales was maintained against Haiti throughout President Aristide's term in office.

Once the thugs had completely surrounded Port-au-Prince, President Aristide was forced to leave Haiti. President Aristide called me on Monday morning and told me that Luis G. Moreno, the Deputy Chief of Mission at the U.S. Embassy in Port-au-Prince, came to his home in the wee hours of the morning with other diplomats and U.S. Marines. He said he was told to leave, and leave now, or he and many Haitians would be killed. He said he was kidnaped.

This certainly has the appearance of a *coup*.

I demand that this Administration explain how they allowed a democratically-elected government to be overthrown by a group of heavily-armed thugs.

RESPONSES FROM THE HONORABLE ROGER F. NORIEGA, ASSISTANT SECRETARY OF STATE, BUREAU OF WESTERN HEMISPHERE AFFAIRS, TO QUESTIONS SUBMITTED FOR THE RECORD BY THE HONORABLE GREGORY W. MEEKS, A REPRESENTATIVE IN CONGRESS FROM THE STATE OF NEW YORK

Question:

I agree that there were many problems with Aristide's government but also strongly believe in democratic and diplomatic solutions and that the US approach was neither of these. It seems to me that nothing Aristide did would have been enough to bring the opposition to negotiate. In hindsight, as the world's superpower working with the poorest country in the hemisphere, is there anything the US could have done to compel the opposition to come to the negotiating plan such that a peaceful and democratic solution involving all political leaders could have been reached?

Response:

The U.S. worked with the United Nations (UN), the Organization of American States, (OAS), and the Caribbean Community (CARICOM) to attempt to resolve the political crisis in Haiti. We did everything we could to bring the two sides to the table, but Aristide had engendered the distrust of the opposition in the political process. His manipulation of violence against the opposition led them to doubt the viability of any power-sharing government led by Aristide. In addition, Aristide had previously refused to take part in any attempts to create a legitimate power sharing government. The opposition and civic society leaders would not engage in an electoral process without good faith actions from Aristide to guarantee their security. Aristide never took these steps.

Question:

It seems that all sorts of sordid figures are coming out of the woodwork to rule in Haiti. Guy Phillipe has taken over the armed forces and is insisting on a role in Haiti's future, Baby Doc wants to return, and Danny Toussaint wants to run for President. What is our current plan for Haiti and will these people be allowed to take office?

Response:

We have been very clear with the interim Government of Haiti that there can be no role in government or the police for anybody who espouses political violence or has committed crimes or human rights abuses in the past. We also encourage the Government of Haiti to pursue justice for any criminal acts through the judicial system.

We are working with the international community to assist Haiti in planning for its elections and in standing up its police force and justice system. The Administration expects to play a role, defined in the context of the other donors in the international community, in Haiti's reconstruction over the next several years to help restore the capacity to govern, develop a professional and independent police force, promote economic development, and support free and fair elections.

Question:

What is the Administration's plan for the future of Haiti? How long do we plan on providing peacekeepers? What actions are being taken to protect the safety and security of innocent citizens in Haiti, in light of the growing threats to public order? What plans exist to help Haiti grow its economy and lift it from the extreme poverty it suffers under today?

Response:

The U.S. military is currently functioning as the lead nation of the Multinational Interim Force (MIF) authorized by UN Security Council Resolution 1529. We expect that the MIF will be replaced by a UN peacekeeping operation on or about May 29. We are pressing the UN Department of Peacekeeping Operations to submit to the UN Security Council its report on recommendations for a follow-on UN peacekeeping force in Haiti. That report will form the basis for deliberations on a second UN Security Council Resolution to authorize a UN peacekeeping force for Haiti.

The MIF in Haiti comprises approximately 3900 personnel from Canada, Chile, France and the United States. Its primary mission is to restore order and to support the Government of Haiti's efforts to re-establish public security and stability. It is supporting the Haitian National Police in the disarmament of illegally armed civilians in accordance with Haitian law. Any illegally armed civilians encountered by presence patrols will be immediately disarmed to ensure force protection of the MIF. Threats to the protection of the MIF will not be tolerated. Additionally, when MIF personnel encounter any acts of violence, they will intervene to protect life. With the presence of the MIF, threats to public order have diminished markedly, although common crime remains an endemic problem in Haiti.

Funding of economic growth programs in recent years has been limited to microfinance and hillside agriculture programs. While these have been successful in creating sustainable economic opportunities for the Haitians they have reached, they are not sufficient to address Haiti's massive unemployment and economic stagnation.

USAID is now considering reallocating some assistance to job creation programs through labor intensive public works to help Haiti re-cover from damage incurred during the political crisis that preceded former president Aristide's resignation.

However, these are necessarily a short-term solution. Sustained economic growth will only be achieved through private sector trade and investment.

The U.S. has provided over $3 million in emergency aid since mid-February in addition to the $55 million in regular assistance budgeted for fiscal year 2004. Since the Haitian government cleared its arrears to the Inter-American Development Bank (IDB), it has approved $398 million in loans. The IDB has distributed $47 million of this amount. All but $30 million of the remainder are project loans that will be disbursed as the projects are implemented, often 5 years or longer. These projects have potential to make a substantial contribution to Haiti's long term development.

Question:

The International Republican Institute is said to have worked with opposition groups, which have not only vetoed the government's attempts to call elections, but have refused to negotiate under CARICOM proposal, or the recent U.S. proposal. Exactly how much was given to IRI since 2000 to work with opposition groups? Did the IRI give this money to opposition groups? What groups were the recipients? Were any of the groups in the Dominican Republic? Did Stanley Lucas work with these groups in Haiti and/or in the Dominican Republic?

Response:

IRI's current grant from USAID is a two-year program, begun in 2002, with an annual project budget of $600,000 per year. From 2000 to 2002, IRI undertook U.S.-based assessments and planning for future activities in Haiti. This involved a few trips to Miami to discuss prospective activities with Haitian political leaders and members of the Haitian diaspora.

Under its current grant, IRI provides training and education in basic skills of democracy, citizenship, and advocacy. Specifically, IRI training focuses on democratic political party development, and communications strategies (public opinion polling, web site development, public outreach).

IRI does not provide financial assistance or material resources to any Haitian political party or group under this grant program. Participants in IRI training sessions receive no fees or payments; only their direct travel, lodging, and food expenses are covered. Since December 2002, IRI's Haiti program has held 26 training sessions. IRI held these sessions in a large public hotel in Santo Domingo, the capital of the Dominican Republic, with direct oversight from USAID. IRI held sessions in the Dominican Republic based on its assessment that security risks in Port-au-Prince were too high.

To foster a level playing field, IRI has concentrated efforts mostly on working with weaker political parties and disenfranchised constituencies such as women and youth. Under its USAID grant, IRI political party training is open to all parties committed to democratic principles. Political parties, groups, and individuals that support violence are not invited to IRI activities. Nor are individuals associated with the former Haitian military. In recent years, reports of links between elements of Fanmi Lavalas and acts of violence discouraged IRI from providing training for them. IRI has not offered or provided training for any groups based in the Dominican Republic.

Stanley Lucas participated in IRI training session noted above held in the Dominican Republic, as part of the IRI Haiti program team.

Question:

What is the legal status of Emmanuel Toto Constant, former FRAPH leader? How did he come to reside in Queens, NY? Does he have CIA connections? Why isn't he considered a risk to Haitians in NY?

Response:

Emmanuel "Toto" Constant arrived in the United States on a B–2 visitor's visa in December 1994, at San Juan, Puerto Rico, with authorization to remain in the United States until June 23, 1995. The Department of State revoked his visa on February 14, 1995. In September 1995, a U.S. immigration judge issued a final order of removal to deport Constant to Haiti. In December 1995, Constant filed a constitutional tort action against the Secretary of State and the Attorney General seeking $50 million in damages. In June 1996, Constant settled his lawsuit. In August 1997, an assessment of the threat to Constant if he were returned to Haiti was prepared. Based on that assessment, reviewed by various government agencies, Constant was not returned to Haiti. There were concerns about Constant's personal safety in Haiti, the inability of Haiti's weak judicial system to guarantee a fair trial, and potential unrest if Constant were returned.

In February 1998, Constant attempted to reopen his case to apply for asylum, but an Immigration Judge denied the motion. In September 2003, the Board of Immigration Appeals upheld the denial. There are at the moment no pending appeals or known legal impediments to Constant's removal. The Departments of State and Homeland Security are evaluating, in light of current country conditions, whether Constant may be removed to Haiti.

We believe that Constant ended up in Queens because of the substantial Haitian community living in New York.

If Constant were considered a threat to Haitians in New York, that would be a law enforcement matter, to be addressed by state authorities and the Department of Homeland Security.

I have no knowledge of alleged connections between Constant and the CIA.

Question:

Noriega suggested that US intervention after the departure of Aristide saved American lives. It seems that pressuring the opposition to accept the CARICOM plan would have prevented American military from having to enter Haiti at all. Why was not pursuing the CARICOM plan, a peaceful and democratic solution, a safer plan for our military than going into Haiti after Aristide's questioned "voluntary" resignation?

Response:

We worked with the international community to pursue a peaceful and democratic solution under the CARICOM plan. However, the armed rebel forces were intent on entering Port-au-Prince and ousting Aristide. These rebels would have marched on Port-au-Prince whether the political opposition had agreed to the CARICOM plan or not. Thousands of innocent Haitian citizens may have been killed in this environment. No one knows if they would have shared power with the political opposition. This would have been a coup d'etat. Aristide chose to resign and leave Haiti, which allowed for constitutional succession and for the international community to pursue the CARICOM plan.

To put U.S. troops on the ground while Aristide was in the National Palace would have been seen by many Haitians, including the rebels, as U.S. support for the Aristide regime. It would have meant putting our troops in the middle of an armed insurgency caused by an unresolved political crisis, largely of Aristide's own making. Armed insurgents would have viewed U.S. protection for Aristide as support for him and would have raised the risk to U.S. troops to an unacceptable level. When Aristide resigned, it became possible for U.S. troops to conduct stability operations without being between armed factions.

Question:

How does US involvement in what happened in Haiti impact the rest of the western hemisphere and how the world sees us?

Response:

I believe it demonstrates that the U.S. acted vigorously to protect the security and welfare of the Haitian people and that our commitment to the democratic process and economic well-being of Haitians remains as strong as ever.

As in the past, the U.S. will continue to support UN, OAS, and other efforts to re-establish a functioning democratic process, good governance, and economic development for the welfare of all Haitians.

RESPONSES FROM THE HONORABLE ARTHUR E. DEWEY, ASSISTANT SECRETARY OF STATE, BUREAU OF POPULATION, REFUGEES, AND MIGRATION, TO QUESTIONS SUBMITTED FOR THE RECORD BY THE HONORABLE GREGORY W. MEEKS, A REPRESENTATIVE IN CONGRESS FROM THE STATE OF NEW YORK

Question:

What is this Administration's plan for the future of Haiti? How long do we plan on providing peacekeepers? What actions are being taken to protect the safety and security of innocent citizens in Haiti, in light of the growing threats to public order? What plans exist to help Haiti grow its economy and lift it from the extreme poverty it suffers under today?

Answer:

The Administration is working with the international community in the wake of the resignation of former President Aristide to ensure that the interim government proceeds in a constitutional, consensus-based manner to restore democratic governance, stability, and economic growth to Haiti. We are doing this by supporting the international plan of action endorsed in OAS Permanent Council Resolution 861 and by taking a leading role in the Multinational Interim Force (MIF) which, pursuant to UN Security Council Resolution 1529, has helped the interim government to restore order and provide security.

As of March 31, the MIF in Haiti totaled over 3,600 uniformed personnel, including over 1,900 from the U.S. UNSCR 1529 provided a 90-day mandate for the MIF and declared the willingness of the Security Council to establish a follow-on UN stabilization force. In addition to protection of dignitaries, static protection of key facilities, and roving patrols, the MIF has extended its operations to the north, central, and southern regions of Haiti as well as Port-au-Prince. It is also supporting the efforts of the Haitian National Police to disarm those who have illegal firearms.

The United States has provided $3.3 million in emergency assistance to Haiti since February 18, when the U.S. Embassy issued a disaster declaration for Haiti. The U.S. remains the largest donor of bilateral assistance to Haiti, and plans to provide at least $55 million under ongoing assistance programs in FY 2004. The U.S. is examining how assistance can be re-oriented to address Haiti's needs for security and economic growth.

The U.S. is by far Haiti's largest trading partner and foreign investor. Haiti is a beneficiary of the U.S. Caribbean Basin Trade Partnership Act and Generalized System of Preferences.

Question:

Our government has been very clear in stating that it will not accept Haitian refugees and repatriated an estimated 1,000 Haitians that have recently fled. It is unconscionable that our government would force innocent people back into the midst of an unavoidable armed conflict when it is clear that conditions are dangerous. Because there clearly exists extraordinary and temporary conditions in Haiti that prevent these nationals from returning in safety. I believe it is necessary to grant Temporary Protected Status to Haitian refugees that reach our shores. Also, why are we not working with UNHCR as we have in the past to offer Haitians fleeing the conflict "temporary protection?"

Answer:

First, it is important to clarify that, per standing U.S. policy, during the recent unrest in Haiti, all migrants who expressed concern about returning to Haiti were interviewed by a trained protection officer from the Department of Homeland Security. The migrants were given a full opportunity to detail their fears, and the United States did not repatriate any migrants who were determined to qualify as refugees.

With respect to Temporary Protected Status (TPS), Congress has provided specific, narrow criteria for TPS designations. After consultation with the appropriate government agencies, the Secretary of DHS may designate a foreign state for TPS based upon: (1) an ongoing armed conflict that poses a serious threat to the safety of returning nationals; (2) an environmental disaster that results in a substantial, but temporary, disruption of living conditions, or (3) extraordinary and temporary conditions that prevent a country's nationals from safely returning to that country, unless the Secretary finds that such designation is contrary to the national interest of the United States.

The United States is actively engaged in efforts to rebuild Haitian democracy. In addition, the United States has placed troops on the ground as the leading contingent of the multinational interim force authorized by United Nations Security Council Resolution 1529, adopted unanimously on February 29, 2004. The level of violence in Haiti has significantly declined as a result.

Given the efforts of the U.S. Government to improve the situation within Haiti, the Department of State does not think it appropriate to recommend to the Department of Homeland Security that it designate TPS for Haitians in the United States at this time. Nevertheless, we will continue to closely monitor events as they unfold.

We maintain a strong working relationship with UNHCR and are its largest contributor. Earlier this year, we supported UNHCR's decision to dispatch experts to assist several Caribbean countries, including Jamaica, the Dominican Republic, and the Bahamas, in their preparations for a potential outflow of migrants in the region. We continue to consult closely with UNHCR on our response to potential outflows of migrants from Haiti and other countries in the region. In addition, we are continuing our discussions with UNHCR to find the best ways to assist the countries of the Caribbean in their preparation for potential outflows of migrants.

Question:

In the past, Haitian refugees were estimated to be in the tens of thousands and provisions were estimated to cost $1.9 million. What provisions if any do we already have in place if a mass exodus takes place? What plans if any do we have for a donor conference, such that, as with Iraq, the American taxpayers would not have to bare *this burden alone? How much do you estimate that the international community would be willing to donate without a conference?*

Answer:

The basic interagency responsibilities for a mass migration emergency are outlined in Executive Order 13276. All appropriate agencies are involved in routine comprehensive contingency planning for a unified response to a mass migration event for the Caribbean. Domestic funding responsibilities are considered a part of this planning.

The World Bank held an informal meeting on March 23, 2004, for donor governments, international financial institutions, and international and regional organizations to exchange views on the situation in Haiti and agree on next steps to ensure a coordinated response to the short and medium-term needs of the country. In this context, donors welcomed the launch by the UN of a Flash Appeal for Haiti to address the urgent needs of the Haitian population in a coordinated manner.

The World Bank reports that donors agreed to propose to the interim government the launch of a joint government/multi-donor assessment of the economic, social, and institutional needs in Haiti. The proposed assessment could result in the preparation of a carefully costed and coordinated national reconstruction plan covering both short-term and medium-term programs. The assessment would build on the ongoing multi-disciplinary rapid assessment mandated by UN Security Council Resolution 1529 to evaluate security, humanitarian, and transitional needs.

Donors also agreed to propose to the interim government to reconvene in Port-au-Prince in three to four weeks to discuss the government's policy priorities and the objectives of the proposed needs assessment mission and to agree on next steps. One of the next steps could be a formal Donor's conference, which could be held in a few months.

The informal donor's meeting on Haiti was attended by high-level delegations from Canada, the CARICOM Secretariat, Chile, the European Commission, France, Germany, the Inter-American Development Bank, the International Organization of la Fracophonie, the International Organization for Migration, the International Monetary Fund, Japan, the Organization of American States, the Pan American Health Organization, Spain, the United States, UNDP, UNDPKO, UNOCHA, UNICEF, the World Bank, and the World Food Program.

RESPONSES FROM THE HONORABLE ADOLFO A. FRANCO, ASSISTANT ADMINISTRATOR FOR LATIN AMERICA AND THE CARIBBEAN, U.S. AGENCY FOR INTERNATIONAL DEVELOPMENT, TO QUESTIONS SUBMITTED FOR THE RECORD BY THE HONORABLE GREGORY W. MEEKS, A REPRESENTATIVE IN CONGRESS FROM THE STATE OF NEW YORK

Question:

What is this Administration's plan for Haiti? How long do we plan on providing peacekeepers? What actions are being taken to protect the safety and security of innocent citizens in Haiti, in light of the growing threats to public order?

Answer:

The U.S. is providing troops to the Multinational Interim Force (scheduled to be in Haiti for 90 days), which will then be replaced by a United Nations Peacekeeping Operation. The Multinational Interim Force is working to contribute to a secure and stable environment in Haiti. The situation in Haiti is returning to normal, with many schools, banks, hospitals, and stores reopening.

The Department of State is in a better position to provide an update on the status of the Multinational Interim Force and the United Nations Peacekeeping Operation.

Question:

What plans exist to help Haiti grow its economy and lift it from the extreme poverty it suffers under today?

Answer:

USAID is continuing its activities in Haiti and has a substantial development and humanitarian network of partners already on the ground. The USG has provided over $3 million dollars in emergency assistance in the last few weeks. Of that amount more than $2 million is from USAID and the remainder from State/PRM.

The planned FY 2004 budget available for economic growth, democracy, health, and food assistance activities in Haiti is now approximately $52 million. We are currently working with other donors to identify additional assistance resources. USAID/Haiti's Draft Emergency Response Plan, currently under development, envisions three phases: (1) Immediate Response (next 6 months), (2) Intermediate Stabilization (months 7–12), and (3) Strategic Development (months 13–24).

- Under the Immediate Response phase, chief priorities are job creation and delivery of critical health and humanitarian services. Illustrative activities would include: (1) jobs programs to help rebuild the nation's badly eroded infrastructure; (2) community water and sanitation programs; (3) human rights monitoring; and (4) provision of humanitarian assistance, especially health services.
- The second phase of Intermediate Stabilization would emphasize: (1) improved health service delivery; (2) returning children to primary school; (3) expanding agriculture, trade, and microfinance activities; and (4) continued job creation, municipal development, and increased investment.
- After one year of intensive donor response, our programs should begin to transition from emergency post-crisis activities to the third phase of longer term strategic development activities. During this period the program would concentrate on further institutional strengthening, longer term expansion of export agriculture, trade, investment and education. Our health and humanitarian programs would, of course, still continue.

Question:

In the past, Haitian refugees were estimated to be in the tens of thousands and provisions were estimated to cost $1.9 million. What provisions if any do we already have in place if a mass exodus takes place?

Answer:

The Coast Guard is continuing to monitor the situation closely and is cooperating with the Haitian Coast Guard. There have been no new interdictions of Haitians by the U.S. since February 27. Out migration is not viewed as a serious problem at this time.

Question:

What plans if any do we have for a donor conference, such that, as with Iraq, the American taxpayers would not have to bar this burden alone? How much do you estimate that the international community would be willing to donate without a conference?

Answer:

Donors have scheduled a meeting with the Haitian interim government in Port-au-Prince on April 22 to discuss the government's policy priorities, the objectives of a proposed needs assessment mission, and to agree on next steps, which will include a donor meeting to pledge funds.

Question:

According to assessments issued by Oxfam International over 140,000 people in Haiti have no access to clean water, many more are short on food, and the threat of disease due to poor sanitation is growing. Oxfam warned that unless a secure environment is created so that humanitarian aid can be delivered, Haiti will be facing a humanitarian crisis. Will this Administration increase humanitarian aid to Haiti and how will it ensure that that aid reaches those it is intended to help?

Answer:

Contrary to reports, food supplies are not scarce in Haiti. However, security and fuel shortages in certain areas of the country remain a problem for food distribution. USAID continues to closely monitor food stocks in country and has been active in providing medicines and supplies. USAID food cooperating sponsors are all working at capacity to make sure that food aid supplies continue to reach those most in need.

USAID is distributing emergency relief supplies, including 12 medical kits each of which will serve 10,000 people for approximately three months, as well as 3 surgical kits and additional medical supplies. We are planning for an additional 10 medical kits under the Draft Haiti Emergency response Plan being prepared by the USAID mission.

We are also working through our NGOs to provide emergency cash grants to support local institutions and provide services for the most vulnerable populations. After providing UNICEF early on with support for emergency vaccines, USAID also will support UNICEF's expanded program on immunizations activities and securing the cold chain. USAID has emergency air transport to conduct assessments and deliver relief supplies in several regions.

Under the Draft Haiti Emergency Response Plan, USAID has proposed several kinds of water purification methods, from the emergency tablet distribution, to more sustainable locally assembled water purification tanks for villages, with chlorine and other purification methods.

USAID also plans to make available, under the Emergency Response Plan, 3,000,000 packets of ORT salts, since diarrheal diseases, endemic in Haiti and a major threat to the lives of those under five years of age, are on the rise, and clean, potable water is in shorter and shorter supply.

Question:

Will U.S. peacekeepers be used to provide safe passage to relief workers and aid?

Answer:

The Multinational Force has deployed beyond the capital and our partners who implement our food programs in Haiti are assessing damages incurred during the last few weeks and are beginning to resume operations.

Question:

Quality of life in the hemisphere's poorest country is abysmal. According to USAID estimates for FY04, approximately 80 percent of the population lives on less that $2 per day; nearly half of Haiti's people are illiterate; and life expectancy is 53. How does the Administration reconcile the vast needs of Haiti against the atrophied requests in the core development accounts for the Caribbean country? How will much needed development programs in Haiti be affected by these cuts?

Answer:

The U.S. Government through USAID is Haiti's largest bilateral donor. From FY 1995 to 2003, USAID provided a total of $850 million in direct bilateral assistance. For FY 2004, USAID has initially planned $52 million in assistance in the areas of health, democracy and governance, education, and economic growth. This planning level, developed as part of the budget cycle two years ago, does show a reduction in the economic growth sector in response to a lack of commitment by the Haitian government to reform. However, at that time, this was counterbalanced with increases in the levels dedicated to HIV/AIDS and other health programs in recognition of the needs of the Haitian people. Under the Draft Emergency Response Plan, efforts will be made to identify additional resources to expand health and education programs and increase income earning opportunities, both through short-term jobs programs as well as long-term sustainable income generating opportunities generated microenterprise, investment promotion, and trade.

Question:

Moreover, given the importance that the U.S. had place on the role of the OAS in Haiti, what is the reasoning behind reducing the request for the OAS Special Mission in Haiti from almost $5 million in FY04 to zero in FY05?

Answer:

The Department of State is in a better position to answer questions pertaining to the OAS.

U.S. DEPARTMENT OF STATE

Country Reports on Human Rights Practices—2003
Haiti
Released by the Bureau of Democracy, Human Rights, and Labor
FEBRUARY 25, 2004

HAITI

Haiti is a republic with an elected president and a bicameral legislature. The 1987 Constitution remains in force, but many of its provisions were not respected in practice. The opposition parties boycotted the 2000 presidential elections, in which Jean-Bertrand Aristide was reelected with extremely low voter turnout. The political impasse and political violence stemming from controversial results of May 2000 legislative and local elections continued during the year. In September 2002, the Organization of American States (OAS) adopted Resolution 822 as a catalyst for resolving the political impasse. Included in the resolution was a provision calling for a legitimate Provisional Electoral Council (CEP), which was to be charged with planning local, municipal, and legislative elections during the year; however, the elections were never held. The Constitution provides for an independent judiciary; however, it is not independent in practice and remained largely weak and corrupt, as well as subject to interference by the executive and legislative branches.

The Government established the Haitian National Police (HNP) in 1995 as the sole security force in the country after disbanding the Armed Forces of Haiti (FAd'H). The HNP is officially an autonomous civilian institution; however, authorities did not maintain effective control of the security forces, and HNP officials at all levels were implicated in corruption and narcotics trafficking. Partisan political leaders increasingly exercised control over elements of the police and influenced it for personal or political gain. President Aristide filled many key HNP positions with political allies lacking experience, training, and credibility. Some parliamentarians, mayors, and members of local government councils (CASECs) exercised arrest authority without legal sanction. The HNP has a variety of specialized units, including a crisis response unit (SWAT); a crowd control unit (CIMOs) serving Port-au-Prince and the Western department; crowd control units (UDMOs) serving each of the remaining eight departments; Special Brigades (BS) attached to certain commissariats; and a small Coast Guard unit. Police "attaches" became increasingly prevalent throughout the country and particularly in certain commissariats. The large and well-funded Presidential Security Unit, officially part of the HNP, had its own budget and remained administratively and functionally independent. Civilian deaths and serious injuries resulted from the inability of HNP units to maintain order. Members of the security forces committed human rights abuses during the year.

The country has a market-based economy and state-controlled utilities, and its economic stagnation continued during the year due to the continuing political crisis and the petroleum price shocks experienced in the second quarter. A small elite controlled much of the country's wealth. Two-thirds of the estimated 8 million citizens worked in subsistence agriculture and were extremely poor. The informal sector accounted for approximately 70 percent of all economic activity, making taxation problematic. Remittances from Haitians living overseas, estimated at $931 million in 2002, were a growing revenue source. Textiles accounted for approximately 80 percent of recorded exports; assembled goods, leather goods, agricultural products, and handicrafts also provided limited export revenue. The Haitian Institute for Statistics calculated real GDP growth of 0.5 percent for the fiscal year, compared with negative growth of 0.9 percent for fiscal year 2002. Inflation was 42.5 percent for the fiscal year, compared with 10.7 percent for fiscal year 2002, largely reflecting the adjustment in fuel prices to world market rates and the decline in the value of the gourde. By year's end, inflation had subsided to an annualized rate in the low teens.

The Government's human rights record remained poor, with political and civil officials implicated in serious abuses. There were credible reports of extrajudicial killings by members of the HNP. Police officers used excessive—and sometimes deadly—force in making arrests or controlling demonstrations and were rarely punished for such acts. Attacks on and threats to journalists and political dissenters by members of Popular Organizations (OPs) and by supporters of the President's party, Fanmi Lavalas (FL), increased. Prison conditions remained poor, and prisoners with valid release orders continued to be held in defiance of these orders. Legal impunity remained a major problem, and police and judicial officials often failed to respect legal provisions or pursue and prosecute suspected violators. The media were largely free and often critical of the Government; however, most journalists practiced some form of self-censorship. Child abuse, violence, and societal discrimination against women remained problems. Internal trafficking of children and child domestic labor remained a problem; however, the Government increased its efforts to address the issue.

RESPECT FOR HUMAN RIGHTS

Section 1. Respect for the Integrity of the Person, Including Freedom From:

a. Arbitrary or Unlawful Deprivation of Life.—There were credible reports of extrajudicial killings by members of the HNP, municipal government officials, and civilian attaches (see Section 1.d.) associated with HNP commissariats.

Individuals involved in the State University protest movement that began in August 2002 continued to be victims of violence and human rights violations. On January 7, assailants shot and killed Eric Pierre, a 27-year-old medical student, while leaving the Faculty of Medicine building. The authorities did not arrest anyone in connection with his death, despite witnesses' allegations that the attackers left the scene in two vehicles, one with official license plates and the other with the state telephone company logo on the side.

On January 8, police shot and killed an anti-government demonstrator as they were breaking up a demonstration in Gonaives. Jean-Dady Simeon, HNP spokesperson, claimed that the man was already dead when police intervened (see Section 2.b.).

On January 27, armed men shot and killed 17-year-old John Peter Ancy Oleus in Carrefour under orders from the wife of the Police Commissioner of Jacmel, Mrs. Cadet. As John Peter and Cadet were arguing over the Oleus family's garbage disposal near her home, Cadet summoned six armed men, one of whom shot and killed Oleus as he ran to lock the front door of his house to protect his sisters inside. The authorities arrested Cadet soon after the crime was committed, but State Prosecutor Josue Pierre Louis released her the following day. Louis claimed that he had to follow the "hierarchy of respect," and that he was simply following orders from the Justice Minister. At year's end, no one had been held responsible for Oleus' death.

On February 4, a group of armed men shot and killed Ronuald Cadet, another student involved in State University demonstrations who had been in hiding since November 2002. This case, remained unsolved at year's end.

On March 27, in Petit-Goave, a police bullet grazed 21-year-old Ginette Pierre, who was believed to be the daughter of a Convergence leader whom the police planned to arrest. After she fell to the ground, the officers put their car in reverse and ran over the woman's head, killing her instantly. The Government provided funds for her wake and funeral, but took no action against the police officers responsible for her death.

On May 18, a civilian attache from the Commissariat in Hinche killed Josue Telusme. On July 8, attaches from Delmas 33 Commissariat riding in a HNP vehicle killed Leon Regois and discarded his body at the State University Hospital.

In October, Municipal Commissaire for Hinche Neguippe Simon shot and killed a woman who accidentally struck his vehicle with a rock during a domestic dispute. Following the incident, Simon disappeared, but was later arrested, then inexplicably released from jail while pending trial in December and was promoted into higher ranks of the HNP leadership.

On October 21, police in Gonaives broke up an anti-Aristide march by the civil society coalition group Union Citoyenne. Police arrested several opposition members participating in the march. Police, in concert with pro-Lavalas "chimeres" (thugs) threw rocks and bottles, preventing the demonstration from taking place; one person was shot and killed and several others were injured.

Sparked by the death of Cannibal Army head Amiot "Cubain" Metayer (see Sections 1.b. and 3), several weeks of intense violence between police and Cannibal Army members were brought to a climax in Gonaives from October 26 to 28. On October 26, Cannibal Army members attacked the home of the Government's representative in Gonaives, Ketlin Telemaque, and burned one of the mayor's vehicles as police responded in kind. Following an attack on the main police commissariat, a gun battle between the police and gang members led to the death of a 12-year-old girl and the injuring of the Departmental Police Director.

From October 27 to 28, police and civilian chimeres mounted a major offensive on the gang-controlled section of Raboteau, Gonaives. While attempting to locate and arrest Cannibal Army members, police burned 10 homes in Raboteau, arrested area residents, and slaughtered livestock. Police efforts were unsuccessful, as the operation only netted civilians not involved with the Cannibal Army. During the siege, a newborn baby was burned to death, a woman was killed, and two other civilians were shot and injured. Reports estimated that there were as many as 50 dead and 80 injured civilians in Gonaives from September through December due to the continued violence.

In May, following a hearing before the Court of Appeals, Deputy Jocelyn Saint Louis of Saint Raphael, who was arrested for his alleged role in the January 2002 murder of mayor Sernand Severe, was released.

In December 2002, armed men dressed in black identified as HNP took three brothers, Angelot, Andy Philippe, and Vladimir Sanon, from their home in Carrefour in Port-au-Prince (see Section 1.c.). Later that day their bodies were found with gunshot wounds and taken to the city morgue. The boys had previously protested the police robbery and shooting of their friend, Marcellus Bongue. The authorities had not arrested anybody, and no examining judge had questioned any of the four policemen whom eyewitnesses identified as the last persons seen with the brothers. The police officers and the civilian attache from the Carrefour Commissariat suspected in the killing of the three brothers had not been brought to justice and were still working in that commissariat at year's end.

There was no progress in several other killings that occurred during 2002, including those of the three youths from Cite Soleil, a farmer in the town of Hinche, and four persons killed in an attack on the Las Cahobas jail.

In September 2002, an investigating judge indicted 10 persons in connection with the 2001 killing of journalist Brignol Lindor; however, he did not indict Petit Goave deputy mayor Duby Bony, who allegedly incited the killing when he said Lindor should be met with "zero tolerance" (a code word for officially sanctioned killings). Out of 27 warrants issued, the authorities arrested only 3 individuals in connection with Lindor's death. Judge Fritzner Duclair determined that the mayor's call did not incite the killing and failed to include the mayor or other local government officials who publicly called for retribution against Lindor (see Section 2.a.). By the end of January, only one person, Masee Zephir, remained in prison awaiting trial.

On March 24, almost 3 years after the killing of popular Radio Haiti-Inter host and journalist Jean Leopold Dominique, Judge Bernard Sainvil issued the final report on his investigation of the journalist's death. The report, criticized by the human rights community for its failure to identify the true authors of the crime, widely suspected to be high-ranking government officials, implicated six men: Dymsley Milien, alias "Tilou," for the actual murder, and five others who have already been in jail for more than 2 years as accomplices. Although Senator Dany Toussaint implicated former deputy mayor of Port-au-Prince Harold Severe during Toussaint's interrogation in January, in the final report, Severe was neither cleared nor implicated in Dominique's death. In August, Judge Jean Bien-Aime released three of the men incarcerated for the crime: Freud Junior Desmarates, Ralph Joseph, and Ralph Leger.

On January 27, the HNP took into custody Herbert Valmond and Carl Dorelien, both former FAd'H colonels returned to the country as criminal deportees. They were turned over to a special police unit who took them to the national penitentiary, where they remained at year's end. On January 29, Justice Minister Calixte Delatour announced that the two would be serving life sentences. In 2000, a criminal court in Gonaives had convicted Valmond and Dorelien in absentia, along with 35 former military leaders, for premeditated homicide in connection with the 1994 Raboteau massacre.

Vigilante killings are a long established practice in the country, and their incidence increased following President Aristide's zero tolerance exhortation to police and citizens to bypass the judicial system if they caught criminals in the act. During the year, human rights organizations, journalists, and opposition groups criticized the Government's support for this practice.

b. Disappearance.—There were credible reports of politically motivated disappearances; however, there were fewer such reports than in the previous year.

Attaches from Delmas 33 police station arrested Junior Jean and Mankes Anelus in front of their neighbors in June. The pair has since disappeared.

On July 15, persons believed to be attaches from the Cap-Haitien Commissariat kidnapped Pierre Franklin Julien, father of Citizen's Initiative founder Denis Julien, and held him for ransom.

Ordonel Paul, a presidential palace employee and widely believed to be the man who betrayed Cannibal Army leader Amiot Metayer, was last seen with Metayer on September 21 (see Section 3).

There were no further developments in the cases of disappearances reported in 2002.

c. Torture and other Cruel, Inhuman, or Degrading Treatment or Punishment.—The 1987 Constitution prohibits the use of unnecessary force or restraint, psychological pressure, or brutality by the security forces; however, members of the security forces continued to violate these provisions. Police officers used excessive and sometimes deadly force in making arrests or controlling demonstrations and were rarely punished for such acts. Torture and other forms of abuse were reported.

Police mistreatment of suspects at the time of arrest and during detention remained common in all parts of the country. Beating with fists, sticks, belts, and "kalot marassa"—a severe boxing of the ears—were the most common form of abuse. Persons who reported such abuse often had visible injuries consistent with the alleged mistreatment. Mistreatment also took the form of withholding medical treatment from injured jail inmates.

A police officer from the Commissariat in Hinche shot Joseline Desroses in the mouth after she refused his sexual advances.

On July 14, the Brigade for Research and Intervention (BRI) arrested opposition militant Judie C. Roy and brought her to the National Police Academy, where she and three colleagues were tortured for 4 days before being transferred to the Delmas 33 police station. While at Delmas 33, they claimed to have been tortured using the kalot marassa method and brutally beaten by civilian attaches before being transferred to Fort National prison. Roy was refused medical treatment and legal counsel upon her initial arrival at Fort National, but eventually was allowed to see a doctor and obtain a lawyer after protest from the National Coalition for Haitian Rights

(NCHR). Roy was eventually transferred to the Petionville police station where she remained at year's end.

On October 14, homeless 16-year-old Jonathan Louima was brutally beaten and tortured in the Port-au-Prince Police Commissariat. After being arrested, Louima was brought to the police station where police beat him and summoned dogs to bite him all over his body. He survived the attack, and HNP Chief Inspector Sainturne promised an investigation. At year's end, no police officers had been held responsible for the attack.

The police were accused of using excessive force against demonstrators and failing to protect demonstrators from violence by pro-Lavalas chimeres (see Section 2.b.).

Prison conditions remained poor. The Penitentiary Administration Management (DAP) made some progress in improving prison administration and warden training. Prisoners and detainees continued to suffer from a lack of basic hygiene, malnutrition, poor quality health care, and, in some facilities, 24-hour confinement. Most prisons periodically suffered from lack of water, especially in the provinces. The incidence of preventable diseases such as beriberi, AIDS, and tuberculosis increased. Some prisoners who were incarcerated for petty crimes were given amnesty and released by the Ministry of Justice during the year. The Government estimated the total prison population to be 3,519, including 116 female and minor (male and female) prisoners. This figure changed somewhat on December 31, when President Aristide issued a decree giving full amnesty to common law criminals still awaiting trial, and commuted the sentences of 66 other prisoners.

Overcrowding prevented the separation of violent from nonviolent prisoners or convicts from those in pretrial detention. Many were incarcerated in temporary holding cells, particularly in the provinces.

Prison officials confirmed reports by international human rights observers of instances of inmate abuse by prison personnel; however, no statistics were available. Prisoners and detainees, ignorant of legal rights or doubtful officials would respond positively, rarely filed official complaints.

The Government commission to investigate the 2001 riot at the National Penitentiary, the country's largest prison facility located in Port-au-Prince, had not yet published a report of its findings.

The Government's Office of Citizen Protection monitored prison conditions and offered training to prison administrators on criminal procedures, particularly the constitutional requirement limiting preventive detention (garde à vu) to 48 hours. The U.N. Development Program (UNDP) continued technical assistance to the DAP, focusing on midlevel warden training and management information. The NCHR actively monitored prison conditions in cooperation with the DAP, which offered a prisoners' rights awareness campaign.

The DAP conducted objective testing of prison physicians and nurses to exclude those who were inadequately trained. Doctors were available in the capital but were less frequently available to those incarcerated in the provinces. Nurses did not conduct daily checkups on the physical condition of inmates. Dispensary supplies were limited, and family members often had to purchase needed medication.

Fort National prison in Port-au-Prince was the only prison facility exclusively for women and juveniles. In other prison facilities, women were held in cells separate from men. However, in 2000, U.N. Special Rapporteur for Violence against Women Radhika Coomaraswamy reported, based on her 1999 visit, that most female prisoners shared living quarters with male prisoners. This subjected women to violence and sexual abuse. Due to overcrowding, juveniles often were held with adults.

On February 14, 18-year-old Natacha Jean Jacques was released from Fort National, following strong protests from civil society organizations. Jacques became pregnant during her incarceration at Fort National while serving time after being arrested in 2000 for killing the man who was raping her. A warrant was issued for the arrest of her rapist in jail, a medical assistant working at the prison, Ilus Denasty. At year's end, he remained at large.

The authorities freely permitted the International Committee of the Red Cross (ICRC), the Haitian Red Cross, and other human rights groups to enter prisons and police stations, monitor conditions, and assist prisoners and detainees with medical care, food, and legal aid. The Director General of the HNP and the DAP cooperated with the ICRC and the UNDP.

d. Arbitrary Arrest, Detention, or Exile.—The Constitution prohibits arbitrary arrest and detention; however, security forces continued to employ both practices. The Constitution stipulates that a person may be arrested only if apprehended during the commission of a crime, or on the basis of a written order by a legally competent official, such as a justice of the peace or magistrate. The authorities can only execute these orders between 6:00 a.m. and 6:00 p.m. and must bring the detainee before a judge within 48 hours of arrest. In practice, officials frequently ignored these provisions. There were also instances of arrests by security forces and local officials lacking proper authority; mayors and members of local CASECs sometimes arrested persons in under-policed rural areas. Judges often issued arrest warrants with little or no evidence.

The HNP is officially an autonomous civilian institution; however, despite a cadre of competent and committed officers trained by U.S., French, and Canadian authorities, HNP officials at all levels were implicated in corruption and narcotics trafficking (see Section 3). While some new cadets entered through a competitive selection process, the Government appointed more than half of the new recruits based on political and personal favoritism. In the spring, the police academy graduated more than 800 police officers, including a record number of female officers. The HNP failed to pursue criminals, promoting a growing condition of judicial impunity. The Special Brigades are small detachments of regular policemen attached to certain commissariats throughout the country. These units, which have no special tactical training, are equipped with assault rifles and dressed in black T-shirts that read "BS." Their job is to provide defense for the commissariats or fill in for SWAT in certain situations until SWAT teams can arrive.

Killings and other abuses (see Section 1.a.) involving civilian attaches in police commissariats increased during the year. Attaches have their roots in the launch of the zero tolerance operation in June 2001. They are not members of the police force, nor have they received any official training at the police academy; rather they act as special units of armed civilian thugs and operate in police stations of large urban areas. They also often provide special security for key political figures. Attaches function under the direct control of the chief commissioner of a police station and are given special identification cards. The most notable commissariats for attache activity were Delmas 33, Carrefour, Cite Soleil, Port-au-Prince, Petionville, Gonaives, Cap-Haitien, and Hinche.

Certain police jurisdictions routinely disregarded the 48-hour requirement to present detainees before a judge, and some detainees were held for years in pretrial detention. Although the 48-hour rule was violated in all parts of the country, it was most often and most flagrantly ignored in Jeremie, Cap-Haitien, Petionville, and the Delmas commissariat of Port-au-Prince. Police or other government officials often apprehended persons without warrants, or on warrants not issued by a duly authorized official. Moreover, arrests sometimes were made on charges such as sorcery or debt with no basis in law. The authorities frequently detained individuals on unspecified charges or pending investigation. The Government often resorted to arrest and detention on false charges or on the charge of "plotting against the security of the State," particularly in political or personal vendettas. Detainees were generally allowed access to family members and a lawyer of their own choosing. Many detainees could not afford the services of an attorney, and the Government did not provide free counsel. Bail is available at the discretion of the investigative judge. Bail hearings are not automatic, and judges usually granted bail only for minor cases and based on compelling humanitarian grounds such as a need for medical attention.

Prosper Avril, former general and head of the military government from 1988 to 1990, remained incarcerated despite the Gonaives Court of Appeals' ruling in October 2002 that his rearrest was illegal, and which ordered his release. However, the district attorney's office in Port-au-Prince did not comply with the ruling. Avril remained incarcerated at year's end.

On March 9, women's rights activist Carline Simon and her husband Serge were brutally arrested, beaten, and held for a week without formal charges brought against them. The couple was arrested after the police rescued them from a failed kidnapping attempt. On March 10, they were transferred from Cite Soleil to the Delmas police station as State Prosecutor Josue Pierre Louis issued a temporary release order for the couple. The Delmas Police Commissioner refused to free them and a HNP spokesperson claimed they were in possession of illegal firearms; those weapons were never found. Due to immense pressure from the human rights community, Simon and her husband were released on March 13.

After spending almost 6 months in the National Penitentiary, Rosemond Jean, head of the movement to reclaim lost money from government-supported cooperatives, was released on March 31. Arbitrarily arrested without warrant in September 2002, attaches beat Jean and accused her of possessing illegal firearms and munitions. Police entered his house without a warrant, claiming that he had weapons and he was plotting against the state. No weapons were ever found in his possession. After pressure from the international community, the authorities cleared Jean of all charges and released him in March.

On February 18, former Army officers Ibert Blanc, Rosalvo Bastia, and Pastor Ceriphin Franck were arrested in the central department of Hinche without charges. On July 29, the three were transported by helicopter to Port-au-Prince. Accused of conspiring against the security of the State, they remained at the National Penitentiary awaiting trial at year's end.

Prolonged pretrial detention was a serious problem. Judicial delays left an estimated 78 percent of the country's prison population awaiting trial. The problem was most extreme in Port-au-Prince, with 88 percent of National Penitentiary inmates in pretrial detention status. Eighty-six percent of females and 95 percent of minor detainees were in pretrial detention. The prolonged detention of persons with valid release orders continued to be a problem (see Section 1.e.).

Since her July 14 arrest, Judie Roy remained incarcerated in a prison in the Port-au-Prince suburb of Petionville, accused of conspiring against the security of the State (see Sections 1.c. and 1.f.).

The Constitution prohibits the involuntary exile of citizens, and there were no reports of its use. Self-imposed internal and external exile were common among opponents of the regime.

e. Denial of Fair Public Trial.—The Constitution provides for an independent judiciary; however, in practice the judiciary was subject to significant influence by the executive and legislative branches. Years of extensive corruption and governmental neglect left the poorly organized judicial system largely moribund. Judges assigned to politically sensitive cases complained about interference by the executive branch.

At the lowest level of the justice system, justices of the peace issue warrants, adjudicate minor infractions, mediate cases, take depositions, and refer cases to prosecutors or higher judicial officials. Investigating magistrates and public prosecutors cooperate in the development of more serious cases, which are tried by the judges of the first instance courts. Thirty appeals court judges hear cases referred from the first instance courts, and the 11-member Court of Cassation, the country's highest court, addresses questions of procedure and constitutionality. In Port-au-Prince, seven judges sit on a special labor court with jurisdiction over labor disputes, but in the provinces courts of first instance adjudicate such cases.

The judicial apparatus follows a civil law system based on the Napoleonic Code; the Criminal Code dates from 1832, although it has been amended in some instances. The Constitution provides for the right to a fair public trial; however, this right was abridged widely in practice. The Constitution also expressly denies police and judicial authorities the right to interrogate suspects unless legal counsel or a representative of the suspect's choice are present or they waive this right; this right was also abridged in practice. While trials are public, most accused persons cannot afford legal counsel for interrogation or trial, and the law does not require that the Government provide legal representation. Despite the efforts of local human rights groups and the international community to provide free legal aid, many interrogations occurred without presence of counsel. However, some defendants had access to counsel during trials. The Constitution provides defendants with a presumption of innocence and the right to be present at trial, to confront witnesses against them, and to present witnesses and evidence in their own behalf; however, in practice corrupt and uneducated judges frequently denied defendants these rights.

Systemic problems including underfunding and a shortage of adequately trained and qualified justices of the peace, judges, and prosecutors created a huge backlog of criminal cases, with many detainees waiting months or even years in pretrial detention for a court date (see Section 1.d.). There was no legal redress for prolonged pretrial detention following acquittal or dismissal of charges.

In most regions, judges lacked the basic resources to perform their duties. Professional competence was sometimes lacking as well. The qualifying yearlong course at the Magistrates' school requires no previous legal training. Judges increasingly conducted legal proceedings exclusively in Creole rather than French, but language remained a significant barrier to full access to the judicial system (see Section 5). UNDP, supported by the Government, provided additional training for many segments of the judicial system, including new judges and attorneys.

The Constitution sets varying tenure periods for judges above the level of justice of the peace. However, in practice the Ministry of Justice exercised appointment and administrative oversight over the judiciary, prosecutors, and court staff. This Ministry can remove justices of the peace and in practice has occasionally dismissed judges above this level.

The Code of Criminal Procedure does not assign clear responsibility to investigate crimes, dividing the authority among police, justices of the peace, prosecutors, and investigative magistrates. Examining magistrates often received files that were empty or missing police reports. Autopsies were conducted only rarely, and autopsy reports seldom issued. The code provides for 2 criminal court sessions ("assizes") per year in each of the 15 first instance jurisdictions for all major crimes requiring a jury trial; each session generally lasts for 2 weeks. Criminal assizes in Port-au-Prince have met only once a year since 1998.

Citizens deported to Haiti after completing prison sentences in foreign countries are detained until a family member agrees to take custody of them and their prison release order is processed, although there is no provision for such detention in the law. This generally takes 1 to 2 months, but has lasted as long as 4 months in unusual instances.

There were no reports of political prisoners.

f. Arbitrary Interference with Privacy, Family, Home, or Correspondence.—The Constitution prohibits such practices; however, police and other security force elements routinely conducted searches without warrants (see Section 1.c.).

Section 2. Respect for Civil Liberties, Including:

a. Freedom of Speech and Press.—The Constitution provides for freedom of speech and of the press; however, the Government did not respect these rights in practice. Several times during the year, the Government publicly expressed support for free expression; however, there were several documented attacks on members of the press. Print and electronic media freely criticized the Government and opposition. However, in practice most media admitted to some form of self-censorship to avoid offending sponsors or the politically influential.

There were two French-language newspapers in the country, Le Nouvelliste and L'Union, with a combined circulation of less than 20,000 readers. L'Union is a government-run newspaper; its editor was the Secretary of State for Communication. Le Nouvelliste and some irregularly printed papers were frequently critical of government policies. There was virtually no Creole-language press.

With a literacy rate of approximately 52 percent and limited access to television, the most important medium is radio, especially those stations broadcasting in Creole. There were 275 private radio stations, with 43 in the capital alone. Most carried a mix of music, news, and talk show programs that many citizens regard as their only opportunity to speak out on a variety of political, social, and economic issues. Uncensored foreign satellite and cable broadcasts were available but limited in impact: most citizens could not afford televisions. The few stations carrying news or opinion broadcasts freely expressed a wide range of political viewpoints.

Although most radio stations and other forms of telecommunications were nominally independent, they are subject to a 1997 law designating the State sole owner and proprietor of the airwaves. The State leases broadcast rights to private enterprises, retaining preemption rights in the event of a national emergency, including natural disasters. The Government did not exercise this right in practice.

There were several attacks on, or threats against, journalists during the year, and the legal system provided limited protection or redress. Journalists were accused of destabilizing the Government and often subjected to anonymous threats of violence, including threats of kidnapping and murder. Police and government officials often failed to protect journalists during civil unrest. The NGO Reporters Without Borders and local journalists' associations continued to protest attacks in prior years and called on the Government to provide security. The Government failed to do so, despite frequent expressions of support for free expression. Pro-government OPs (loosely organized neighborhood-based groups that often functioned as politically-affiliated gangs) sometimes threatened journalists covering protests, civil unrest, and other large group events. In such cases, the Government's inability or unwillingness to provide adequate security to media outlets and journalists contributed to an increased sense of vulnerability among members of the media who criticized the Government or Fanmi Lavalas.

According to a report released on August 15 by the Committee to Protect Journalists, in less than 3 years, 2 journalists, Brignol Lindor and Jean Dominique, had been killed and nearly 30 others had fled into exile. At year's end, only one person remained in prison awaiting trial for the December 2001 killing of Petit-Goave journalist, Brignol Lindor (see Section 1.a.).

On February 4, assailants shot Reverend Manes Blanc, the director of Radio Shekina in St. Marc, twice in the stomach. His assailants said he was too vocal in his anti-Lavalas comments, and that they intended to kill him. The gunshots were not fatal, and no one was charged with the crime.

On February 14, veteran reporter Goudou Jean Numa was warned about returning to his home as unknown persons had visited earlier in the day inquiring about him. Arsonists returned later and set fire to the reporter's vehicle. Goudou left the country.

On February 18, pro-Lavalas forces burned the home of Voice of America stringer Montigene Sincere and arrested, then released, his two sons, who were also journalists. Sincere was attacked in the past by persons believed to be acting on behalf of FL.

That same day, Radio Metropole, a pro-opposition radio station in Port-au-Prince, observed a 24-hour pause in news reporting to protest attacks on several of its staffers in weeks prior. Two days before, shots were allegedly fired at the home of the mother of Radio Metropole political columnist Nancy Roc.

On October 28, several armed and masked individuals in a truck with government service license plates opened fire on Radio Caraibes in Port-au-Prince. The attack occurred the day before a court hearing on the case of a Radio Caraibes journalist who was killed in a traffic accident involving a vehicle and employees from the Interior Ministry. No one was injured in the attack. While he did not denounce the attack, government spokesperson Mario Dupuy promised an investigation of the event. The case remained unsolved at year's end.

Radio Maxima in Cap-Haitien, a prominent anti-Aristide station was attacked a number of times since December 2002, leaving all three of its transmitters destroyed. Staff also reported verbal threats against their lives before and after the anti-Lavalas demonstrations planned for October 24–25 in Cap-Haitien.

In September 2002, Radio Kiskeya temporarily went off the air after receiving threats that an OP was going to attack the station. On April 30, Liliane Pierre Paul, the Program Director for the station, received a threatening letter with a bullet inside. The letter instructed her to broadcast a message on the radio by May 6 calling for French President Chirac to pay financial reparations to Haiti, threatening to kill French citizens in the country and Pierre Paul if she did not oblige. The letter was signed by members of various OP Lavalas groups, including the group believed to be responsible for the murder of Brignol Lindor. Nothing happened on May 6.

On March 20, the investigative report by Judge Sainvil on the 3-year-old murder of radio journalist Jean Dominique was released. The report indicted six men who have been in prison for 2 years on unrelated charges (see Section 1.a.). In December 2002, armed men attempting to enter the home of Michele Montas, Dominique's widow, shot and killed Maxime Seide, her bodyguard. Montas left the country. On April 3, the third anniversary of Dominique's death, major radio and print media staged a blackout refraining from all news reporting, broadcasts, and analyses to demonstrate what a country would become without a free press.

Foreign journalists generally traveled without hindrance from the authorities. The Government did not censor books or films.

The Government did not limit access to the Internet.

The Government did not restrict academic freedom.

b. Freedom of Peaceful Assembly and Association.—The Constitution provides for freedom of assembly; however, the Government's increasing repression of planned events and periodic prohibition of demonstrations flagrantly ignored that freedom. Although some organizations were able to exercise this right without hindrance throughout the year, numerous violations of this freedom frequently occurred in the capital as well as in the provinces. Authorities frequently failed to provide police protection for opposition parties, student groups, and women's groups conducting peaceful demonstrations. Authorities often transported pro-Aristide supporters, armed and unarmed, to announced opposition events and failed to arrest them for throwing rocks or bottles at the demonstrators and brutally beating them with clubs.

The HNP and governmental authorities continued to suppress citizens' fundamental rights to demonstrate, protest, and express their opinions. There were a series of general strikes in January promoting a variety of causes that often ended in confrontation or death (see Section 1.a.). Transportation unions and the opposition called for strikes and demonstrations throughout the month of January to protest the price increase for fuel and continued to urge President Aristide to resign.

Activists and women's organizations took to the streets of Port-au-Prince on March 10 to commemorate International Women's Day and to call for justice in cases where women's rights had been violated. The HNP attempted to break-up the demonstration, claiming that the women were not authorized to hold a march. Police confiscated the keys to the vehicle carrying the sound system and cut the connection from the system to the generator, yet the women were able to continue marching without further incident.

For several years, the Central Plateau and the city of Hinche have been plagued with political violence. In March, the pro-opposition Papaye Peasants Movement cancelled its march, marking its 30th anniversary in Hinche, due to warnings of security problems, and read its resolutions on the radio instead. Armed Lavalas OP's, unaware of the cancellation, blocked the road between Hinche and Papaye and assaulted anyone who attempted to travel that road. They injured more than 10 persons in the attacks.

On July 12, the civil society Group 184 (G184) led a "Caravan of Hope" on a march into the pro-government stronghold of Cite Soleil. The group planned to unveil a new social contract, but the event turned violent when the meeting place was overrun by a mob of pro-Lavalas chimeres. Police put forth little effort in stopping the chimeres and appeared to have incited hostilities. Personnel from foreign embassies and the OAS were on hand to observe the rally and were unharmed.

On August 30, in the north, Cap-Haitien police, apparently responding to government instructions, violently repressed the opening event of a planned opposition/civil society "Weekend of Solidarity," using tear gas and automatic weapons to disperse the peaceful open-air meeting. Pro-government popular organizations used barricades of burning tires to block access. The march scheduled for August 31 was then cancelled.

On September 14, another opposition march in Cap-Haitien was broken up a half a kilometer from its starting point by another group of chimeres throwing rocks and bottles at 2–5,000 demonstrators. Police launched tear gas at both the Lavalas aggressors and then at the opposition crowd. The confrontation occurred after police allowed 1,000 pro-FL counter-demonstrators to breach their assigned route and confront the oncoming opposition demonstration.

On October 25, in Cap-Haitien, pro-Lavalas chimeres constructed barriers and blocked road and air entry into the city in anticipation of an opposition march planned for October 26. Despite police efforts at dismantling the barricades, rock-throwing chimeres went on a rampage through the city effectively causing the opposition to cancel the demonstration.

On October 29, two nonpolitical demonstrations staged by women's groups, one to protest the climate of violence in the country and one to plant trees, were broken up by Lavalas chimeres. In both cases, police failed to prevent the disruption of the demonstrations, and little afterward to constrain the chimeres.

The G184 planned November 14 rally, to discuss its social contract and to present its political proposal, in downtown Port-au-Prince foundered in the face of a governmental campaign of obstruction and repression. Long before the rally was to begin, police impeded access to the area by constructing roadblocks and searching private vehicles. The rally failed to commence as OP members attacked the G184's stage equipment while police arrested 25 G184 members, including the brother-in-law and nephew of G184 leader Andy Apaid. As G184 members tried to move to the staging point, they were confronted by rock-throwing pro-Lavalas OP members. Crowd-control police intervened using tear gas and firing warning shots into the air. In an effort to avert further violence, Apaid called an end to the gathering in the early afternoon as OP members chased G184 partisans from the scene. Most of the G184 members were released on November 18, but the Apaid family members remained in prison until December 1 on false weapons charges.

On December 5, pro-Lavalas chimeres violently disrupted an anti-Aristide demonstration planned by State University students. An estimated 30 students were injured, at least 10 by gunfire. The University Rector suffered 2 broken kneecaps as a result of clubbing by the chimeres. Police on the scene were complicit with the chimeres throughout and did nothing to curb the violence, reacting only when the Rector was clubbed, and only then assisting in the evacuation of the students. Human rights groups and government officials widely criticized the attack, which led to the resignation of the Minister of Education, Marie-Carmel Paul Austin.

On December 8, several thousand students demonstrated in Gonaives, demanding justice for Port-au-Prince university students attacked by pro-Lavalas chimeres on December 5 (termed "Black Friday"). Police used tear gas to disband the demonstrators and indiscriminately fired into the crowd injuring several civilians and two police officers. One journalist on the scene reported that police shot and injured several journalists attempting to verify how many protesters died during the event.

On December 12, State University student protesters in Port-au-Prince joined forces with Apaid's 184 and members of the city's business, legal, academic, and artisan community to launch a massive anti-government demonstration. Early morning police barricades and burning tires erected by chimeres, some carrying arms, attempted to thwart the crowds that had gathered in various sections of the city. Police fired into the air and used tear gas in an attempt to disperse the demonstrators, who regrouped later in another location; this pattern continued throughout the day. There were no reported fatalities.

Following a student demonstration on December 15, HNP officers injected 21-year-old Josue Alcenat with an unknown substance while holding him at the police station in Canape Vert section of Port-au-Prince. Alcenat spent 5 days in a local hospital undergoing tests to determine the nature of the substance. Alcenat was sent to a medical facility abroad to undergo further testing after the hospital was unable to arrive at any concrete conclusion.

On December 17, small groups of students attempted to mobilize in Port-au-Prince, but low numbers and aggressive police intervention combined to prevent a major demonstration. Lavalas chimeres reportedly opened fire on several journalists and protesters in different parts of the city as police used large amounts of tear gas to disperse students assembled at various points. Simultaneously, police employed similar tactics to halt anti-government demonstrations in cities outside the capital, such as Jacmel, St. Marc, and Cap-Haitien. During one protest in Trou de Nord, police fired into a crowd attempting to break-up a protest and killed a young girl. Protesters responded by attacking several government office buildings and burning the house of the police officer who shot the girl.

The Constitution provides for freedom of association, and the Government generally respected this right in practice. The Penal Code requires prior government approval for any association of more than 20 persons that seeks tax benefits and official recognition from the Government.

c. Freedom of Religion.—The Constitution provides for the right to practice all religions and faiths, provided that practice does not disturb law and order, and the Government generally respected this right in practice.

In many respects, Roman Catholicism retained its traditional primacy among the country's religions. Precise figures were difficult to obtain, but it was estimated that 80 percent of the population were Catholic. However, Protestant denominations (primarily Methodist and Baptist) were growing in terms of number of active members, in comparison to the Catholic Church membership. A large segment of the population practiced Christianity as well as Voodoo, a traditional religion derived in part from West African beliefs. While there were associations of Voodoo practitioners and priests, there was no organized hierarchy. Official recognition by the Ministry of Religious Affairs gives religious organizations legal standing and tax-exempt status, and extends civil recognition to church documents. In 2001, the Ministry of Religion officially recognized the first Voodoo church, the Eglise Vodou d'Ayiti, and in April, the Government officially recognized Voodoo as a religion.

Accusations of sorcery, particularly in rural areas, led to mob violence and killings, and Voodoo practitioners were targeted in some cases.

For a more detailed discussion, see the 2003 International Religious Freedom Report.

d. Freedom of Movement within the Country, Foreign Travel, Emigration, and Repatriation.—The Constitution provides for these rights, and the Government generally respected them in practice.

An unknown number of undocumented migrants left the country by sea or land to seek better economic opportunities. The Government's National Migration Office (ONM) was responsible for assisting citizens repatriated from other countries and frequently provided small sums of money to repatriated migrants for transportation. During the year, the ONM assisted 17,323 repatriated citizens. There were reliable reports of family separation and maltreatment of Haitians by Dominican soldiers during the year. There were no credible reports of government mistreatment of repatriated migrants.

The law includes provisions for the granting of refugee status or asylum to persons who meet the definition in the 1951 U.N. Convention Relating to the Status of Refugees or its 1967 Protocol. In practice, the Government provided protection against refoulement, but did not routinely grant refugee status on asylum.

Section 3. Respect for Political Rights: The Right of Citizens to Change Their Government

The Constitution provides citizens with the right to change their government peacefully. In practice, the political system remained in transition from a dictatorial system to a more open and competitive one, and the political crisis stemming from flawed 2000 elections continued to hinder the implementation of this right. The dominant Fanmi Lavalas (FL) political party, which controls all branches of government, manipulated legislative elections in May 2000 and exaggerated electoral participation in the November 2000 presidential elections. OAS efforts since then to resolve the crisis have been unsuccessful.

In September 2002, the OAS unanimously approved Resolution 822, delinking international economic assistance from the signing of an FL/Convergence Democratique (CD) accord between FL and opposition parties. It called on the Government to implement previous OAS resolutions, expressed the expectation that the Government would hold legislative and local elections in 2003, and called on the Government to create a favorable security climate, implement a disarmament plan, strengthen independent police and judicial institutions to combat impunity, and participate in the formation of a credible Provisional Electoral Council by November 4, 2002, and an Electoral Guarantees Commission by December 4, 2002. The resolution broadened the mandate of the OAS Special Mission to assist the Government in undertaking its obligations and to monitor and evaluate those efforts. By November 20, 2002, seven of the entities comprising the CEP had nominated a representative, although not officially sworn them in. CD, the main opposition block, had not put forth a representative.

OAS policy remained focused on implementation of Resolution 822, the main thrust of which was the formation of a legitimate CEP, which was to be charged with planning local, municipal, and legislative elections during the year. However, elections did not take place, largely due to the inability to form the consensus CEP.

The Government had invited a three-member OAS special inquiry commission to investigate the 2001 attacks on members of opposition parties, which were triggered by an apparent attack on the presidential palace. Under international pressure, the Government agreed to pay reparations to the victims and publish a report of actions taken against persons implicated in the events. An agreement was reached between the two largest opposition political parties, the Struggling People's Organization (OPL) and the New Christian Movement for a New Haiti (MOCHRENA), and the Government paid reparations during the year.

Resolution 822 also called for a thorough inquiry into all politically motivated crimes and cited the need to strengthen independent police and judicial institutions to combat impunity. In particular, the OAS requested the arrest of Amiot "Cubain" Metayer, also the leader of the Cannibal Army in Gonaives, for his part in the violence of December 2001. After failing for 7 months to rearrest Metayer, and following the exile of the judge assigned to the case due to threats and pressure, the State Prosecutor's office in Gonaives exonerated Metayer and declared his initial arrest illegal on May 14. On September 23, Metayer's body was found in St. Marc. Although the Government promised a full investigation, many opposition groups, and even Metayer's own Cannibal Army, accused authorities of ordering the murder to ensure Metayer's silence about official involvement in the violence.

On the occasion of the high-level OAS/CARICOM meeting on March 19–20, the OAS emphasized replacing the leadership of the HNP for the Government to further demonstrate its willingness to combat impunity. On March 25, Jean Claude Jean-Baptiste replaced Jean Nesly Lucien as Director General (DG) and Evans Pierre Sainturne replaced Victor Harvel Jean-Baptiste as HNP Chief General Inspector. These appointments immediately sparked controversy among human rights organizations and the international community because of numerous and credible reports of criminal activity by both officials. There was photographic evidence of Jean-Baptiste participating in the brutal beating and burning murder of Pastor Sylvio Claude, leader of the Parti Democrate Chretien Haitien, one of the political parties that ran against FL in the 1990 elections. Additionally, Jean-Baptiste was named as DG without consultation with the OAS, as required by Resolution 822.

Under significant international pressure, the authorities replaced Jean-Baptiste with Jean-Robert Faveur, who was sworn in on June 6, as DG of the HNP. On June 21, Faveur resigned his position, citing government intimidation and interference in his decision-making, and his unwillingness to execute illegal orders. Faveur fled the country fearing retribution for public statements he made on the radio about his experience as DG. In July, former civil court senior judge (Doyenne) Jocelyne Pierre replaced Faveur as DG. Sainturne was implicated in the 2001 murder attempt on the investigating judge of the Jean Dominique murder investigation, but remained the Chief General Inspector at year's end.

Affiliation with the FL was increasingly required for government employment, and political patronage was widespread. It was common for political appointees to use their positions for personal enrichment. Many of the 2,500 to 3,500 officers on the official HNP payroll were ghost officers who did not actually work (see Section 1.d.).

The Government continued to accuse opposition supporters of plotting against the State. Members of opposition parties and their supporters faced the constant threat of arrest (see Section 1.d.). Most remained in jail for months despite the widespread perception that the charges were without foundation.

On December 14, two prominent critics of the Government, Senator Pierre Prince Sonson and Catholic Bishop Pierre Andre Dumas, were shot at in what appeared to have been murder attempts or intimidation. Another vocal critic of the Government, Evans Lescouflair, also reported a December 11 attempt on his life. An opposition politician accompanying Prince Sonson at the time of the attack identified Lavalas Deputy James Desrosins as driver of the vehicle used in the attempt on Sonson's life. The attack on Sonson came days after a Lavalas Deputy issued an incendiary call to arms to Lavalas supporters.

There are no legal impediments to women's participation in politics or government. The monetary deposit required of female candidates for political office (if sponsored by a recognized party) is one-half that required of male candidates. At year's end, 3 of the 81 deputies were women, and there were 6 women among the 19 senators. Five of the 16 ministers in the Government were women.

Section 4. Governmental Attitude Regarding International and Nongovernmental Investigation of Alleged Violations of Human Rights

A number of domestic and international human rights groups generally operated without government restriction, investigating and publishing their findings on human rights cases. Government officials generally acknowledged their views but often failed to implement recommendations. The Government permitted special missions and the continued presence of U.N. bodies and other international organizations such as the ICRC, the U.N. Independent Expert on Human Rights, the UNDP, the IACHR, and the OAS Special Mission's human rights office. However, threats and intimidation from unknown sources against domestic NGOs continued during the year.

In a report released before the April 17 session of the U.N. Human Rights Commission, independent observer Louis Joinet cited the steady decline in the human rights situation since his September 2002 visit and recommended establishment of an office of the U.N. High Commissioner for Human Rights in the country. Joinet noted that security had deteriorated and violence against human rights defenders increased; arrests, illegal detentions of political activists, police brutality, and cases of intimidation had been widely publicized; and the judicial system continued to be deficient as judges had been subjected to attacks, causing some to go into exile. Joinet's report also recommended a national commission on reparations for the victims of the 1991 coup d'etat and legislative reform of three bills concerning the judiciary as a means of combating impunity. At year's end, the proposed office had not been established, but the U.N. High Commission on Refugees (UNHCR) opened an office in the neighboring Dominican Republic, which began to handle cases of Haitian political asylum seekers.

Human rights organizations increasingly turned to issues that they had not previously addressed, including prison conditions, the widespread lack of health facilities, and impunity for criminals. Local officials often attempted to control and sought money from domestic human rights groups, as well as other local NGOs. Especially in Gonaives, the Les Cayes region, and in the Central Plateau, local officials and their supporters often harassed, refused permits to assemble, and threatened NGOs.

No investigations were opened in the 2002 cases of Patrick Merisier, a human rights field monitor who was shot, or human rights attorney Fleury Lysias who was illegally arrested and beaten.

At the national and international levels, human rights organizations have been active and effective in monitoring human rights issues, and met frequently with government officials. Human rights organizations, including the Platform of Haitian Human Rights Organizations, the NCHR, the Lawyers' Committee for the Respect of Individual Rights, the Ecumenical Center of Human Rights, and the Catholic Bishops' National Commission on Justice and Peace, made frequent media appearances and published objective reports on violations. All reported receiving threats as a result of their work.

In February, Marie-Yolene Gilles, coordinator of NCHR's Human Rights Monitoring Program, was targeted by a campaign of intimidation. While working on the December 2002 triple murder case of the three brothers killed by police in Carrefour (see Section 1.a.), Gilles received phone calls with threats to kill her and her family and burn down her home. She was threatened again in August for her work investigating attaches in police stations.

The Office of the Protector of Citizens (OPC), an ombudsman-like office provided for by the Constitution, received complaints of abuse at all levels of government. The Government did not directly impede OPC investigations but did not always respond to its requests for information. In the past, local human rights organizations did not view the office as an advocate or interlocutor with the Government and often did not file complaints with the OPC, reporting that OPC did not play an active role following up on human rights complaints. This perception changed, however, with the appointment of Necker Dessables, a respected human rights advocate, as the OPC ombudsman in 2002. Relations between the OPC and major human rights organizations such as the Platform for Human Rights and the Lawyers Committee for the Respect of Individual Rights improved and continued to be positive. The OPC had budgetary problems and employed only four investigators and was therefore unable to be very active in investigations of human rights abuses.

The Parliament's Justice and Human Rights Committee did not have a high profile and focused largely on judicial issues.

Section 5. Discrimination Based on Race, Sex, Disability, Language, or Social Status

The Constitution does not specifically prohibit discrimination on the grounds of race, sex, disability, language, or social status. It does provide for equal working conditions regardless of sex, beliefs, or marital status. However, there was no effective governmental mechanism to administer or enforce these provisions. Societal discrimination occurred against persons with HIV/AIDS, particularly women, but educational programs and HIV/AIDS activists were fighting to change that stigma.

Women.—The law provides penalties for rape and domestic violence; however, the Government did not enforce these provisions adequately. According to women's rights groups, rape and other abuse of women was common, both within and outside marriage. Women's shelters and organizations reported that local armed thugs frequently raped and harassed girls and women in the "quartiers populaires" (slums) like Cite Soleil and Martissant. Police authorities rarely arrested the perpetrators or investigate the incident, and the victims sometimes suffered further harassment in retaliation. There were no government-sponsored programs for victims of violence. The Criminal Code excuses a husband who murders his wife or her partner upon catching them in the act of adultery in his home, but a wife who kills her husband under similar circumstances is not excused.

The law does not specifically prohibit sexual harassment, although the Labor Code states that men and women have the same rights and obligations. Sexual harassment of female workers was a problem, especially in the assembly sector (see Section 6.b.).

Women do not enjoy the same social and economic status as men. In some social strata, tradition limits women's roles. A majority of peasant women remained in traditional occupations of farming, marketing, and domestic labor. Very poor female heads of household in urban areas also often find their employment opportunities limited to traditional roles in domestic labor and sales. Laws governing child support recognize the widespread practice of multiple-father families but were rarely enforced. Female employees in private industry or service jobs, including government jobs, were seldom promoted to supervisory positions. However, well-educated women have occupied prominent positions in both the private and public sector in the past several years.

The Ministry of Women's Affairs is charged with promoting and defending the rights of women and ensuring that they attain an equal status in society, but had few resources at its disposal and was able to accomplish little in this regard.

Domestic women's rights groups were small, localized, and received little publicity.

Children.—Government health care and education programs for children were inadequate. Malnutrition was a problem; approximately 23 percent of all children under 5 were chronically malnourished. The Government has a school nutrition program, administered through the Office of National Development and supported by foreign donors. Through this program, health clinics and dispensaries have begun to distribute donated food to children.

The Constitution and the law provide for free and compulsory primary education; however, in practice most rural families had no access to public schools. The costs of school fees, books, materials, and uniforms, even in public schools, were prohibitive for most families, and an estimated 90 percent of schools were private. Schools were dilapidated and understaffed. According to the Government, 40 percent of children never attend school; of those who do, less than 15 percent graduate from secondary school. The Ministry of Education estimated primary school enrollment at 65 percent. Poorer families sometimes rationed education money to pay school fees only for male children.

Child abuse was a problem. Government-sponsored radio commercials urged parents not to abuse their children physically or mentally. There was some anecdotal evidence that in very poor families, caretakers deprive the youngest children of food to feed older, income-generating children.

In early January, a 10-year-old girl was lured into an alley, raped, and became pregnant by a 16-year-old male. On April 16, the victim's family filed a complaint against the male with the Justice of the Peace of Carrefour. On January 17, police arrested him and released him the following day, but then rearrested him on April 28 after the family filed a complaint with the State Prosecutor's office. After discussion between the assistant prosecutor and the defendant's lawyer, the defendant was released, provided he would return for the hearing in May; he never appeared and neither did the Assistant Prosecutor. The lead State Prosecutor highlighted the apparent collusion between the defendant's lawyer and the assistant prosecutor. Following significant press coverage and interventions by human rights and women's organizations, the defendant was arrested for a third time on May 16. He spent only a few days in prison at Fort National and was subsequently released due to his age. The prosecutor's investigation of the case continued at year's end.

The law prohibits corporal punishment of children, and all schools must post clearly their disciplinary policies. It also called for the establishment of a commission to determine appropriate school disciplinary measures. In practice, corporal punishment was accepted as a form of discipline.

Port-au-Prince's large population of street children included many domestic servants, or "restaveks" ("to stay with" in Creole) who were dismissed from or fled employers' homes (see Section 6.f.). The Ministry of Social Affairs provided some assistance to street children.

Several international and local NGOs worked on children's issues. UNICEF and Save the Children Canada and UK, in conjunction with local NGOs such as the Haitian Coalition for the Defense of the Rights of the Child (COHADDE), promote children's rights by conducting studies of children's issues, most notably a study on child domestic labor (see Section 6.f.), and awareness raising activities in the country.

Persons with Disabilities.—The Constitution provides that persons with disabilities shall have the means to ensure their autonomy, education, and independence. However, there was no legislation to implement these constitutional provisions or to mandate provision of access to buildings for persons with disabilities. Given the severe poverty in which most citizens live, those with disabilities faced a particularly harsh existence even though they did not face overt mistreatment. Disabled beggars were common on the streets of Port-au-Prince and other towns.

National/Racial/Ethnic Minorities.—Approximately 99 percent of Haitians are descendants, in whole or in part, of African slaves who won a war of independence from France in 1804. The remaining population is of European, Middle Eastern, North American, or Latin American origin. The law makes no distinction based on race. However, longstanding social and political animosities were often tied to cultural identification, skin color, and overlapping issues of class in a starkly nonegalitarian society. Some of these animosities date back to before the country's revolutionary period.

Racial distinctions tend to parallel social and economic strata. Mulattos generally belong to the wealthiest classes of society. Mulattos historically have been targets of sporadic attacks and kidnappings because they were perceived as wealthy.

The Government recognizes two official languages: Creole, spoken by virtually all Haitians; and French, limited to approximately 20 percent of the population including the economic elite. Lack of French-language skills limited access to political and economic opportunities for the majority of the population. Although Creole was used in parliamentary debate in the Lower House of Parliament, the Government prepared most official documents only in French. Language also remained a significant barrier to full access to the judicial system (see Section 1.e.). Despite the Government's literacy promotion, many Creole speakers were illiterate.

Section 6. Worker Rights

a. The Right of Association.—The Constitution and the Labor Code provide for the right of association, which was generally respected in practice; however, the Labor Code dates from earlier governments and is far more restrictive. For instance, there is no legislation protecting the right of public employees to organize.

The law protects union activities and prohibits a closed shop. For legal recognition the law also requires that a union, which must have a minimum of 10 members, register with the Ministry of Labor and Social Affairs within 60 days of its formation. The Labor Code does not require prior approval before any association is established. Unions are subject to the same registration requirements as other associations (see Section 2.b.). The law prohibits employers, management, and anyone who represents the interests of employers from joining a union.

In theory unions are independent of the Government and political parties. Nine principal labor federations represented approximately 5 percent of the total labor force of approximately 2.8 million persons, including the approximately 2 to 3 percent working in the industrial sector. Union membership decreased significantly, but unions remained active in the public sector. Some union representatives asserted that union activists not affiliated with the Government felt themselves forced into self-exile.

Several unions have grievances pending against the Government over unfair labor practices and other worker rights violations before the International Labor Organization (ILO) and the International Confederation of Free Trade Unions.

Labor unions reported several cases of threats and arrests during the year. Leaders of several major labor confederations reported receiving threats and demands to support the FL party. On July 29, armed men visited the home of Petit-Frere Jean-

Louis, Secretary General of the General Independent Organization of Haitian Workers. Jean-Louis had spoken out against the corruption among Lavalas officials in Port de Paix and in the Northwest Department. He was not home at that time but upon hearing of the incident, he left Port de Paix and went into hiding in Gonaives.

On July 30, the office of Fignole St. Cyr, Secretary General of the Autonomous Central of Haitian Workers, was the target of similar harassment. While he was out, armed thugs entered St. Cyr's office and demanded his staff divulge his arrival time. The truck circled the office for the remainder of the morning but eventually left when St. Cyr failed to appear. St. Cyr had taken part in the G184 demonstration in Cite Soleil (see Section 2.b.) and had criticized the Government on unemployment, the political crisis, and interference with the press.

Union leaders asserted that some employers in the private industrial sector dismissed individuals for participation in union organizing activities. In 2000, the ILO criticized the Labor Code for its failure to include a specific provision providing protection against anti-union discrimination at the time of hiring.

Unions may freely form or join federations or confederations and affiliate with international bodies. Each of the principal labor federations maintained some affiliation with various international labor organizations.

b. The Right to Organize and Bargain Collectively.—The Labor Code protects trade union organizing activities and stipulates fines for those who interfere with this right but does not provide for reinstatement of workers fired for trade union activities. No fines were issued during the year, or in previous years. Unions generally were free of government and employer interference to pursue their goals, although the Government made little effort to enforce the law.

Organized labor activity was concentrated in the Port-au-Prince area, in state enterprises, and in the civil service. High unemployment rates and anti-union sentiment among some factory workers and most employers limited the success of union organizing efforts.

Collective bargaining was nonexistent, and employers set wages unilaterally. The Labor Code does not distinguish between industries producing for the local market and those producing for export. Employees in the export-oriented assembly sector enjoyed better than average wages and benefits. However, frequent verbal abuse and intimidation of workers and organizers were problems in the assembly sector. Female workers in the assembly sector reported that some employers sexually harassed female workers with impunity. Women also reported that while most assembly sector workers were women, virtually all supervisors were men. Workers had access to labor courts (Tribunaux de Travail) set up to resolve common labor-management disputes; however, the courts' judgments were not enforced. The courts function under the supervision of the Ministry of Labor and Social Affairs and adjudicate minor conflicts, but unions stated that the process was inefficient. Seven labor courts operate in Port-au-Prince, and in the provinces plaintiffs utilize municipal courts.

The Labor Code provides for the right to strike, except for managers, administrators, other heads of establishments, and public utility service workers. The Labor Code defines public utility service employees as essential workers who "cannot suspend their activities without causing serious harm to public health and security." There were few public sector strikes during the year. In May 2002, hospital residents went on strike to protest lack of supplies and the diversion of existing supplies to administrators. When the Government intervened and provided additional materials, residents resumed work.

There are no export processing zones (EPZs) outside of the metropolitan area. Legislation governing free trade zones provide that the Labor Code applies in the EPZs, and the Government signed an agreement with Grupo M, a Dominican textile company, to build a production facility in a newly established free trade zone on the border near Ouanaminthe. On October 9, the International Finance Corporation (IFC) approved a loan to the company; its provisions stipulated a social compensation plan for farmers and landowners displaced by the project. The IFC called for independent investigations into allegations of Grupo M abuse of workers and union organizers. Nevertheless, Batay Ouvriye, an organization of peasant workers, strongly opposed the project, and progress has stalled pending legislative authorization of the land concession, which had not been granted at year's end.

c. Prohibition of Forced or Bonded Labor.—The Labor Code prohibits forced or bonded labor for adults and minors; however, the Government failed to enforce this law for children, who continued to be subjected to forced domestic labor as restaveks in urban households, sometimes under harsh conditions (see Sections 5 and 6.f.).

d. Status of Child Labor Practices and Minimum Age for Employment.—The minimum employment age in all sectors is 15 years, with the exception of domestic service, for which the minimum is 12 years of age. There is also a legal provision for employment of children between the ages of 12 and 16 as apprentices. The Labor Code prohibits minors from working under dangerous conditions and prohibits night work in industrial enterprises for minors under 18. Fierce adult competition for jobs ensured child labor was not a factor in the industrial sector; however, children under the age of 15 commonly worked at informal sector jobs to supplement family income. Children also commonly worked with parents on small family farms, although the high unemployment rate among adults kept children from employment on commercial farms in significant numbers. Government agencies lacked the resources to enforce relevant laws and regulations effectively. According to COHADDE, children worked primarily as domestic servants (restaveks); however, some worked on the street as vendors or beggars, and some were involved in prostitution.

The Government has not ratified and does not adhere to ILO Convention 182 on elimination of the worse forms of child labor. It has not defined "worst forms of child labor" or "hazardous work."

The Government designated the Ministry of Labor and Social Affairs' Social Welfare and Research Institute (IBESR) to implement and enforce child labor laws and regulations. The Government has begun to place a high priority on the eradication of child domestic labor (see Section 6.f.). Despite the Government's efforts, the budget for the Ministry remained below what is needed to fund adequately programs to investigate exploitative child labor cases throughout the country.

The IBESR coordinated efforts with the Ministries of Justice, Education, and Foreign Affairs, as well as local and international agencies, to formulate and enforce child labor policies. The Government signed a Memorandum of Understanding with ILO's International Program for the Elimination of Child Labor (IPEC) in 1999. IPEC began a Child Labor Project in 2000, which was scheduled to end in December 2002 but continued through the spring and developed a framework focusing on institutional capacity building, prevention through awareness-raising, and direct assistance to victims of child labor. A much-lauded government-sponsored hotline for children in crisis operated only during regular business hours and had limited resources and access to safe shelters. In August 2002, NCHR-New York inaugurated a program to prevent the restavek practice, improve living conditions for and rescue these children, and reintegrate them into society (see Section 6.f.).

e. Acceptable Conditions of Work.—The legal minimum daily wage, established in 1995 by the Tripartite Commission of Salaried Workers, whose six members were appointed by the President (two representatives each of labor, employers, and government), is approximately $0.96 (36 gourdes). This wage was insufficient to provide a decent standard of living for a worker and family. Some workers were paid on a piece-rate basis and may earn more than the minimum wage. The majority of citizens worked in the informal sector and subsistence agriculture, where minimum wage legislation does not apply and wages of $0.40 (15 gourdes) a day were common. Many women worked as domestic employees, where minimum wage legislation also does not apply.

The Labor Code governs individual employment contracts. It sets the standard workday at 8 hours and the workweek at 48 hours, with 24 hours of rest on Sunday. However, HNP officers worked 12-hour shifts 6 days per week, in apparent violation of the Labor Code. The code also establishes minimum health and safety regulations. The industrial and assembly sectors largely observed these guidelines. However, the Ministry of Social Affairs did not enforce work hours or health and safety regulations.

The assembly sector published a voluntary code of conduct in 1999, committing signatories to a number of measures designed to raise industry standards, including payment of the minimum wage and the prohibition of child labor. Employers in the assembly sector generally paid the minimum wage or higher. In this sector, working conditions were also generally better and there were no reports of child labor.

There were no formal data, but unions alleged that job-related injuries were prevalent in the construction industry and public works sectors. With more than 50 percent of the population unemployed, workers were not able to exercise the right to remove themselves from dangerous work situations without jeopardy to continued employment.

f. Trafficking in Persons.—The Government passed a law in June prohibiting trafficking in women and children; however, trafficking in women and children was a problem. Internal trafficking of children for domestic labor remained a problem in the country. On October 8, a new, more comprehensive law was introduced before Parliament that would render trafficking in all persons illegal. The Chamber of Deputies approved it and it was waiting Senate passage at year's end.

Haitians trafficked overseas were sent largely to the Dominican Republic, the U.S., Europe (mainly France), and Canada. The results of the most recent study of trafficking across the border conducted by UNICEF in August 2002 reported that between 2,000 and 3,000 Haitian children were trafficked to the Dominican Republic each year. The findings were the result of a joint UNICEF/International Organization for Migration study. However, most trafficking occurs within the country's borders and involves children. In June, the Government created a Brigade for the Protection of Minors (BPM), a special unit under the HNP charged with investigating cases of child trafficking and monitoring movement of children across the Haitian/Dominican border. The BPM was functional; however, resource issues remained a barrier to its operational capacity.

Rural families continued to send young children to more affluent city dwellers to serve as unpaid domestic labor in a practice called restavek. In May, the country's first lady, Mildred Aristide, authored a book documenting the restavek phenomenon in Haiti, its historical background, and the steps that the Government should take to combat the practice. The practice of sending children, mainly girls, to work as domestic servants in exchange for that child's room and board has existed in the country for centuries. While some restaveks received adequate care including an education, the Ministry of Social Affairs believed that many employers compelled the children to work long hours, provided them little nourishment, and frequently beat and abused them. The majority of restaveks worked in homes where the yearly income was very low, so conditions, food, and education for nonbiological children were not priorities.

In May, the Ministry of Labor and Social Affairs held a conference to unveil the results of a study that the Government co-sponsored with UNICEF, ILO/IPEC, UNDP, and Save the Children Canada and UK to determine the fundamentals of child domestic labor practice. The study, which covered the fiscal years 2001–02, noted that 173,000 children, or 8.2 percent of children between the ages of 5 and 17 years of age, worked as domestic household labor. Of that 8.2 percent, girls comprised the majority of child domestics at 59 percent and boys at 41 percent. Labor laws require anyone who has a child domestic in their employ to obtain a permit from IBESR and to ensure the overall welfare of the child until they reach 15 years of age. Additionally, the law requires that restaveks 15 years of age and older be paid not less than one half the amount paid to an adult servant hired to perform similar work, in addition to room and board. To avoid this obligation, employers dismissed many restaveks before they reached that age.

The Government acknowledged the problem of internal trafficking and took steps to address it, despite severe resource constraints. The Government devoted the bulk of its entire social welfare budget to combating trafficking of children. Since its establishment in 2000, the hotline for child abuse victims received over 720 calls leading to action on 158 cases, either through initiation of criminal action against an abusive adult or removal of the child from an abusive situation. Eighty-three percent of the children involved in these cases were in domestic service, many were under the age of 12, and many reported abuses such as beatings, rape, and malnutrition. In August, IBESR hired four additional monitors to rescue children believed to be working in forced labor situations. Government officials placed rescued victims in shelters and in the care of local NGOs, such as Foyer Maurice Sixto, a children's shelter located in Port-au-Prince.

In August, the Ministry of Foreign Affairs approved the creation of three additional consulates along the Haitian/Dominican border, which were charged with monitoring the movement of Haitian children across the border. The Ministry of the Interior also reinforced agents at border control points at the three international airports to watch for children who might be traveling unaccompanied or without their parents. The Ministry of Justice circulated memorandums to magistrates around the country in an awareness-heightening campaign on the new anti-trafficking law and on child labor laws. To address some of the social aspects of the restavek practice, the Government provided a subsidy of 70 percent for educational supplies, including books and uniforms. The Government also called on employers of child domestics to release them from their duties in the afternoon to allow them the opportunity to attend school.

There was no evidence that the authorities were complicit in trafficking of persons.

U.S. DEPARTMENT OF STATE

International Narcotics Control Strategy Report—2003

Released by the Bureau for International Narcotics and Law Enforcement Affairs

MARCH 2004

HAITI

I. Summary

Haiti's geographical position, weak institutions, and subsistence economy have made it a key conduit for drug traffickers transporting cocaine from South America to the United States and, to a lesser degree, Canada and Europe. The Haitian National Police (HNP) lacks discipline and is riddled with corruption. The judicial system is equally weak, its prosecutors and judges susceptible to bribes and intimidation.

The Government of Haiti (GOH) made slow progress toward implementation of the May 2002 counternarcotics Letter of Agreement with the United States. A new facility for the Haitian Coast Guard (HCG) in Cap Haitien was completed and staffed. However, operational funding remained inadequate. The Bureau de Lutte contre le Trafic Illicite de Stupefiants (BLTS), the counternarcotics unit of the HNP, restricted to the capital by lack of transport resources, did little without DEA leadership and involvement.

Corruption, weak law enforcement capability, and lack of GOH commitment combined to limit cooperation in general, although Haitian officials have cooperated in some specific cases. The GOH's major achievement was its expulsion of four drug traffickers, including the notorious Jacques Beaudoin Ketant, to the U.S. for prosecution. Haiti's ongoing political and economic crises continued to grip the country in 2003, eclipsing the fight against drug trafficking. Serious allegations persisted that high-level government and police officials are involved in drug trafficking.

Haiti remains highly susceptible to money laundering due to its weak legal system and pervasive corruption. The money laundering law passed in 2002 has not been implemented. The anti-money laundering commission finally submitted candidate lists for Director General and deputy DG to the President and the Minister of Justice. On December 11, 2003, the GOH inaugurated the Financial Intelligence Unit (FIU) to serve as a clearinghouse for information relating to money laundering and other misuses of the financial system. The FIU will simultaneously serve as a conduit for the transfer of seized assets to the Ministry of Finance. Haiti is a party to the 1988 UN Drug Convention.

II. Status of Country

The political disconnect between supporters and opponents of President Aristide deepened in 2003 and took on violent overtones. The economy remained stalled and attracted little foreign investment, and trafficking in drugs and aliens remained one of the few reliable avenues to wealth. The currency fluctuated around 40 to one against the dollar. Fuel price controls were lifted just before January 2003, doubling prices overnight and affecting law enforcement's ability to conduct operations. In December 2003, months of unrest erupted in demonstrations by the political opposition and by Lavalas supporters, the latter strengthened by roving gangs of "chimeres" (thugs).

The HNP continued to lose mid-level and senior officers but retained overall membership levels with the graduation of about 850 new agents in 2003. Under Lavalas pressure, unqualified Aristide loyalists were placed in key HNP positions, which relegated U.S.-trained officers to secondary positions. For instance, the 14th police academy class is almost entirely composed of Aristide loyalists, including many who are totally illiterate. The government does not provide adequate resources to the police. The GOH routinely pays HNP officials late or not at all, and new recruits are often assigned without uniforms, firearms, training, or supervision. Severely limited international assistance has damaged both the HNP and the judiciary and contributed to their erosion in numbers and effectiveness. The Organization of American States assigned 24 foreign police advisors mid-year, but a lack of GOH support for their mission limited its impact.

III. Country Actions Against Drugs in 2003

During the year, the GOH moved cautiously toward fulfillment of its commitments made in the Letter of Agreement of May 15, 2002. A National Drug Control Strategy Bill, developed with OAS support, is still being debated in Congress. The GOH has not yet ratified the 1971 UN Convention on Psychotropic Substances. The GOH occasionally permitted U.S. hot pursuit into territorial waters and assisted in one pursuit in January 2003. A few investigations of official drug-related corruption were started, but none were carried through. Seizures remained low. No major drug trafficker was prosecuted or extradited, but four well-known traffickers were expelled to the U.S. Haitian law enforcement remained starved for resources. The

GOH did increase the number of HNP agents assigned to the BLTS and the HCG, and the new Coast Guard station at Cap-Haitien is staffed and operating.

DEA provided a basic drug enforcement seminar for 32 BLTS agents in March 2003. DEA polygraphed 26 BLTS agents in August 2003, and the four who failed were reassigned. The Embassy proposed establishment of a special drug court to the Prime Minister and Minister of Justice, but GOH officials took no action.

On February 3, leading daily Le Nouvelliste published a list of ten officials who allegedly had their U.S. visas canceled. On the list were two highly placed HNP officials, National Police Superior Council member Carel Alexandre and BLTS commander Evintz Brillant. Both were soon relieved of their posts. Brillant's supervisor, Jeannot Jean-Francois, sought asylum in the French embassy and eventually fled to Miami. In March, Jean-Claude Jean Baptiste, unofficial liaison between the Palace and violent gangs, was named head of the HNP, and soon was linked to a previous political murder and criminal activity. International protests led to his replacement in June by Jean-Robert Faveur, an uncorrupted, professional officer who fled the country within ten days of his appointment following political pressure that undermined his authority. The current head of the HNP is Jocelyn Pierre, a senior judge with no prior law enforcement experience, known for having bowed to political pressure in a high profile case.

Corruption. There was no effort to curb drug-related corruption, and no prosecutions or convictions of major traffickers took place in Haiti. Involvement of government and HNP officials in drug trafficking continued to hamper cooperation and erode trust between Haitian and foreign law enforcement agencies. There is strong evidence of interference by Haitian law enforcement officials, particularly leaking information on planned operations, as well as considerable involvement in trafficking.

On October 5, 2003, a twin-engine Aztec aircraft landed near Cap-Haitien and offloaded 500 kilograms of cocaine. The Secretary of Public Security refused to take action to apprehend three traffickers lodged at the Continental Hotel until DEA pressure forced their arrest. Witnesses have often observed light aircraft landing with drug cargoes on Route 9 in Port-au-Prince. Typically, HNP officers will block traffic and help with off-loading and ground transport.

Law Enforcement Efforts. On June 18, Jacques Ketant, one of Haiti's most notorious drug traffickers, was expelled by the GOH. The GOH subsequently expelled three other traffickers in similar fashion. With Haitian cooperation, DEA has seized several large houses belonging to Ketant. Haitian citizen Salim Jean Batrony, arrested in 2002 with 58 kilograms of cocaine, was released, causing a scandal in which the judge was dismissed, but Mr. Batrony was not re-arrested.

There were no joint large-scale U.S.-Haiti law enforcement counternarcotics operations in 2003 in part because of the disappointing results of Operation Hurricane in 2002.

The HCG was involved in three significant law enforcement cases during the year. On September 18, Cap-Haitien officers seized $400,000 from the M/V NIKLAS II. On October 13, the Cap-Haitien detachment stopped a boatload of migrants who reportedly intended to smuggle drugs to Miami. In November, the Coast Guard intercepted a boat carrying 40 pounds of marijuana.

During 2003, the U.S. invoked the 2002 Bilateral Agreement to Suppress Illicit Maritime Drug Traffic eight times, pursuing suspect vessels into territorial waters and sometimes boarding them. In all cases, Haitian authorities have permitted search of Haitian-flag vessels, sometimes without the presence of a Haitian law enforcement official.

Haitian drug trafficking organizations continue to operate with relative impunity. The arrival of cocaine from South America is generally unimpeded, due to the HNP's lack of human and material resources. Haiti's roads are very poor, and the HNP has no air assets. The HCG has no presence on the south coast and, even with assistance from the U.S. Coast Guard, its ability to patrol in other areas is limited by frequent vessel breakdowns. The BLTS has no permanent presence outside Port-au-Prince and no effective means of transport. The GOH does not provide the HCG or BLTS with necessary equipment, maintenance, or logistical support.

Agreements and Treaties. Haiti is a party to the 1988 UN Drug Convention. Haiti's law on the control and suppression of illicit drug trafficking reflects most of the Convention's provisions; however, there has been no serious effort to implement it. Extradition is carried out under the 1905 U.S.-Haiti extradition treaty. Haitian law prohibits the extradition of its nationals. The GOH has cooperated with specific requests for expulsion of non-Haitians, and this year for the first time expelled Haitian drug traffickers. The GOH has not yet ratified the OAS mutual legal assistance treaty. Haiti has signed, but not yet ratified, the Inter-American Convention Against Corruption.

Cultivation/Production. Illicit cultivation in Haiti is limited to minor amounts of marijuana. There is no information on drug production or use of precursors.

Domestic Programs (Demand Reduction). There are no viable demand reduction or rehabilitation programs. Polling data indicate that domestic marijuana and cocaine use, while low, continues to rise.

Drug Flow/Transit. Embassy Port-au-Prince estimates that the flow of cocaine through Haiti has continued to increase, with some cocaine going to the U.S. through the Dominican Republic, whose 225-mile (360 km) border with Haiti is largely uncontrolled. Approximately 8 percent of the cocaine destined for the U.S. transited Haiti and/or the Dominican Republic. Cocaine arrives in the country by maritime or air conveyances. Traffickers forward these shipments onward using maritime vessels or over land to the Dominican Republic. During 2003, United States authorities seized drugs concealed on five different commercial vessels arriving in Miami from Haitian ports, totaling 1,214 pounds of cocaine.

IV. U.S. Policy Initiatives and Programs

The U.S. plan for combating illegal drug trafficking via Haiti remains one of interdiction along with police and judicial institution-building. However, several factors work against successful implementation of that plan-forewarned smugglers elude the HNP, and low or no response by the HNP to DEA intelligence allows suspected air and sea deliveries to be completed without challenge. The GOH's slow implementation of the bilateral counternarcotics assistance agreement also hinders significant achievement, and lack of resources and lack of political will are equally to blame.

The Road Ahead. Stemming the flow of illegal narcotics through Haiti remains a cornerstone of U.S. counternarcotics policy. Key preconditions to stemming the illegal flow remain improving the effectiveness of GOH law enforcement and judicial institutions and strengthening the GOH's ability to fund these institutions by encouraging development of an effective system of liquidating assets seized from arrested smugglers. The new HCG base at Cap-Haitien must be supplemented with a small BLTS detachment and eventually replicated on the south coast. The road ahead is obstructed by the politicization and corruption of the police and judiciary, and further obscured at this time by social disorder and political violence.

MARC ASHTON
825 Parkside Circle North
Boca Raton, FL. 33486

Rep. Cass Ballenger
2182 Rayburn House Office Building
Washington, DC 20515
Fax No: (202) 225 0316

Sir,

As a US Citizen, having lived in Haiti for more than fifty years and still engaged in business there, I wish to voice my full approval of the efforts of our Government to find a solution to the Haitian dilemma.

The departure from Haiti of Mr. Aristide was the only way of avoiding a blood bath, and even today, we are still witnessing his violent mode of operation. One of his two main "henchmen", Jonas Petit, declared today that he was given enough money to continue to destroy all the commerce and industry in the country.

The Jonas Petits and the Paul Raymonds are still actively pursuing their systematic destruction of what little is left.

All one needs to do is to refer back to one of Aristide's early speeches, in which he clearly stated that what needs to be done in Haiti is what the peasant farmers do when they have a bad crop, which is to burn off the crop to the ground, and let a new crop grow to replace it. This, he made clear, was in reference to the actual businesses and business sector, at the time.

The Lavalas movement is predicated on destruction, violence, intimidation and absolute power. Aristide recently said in another speech that he intended to remain in power at least until the year 2015.

When Aristide came to power, he had the support of the vast majority of Haitians of all classes and the vast majority of the International donor organizations and foreign governments, but he failed miserably in everything but making himself very rich and the country poorer.

It would be a shame to allow him to live in exile and not face the judicial system that Manuel Noriega of Panama was forced to face. The evidence is certainly available to have him answer to his many accusations.

At the very least, a thorough investigation of his finances should be undertaken.

Respectfully yours,

Marc Ashton

E-mail: MAs6811803@aol.com. Tel: (561) 362 7120 or (954) 425 2063

March 3, 2004

Ref: Haiti

Rep. Cass Ballenger, Chairman
Washington Office
2182 Rayburn House Office Building
Washington, DC. 20515

Dear Mr. Ballenger:

Let me think Mr. Collin Powell and President Bush for rescuing the Haitians. The work just begins in Haiti there is a lot more to be done. Aristide is gone for his own good, his life and that many more Haitians were in great danger.

I am a Haitian-American and I love Haiti dearly and ¾ of my family still in Haiti facing danger every day since 1994. I am not a politician but a concerned and proud Haitian-American. It appears that the **Black Caucus and Mr. Ira Kurzban** ignore the suffering of the Haitians all they care about is Mr. Aristide who contributes to their financial needs while he is bringing the country to very less level of poverty. **Mr. Ira Kurzban is Mr. Aristide private lawyer he is lobbying for his fixed salary like some members of the Black Caucus.** Where was the Black Caucus when Mr. Aristide elected himself president by paying people to vote more than normal and to have the dead came back just to vote for him in 2000. Where was the Black Caucus when Mr. Aristide formed a cooperative and asked all the Haitians living abroad to invest in his coop at the rate of 100% interest and after few months declared to the investors that he did not know what happen to their money. Where was the Black Caucus when Mr. Aristide authorized his supporters to kill the businessmen and took their goods. Where was the Black Caucus when Mr. Aristide turned the national airport into a drug market.

After 200 years the Haitians are still living in mud house and pit latrine or the forest. It is said that President Bush kidnapped Mr. Aristide for which we are very grateful but now the Black Caucus needs to go to Haiti solve the rebels' problems. They have no place in the new Haiti. Mr. Guy Philippe and Jodel Chamblain should never return to Haiti. They were members of the previous government death squad.

Please do not waste time with Mr. Ira Kurzban and the Black Caucus now because Haiti does not know its true color or does not have color. If the Black Caucus cares so much they should go to Haiti and take the rebels out. Please encourage your colleagues to continue to support President Bush and Mr. Collin Powell in their willingness to liberate Haiti. Investigation should focus on Jesse Jackson, Ira Kurzban, the late Ron Brown, and the Clinton involvement in Haiti.

Thank for your support.

Marie D. Alexandre MAlexandre

God bless

In support of the recent US government actions in Haiti

DECLARATION FOR DEMOCRACY IN HAITI

Miami, Florida, -

On the 18th anniversary of what should have been the end of dictatorship in Haiti, Haitians today are facing another arbitrary, autocratic government. The Aristide regime is systematically violating human rights, destroying civil society, ignoring the fundamental principles of the separation of powers enshrined in the Haitian constitution of 1987, and is pushing the country toward civil confrontation.

Tens of thousands of Haitian citizens have taken to the streets in recent weeks to peacefully demonstrate against President Aristide's repeated attacks on the free press, the university, opposition parties and civil society.

The country is now on the brink of political, economic, ecological and social chaos. Four years of tireless national and international mediation efforts have been met with intransigence and blatant bad faith on the part of President Aristide.

It is now time for action.

The Haitian American community joins its brothers and sisters in Haiti, students, religious leaders, and members of civil society throughout Haiti in condemning:

- the state-sponsored violence against students and demonstrators,

- the imprisonment of Haitian citizens without due process

- the systematic violation of human rights and political rights guaranteed by the Haitian constitution

- the systematic destruction of the judiciary and legislative institutions

- acts of repression against all the media

- the use of "chimères" or thugs to repress the masses

- the illegal intrusion of the police force in churches, schools and hospitals and

- all attempts to suppress the people's right to life, liberty and the pursuit of happiness as guaranteed by the Declaration of Independence of 1804 and the Universal Declaration of Human rights of 1948.

Through his abuse of power and disregard for constitutional rule of law, President Aristide has broken faith with the very people who elected him. President Aristide was elected to uphold the constitution and the rule of law. During his tenure, President Aristide failed to do either. He has violated his covenant with the Haitian people. Therefore all Haitians, in Haiti and in the Haitian Diaspora, have a responsibility to stand up for their rights and even call for President Aristide's resignation.

The Haitian American community believes that the only way to break the impasse, restore democratic government and provide a peaceful and prosperous future for all Haitians is for President Aristide to place the future of our country before his own interests.

The Haitian American community also calls upon all Haitians – including those within the Haitian government and the United States who seek true democracy – to unite and work together to build democratic institutions and strengthen civil society such that the ideals of February 7, 1986 will finally become a reality.

Signatories:

Civic and Professional Organizations

Haitian-American Doctors Association

Haitian-American Nurses Association

Haitian-American Engineers and Scientist Association

Alliance of Haitian American Law Enforcement Fraternal Organization

Coalition for the Advancement and Development of Haiti (CADH)

Movement for National Unity (MOUN)

Haitian American Republican Club of South Florida (HARC)

Society of Haitian-American Professionals and Entrepreneurs (SHAPE)

Patriote Unis Pour la Démocratie en Haiti (PUDH)

Organization for the Protection of Haitian Rights (OPHR)

League of Young Haitian-American Professionals (LIJECH)

Haitian American Nationalists for Democracy (HAND)

Haitian Democracy Project (HDP)

PATRI

HACHO of South Florida Community Outreach Health Organization

Parti Social Chrétien D'Haiti (PSCH)

Haitian Organization of Women of Miami

Haitian Alternate Liberté Travaille Espoire (HALTE)

Haiti for All

National Association for the Advancement of Haitian Descendants (NAAP)

Civic and Professional Organizations

Haitian-American Republican Caucus

Syndicate des Magistrats a L'étranger

Coalition for Justice

Coalition des Forces Civiques et Morales de Miami

Association of Police Officers Living Abroad

FIU Student Organization

American Foundation Liberty and Democracy (AFLD)

Organization for the Protection of Haitian Rights (OPHR)

Haitian-American Alliance for Progress (HAPP)

Exotic Haitian Enterprises, Inc.

Forgotten Children of Haiti

Artists /Musicians

Wyclef

Sweet Mickey

Lolo, Boukman Esperyans

Radio Club Culturelle

Churches

Pasteur Gornel Joseph, Bereca I and II

Rev. J. Bonhomme,

Haven of Pasteur Jacques O. Michel

Radio/T.V. Personalities

Ménard

Carine Sylvain

Leslie Jacques

For additional information - 305-613-3067

FAX 202-225-2574 B 7485 Page 1 of 2

Cc: Rep. Cass Ballenger Chm. Cong'l Sub. Com on W. H Thank you

Subj: **PLS EXCUSE MY TYPOS - MARIE-EDLYN**
Date: 3/1/2004 5:36:10 PM Eastern Standard Time
From: Mie Edlyn
To: PRESIDENT@WHITEHOUSE.GOV
CC: jocedito516@hotmail.com, tatietou58@yahoo.com, Monfleu, MAllen9644, pbatraville@hotmail.com, marysebayard@hotmail.com, fbellande14@hotmail.com, dickcamera@hotmail.com, cagnat@avantel.net, calixtef@bellsouth.net, ccolette41@hotmail.com, Cassmaud, Bernard_Cassagnol@hotmail.com, edwige7@msn.com, clearco1patrick@hotmail.com, ddmaryline171@hotmail.com, soniadeneffe@yahoo.com, edeshauteurs@pololeather.com, kdeutsch@herald.com, smdrouin@facstaff.wisc.edu, gernancy@hotmail.com, French_Carmel/ME/FDS@FDS.com, gagneron@plazacolon.com, GJWGerdes@cs.com, glaude@un.org, lhermantin@hotmail.com, Asterix107, Jean Elie, decostejeudy@yahoo.com, Johndanies, Tiden@adelphia.net, diasfree@hotmail.com, Alelidan@yahoo.com, lespes@un.org, tiquine@hotmail.com, Lyssabelle15, edmangones@hotmail.com, nicole@blickmanjewelers.com, ansedazur@hotmail.com, jnicolas@pap-co.ht.dhl.com, h9112p@excite.com, racheldenis54@hotmail.com, rameau 1@hainet.net, mh-r@bluewin.ch, hg.rey@wanadoo.fr, lrigaud@nyc.rr.com, ourladyp99@yahoo.com, Azzmr1, Psesesq, philippe.talon@mageos.com, fthomas@nyc.rr.com, rolftippen@hotmail.com, szechman@hotmail.comso

DEAR MR. PRESIDENT,
TO THE U.S. SENATE,
TO THE U.S. CONGRESS,

A QUICK NOTE TO THANK YOU FOR YOUR UNDERSTANDING AND FOR YOUR GREAT HELP (ALONG WITH THE FRENCH GOVERNMENT) **IN DELIVERING THE HAITIAN PEOPLE FROM THE SO-CALLED PRIEST TURNED DEMON, ARISTIDE.**

FROM THE BOTTOM OF MY HEART AND IN THE NAME OF THE HAITIAN PEOPLE HERE AND ABROAD, I ACKNOWLEGE OUR GRATEFULNESS. THE FACTS OBVIOUSLY SPOKE FOR THEMSELVES.

1) ARISTIDE IN WHOM SO MANY PUT THEIR TRUST DISAPPOINTED ALMOST EVERYONE.

2) WE FORGET, BY THE WAY, THAT WHEN HE TOOK OFFICE HE WAS ALREADY ADVOCATING CLASS WARFARE IN KEEPING WITH THE THEOLOGY OF LIBERATION. BY THE WAY, **HE WAS SO ANTI-AMERICAN, HOW HAS HE DARED ASKED FOR THE U.S. GOVERNMENT TO COME TO HIS RESCUE?**

2) **WHAT HAS ARISIDE DONE WITH THE MILLIONS INFUSED INTO HAITI OVER THE PAST YEARS IN ORDER TO IMPROVE THE LIVING CONDITIONS OF OUR PEOPLE? CAN WE NAME EVEN ONE OF HIS ACCOMPLISHMENTS? MAYBE THE BLACK CAUCUS AND IRA KURZBAN CAN PROVIDE US AN ANSWER!**

3) HAITI'S TREASURY IS TOTALLY DEPLETED. FOREIGN HELP, MOSTLY U.S. GOVERNMENT'S, WENT INTO HIS LAVISH LIVING AND THAT OF HIS ENTOURAGE, ACQUIRING PRIVATE MULTI-MILLION DOLLAR PLANES AND HELICOPTERS, CHANNELING EXTRAORDINARY AMOUNTS OF MONIES IN PAYING AMERICAN SECURITY GUARDS (A MAN SO POPULAR WITH "HIS PEOPLE"!), PAYING AMERICAN LAWYER(S), LOBBYISTS, AND OTHER HIGH-CALIBER GROUPS TO PROMOTE HIS INFAMOUS CAUSE. FORTUNATELY, THEY WERE NOT SUCCESSFUL - THE REALITY IS TOO BLATANT. AS YOU KNOW, HAITI HAS BECOME TO BE KNOWN AS A NARCO-STATE.

3) ARISTIDE HAS NOT MPROVED THE ECONOMY AND SOCIAL CONDITIONS EVEN AN IOTA. HE MADE SO MANY PROMISES! HAITI REACHED ROCK-BOTTOM!

4) ARISTIDE PROVED HIMSELF ALONG WITH HIS ENTOURAGE, INCLUDING UNFORTUNATELY SOME ALREADY WELL-OFF UNPATRIOTIC HAITIANS (OPPORTUNTISTS), TO BE ONE OF THE BIGGEST DRUGDEALERS AND ASSASSINS IN THE WORLD. INDEED, HE PROVED TO BE VERY SUCCESSFUL AT STEALING, DRUGDEALING AND KILLING, WHILE THE HAITIAN PEOPLE PLUNGED EVEN MORE DEEPLY INTO THE MOST ABJECT POVERTY AND DESPAIR. HE PROVED TO BE A SUPER-EXPERT AT MANIPULATING THEIR FEELINGS! BUT, MANIFESTLY, THEY COULD NO LONGER BE DUPED AS THEY TURNED OVERWHELMINGLY AGAINST HIM AND CONTRIBUTED LARGELY TO HIS OVERTHROW.

5) THE HAITIAN PEOPLE IS IN ESSENCE A VERY GOOD PEOPLE AND VERY TALENTED ONE. THEY ONLY NEED DIRECTIONS AND OPPORTUNITIES PROVIDED BY A GOVERNMENT WITH STRONG STRUCTURES, AND INSTITUTIONS OVERLOOKING AND ENSURING THE RESPECT OF THE CONSTITUTION AND THE LAWS, THEREBY GUARANTEEING THEIR WELL-BEING.

WE SHOULD BE ABLE TO SEND A MESSAGE TO ARISTIDE'S ILLITERATE AND HIGHLY-EMOTIONAL SUPPORTERS HERE IN THE STATES THAT IN VIEW OF THEIR ALLEGIANCE TO HIM, THE WORLD LOOKS UPON SORROW UPON THEM. BECAUSE THEY APPARENTLY BELIEVED IN HIM, THEY SHOULD HAVE BEEN AT HIS SIDES TO EITHER HELP HIM REBUILD A BETTER HAITI BY COOPERATING WITH HIM AND ALSO HELP HIM DEFEND HIMSELF AGAINST THE SO-CALLELD "TERRORISTS" WHOM HE CLAIMS HAVE BEEN HAMPERING THE SO-CALLED "DEMOCRATIC PROCESS." WHAT AN ABERRATION! HE WAS CONFUSING "DEMOCRATIC" WITH "AUTOCRATIC."

MR. PRESIDENT, YOUR GOVERNMENT WILL NOT BE DISAPPOINTED IN THEIR DECISION. SOMETIMES, MISTAKES ARE MADE, BUT THEYCAN ALWAYS BE CORRECTED. OR SOMETIMES, WHEN THINGS GO WRONG OR NOT WORKING AS PLANNED, ONE SHOULD BE ABLE TO CHANGE THEIR COURSE. IN THE CASE OF ARISTIDE, TWO MORE YEARS WOULD HAVE BEEN UNCONCEIVABLE.

SHAME ON THE BLACK CAUCUS, CARICOM, ET AL!

THANK TO ROY INNIS, CONGRESSMAN MARK FOLEY, SENATOR BILL NELSON AND MANY OF THE OTHERS WHO ARE FOR JUSTICE AND DEMOCRACY IRRELEVANT OF THEIR POLITICAL AFFILIATION(S). AS I BELIEVE THE GREAT MARTIN LUTHER KING ONCE SAID, "INJUSTICE ANYWHERE IS A THREAT TO JUSTICE EVERYWHERE."

LET'S HOPE THAT THE MISTAKES OF THE PAST WILL NOT BE REPEATED. IT IS THE WISH OF ALL DECENT AND CONCERNED HAITIANS THAT THIS YEAR, THE YEAR OF THE COMMEMORATION OF HAITI'S BI-CENTENNIAL, WILL BE A NEW CHAPTER IN THE HISTORY OF HAITI, A CHAPTER IN WHICH THE HAITIAN PEOPLE WILL BE DESERVING OF THE HEROIC EFFORTS OF OUR ANCESTORS IN THEIR FIGHT FOR FREEDOM AND HUMAN RIGHTS.

GRATEFULY AND RESPECTULLY,

MARIE-EDLYN THOMAS
A NATURALIZED U.S. CITIZEN (HAITI-BORN)

CORRECTIONS: PLEASE READ ARISTIDE (BUT WHO CARES), WITH SORROW, AND INCONCEIVABLE. SORRY AND TKS.

PREPARED STATEMENT OF REVEREND WALTER FAUNTROY, FORMER DELEGATE TO THE U.S. HOUSE OF REPRESENTATIVES FROM THE DISTRICT OF COLUMBIA

WALTER FAUNTROY PLAN

- There is one issue that is at the core of the problems in Haiti that few people are talking about. In the last ten years, Haiti has become a major illegal drug transshipment center for the Cali, Medellin and Baranquilla drug cartels in South America.

- The cartels are treating Haiti the way they always treat black communities in this country: they market their stuff through poor black communities by supplying groups of poor black kids whom they arm to fight drug wars as a way of making sure that the lion's share of the money gets passed back to them in Columbia and Bolivia.

- Think of it, there's no gold or diamonds in Haiti for major corporations to exploit as in Africa. They'd rather out-source their jobs in the textile industries and now their computer technology jobs to far off Korea, Taiwan, China and India than to give wretchedly poor black people on an island just off our shores of the United States. And God knows there is no more mahogany or other valuable lumber for them to exploit. For what forestry the French did not ripped from the mountainsides in their time, the U.S. did in a vain effort during World War II to get the soil to grow rubber trees for the war effort. The result is that the good soil has been washing to the sea for decades making it hard to grow crops for export and robbing the beaches of their attractiveness because there is so much mud around.

- Who is supplying the money it takes to arm all of those murderous gangs in Haiti? Where are all of these powerful, sophisticated weapons coming from and who is giving them to the gangs? All you have to do is to look in on any drug-infested black community in America and you see there the very same phenomenon that is destroying our families, our neighborhoods, our young people and our future.

- In Haiti in the Duvallier Era – get this – the Army, the President and the business elite were the Drug Lords! What did they need an army for? They had not had to fight a foreign invader since they kicked the French out 200 years ago. The army was one big drug gang. Reverend Fauntroy tells me that when he was chair of the Bi-partisan/Bicameral Congressional Task Force on Haiti in the 1980s, and a member of the House Select Committee on Narcotics Abuse and Control, they identified a high ranking Army General named Jean-Claude Paul who got $100,000 a day for allowing Cali Cartel planes to land on an airstrip on his farm to "refuel" on their runs to the Florida coast line to drop their stuff off-shore for the distributors to pick up in their small recreational boats. From there the drugs are systematically delivered to pushers straight up east coast our country from Maine to Florida: crack, cocaine, heroine and everything else that poor black kids market for them.

- When in 1994, the U.S. and Aristide dismantled the Army, the guys who were the foot soldiers in this criminal enterprise just re-grouped and called themselves FRAPH, the **F**ront for the **A**dvancement and **P**rogress of **H**aiti and resumed their killing in an effort to reclaim the presidency for the criminal enterprise.

- Aristide countered by getting into the game himself. He organized his own gang of thugs. Fauntroy tells me that they were the "Cannibal Army" in Gonaive; the "Clean Sweep" in St. Marc, the "Red Army in Cite Solie; "The Sleep in the Woods" in Petit Goave and the "Saddam Hussein Army" in the north. They divided the turf with FRAPH and went about the business of checkmating one another in the patented way the cartels supply gangs in the black ghettoes of America.

- Two things happened that created the current crisis. First, Aristide used his gangs to intimidate political opponents and steal the legislative elections in 2000 with the result that the international community, not the United States alone, had no choice but to declare the elections a fraud and withhold $500 million in foreign aid until they organized new elections. The second thing that happened was that both FRAPH's drug gangs and some of Aristide's drug gangs turned on Aristide and his high level cronies who were creaming the money at the top and living in the lap of luxury while, according to Fauntroy's sources, money contributed by the cartels to the Steele Foundation was funding and supplying the disgruntled drug gangs on both sides.

- It came to a head with "Second Massacre of Raboteau" in October of 2003. Because Amoit Metayer, the leader of Aristide's "Cannibal Army" in Gonaive, began attacking Aristide and his new "elite cronies" for the maldistribution of the wealth, Aristide loyalists assassinated him for turning against Aristide. Metayer's brother, Buteur, then rallied his assassinated brother's forces to resist the new tyranny and before you knew it, FRAPH and some of the other Aristide gangs - "Clean Sweep" in St. Marc, the "Red Army in Cite Solie; "The Sleep in the Woods" in Petit Goave and the "Saddam Hussein Army" in the north - came together in a united rebellion to get rid of Aristide. Fauntroy believes that these rebels used the desperate situation of the masses to justify their actions, their real purpose is to take over the drug criminal enterprise for themselves an spread the income more evenly among themselves.

- That's why the Fauntroy Plan calls first for rooting out of Haiti the drug cartels that have made a whole "broken glass" nation a major drug transshipment with all of the familiar negatives that blacks witness every day in the "broken glass" neighborhoods where generation after generation of our young are programmed for addiction, gang warfare and prison.

- The steps of the plan are:

(1) Get humanitarian aid in there immediately to feed, clothe and house the war ravaged masses.

(2) Get our law enforcement and intelligence agencies to come clean, prosecute the known drug lords, and serve notice on the cartels that Haiti is now "off limits" for their activities just like the affluent communities of America that buy most of the stuff from the African American drug war zones.

(3) Get a truck load of national and international aid into the place to disarm and re-train the combatants and train them with the millions of unemployed workers to build the roads, bridges, hospitals, schools, houses and businesses that provide for the "general welfare" that, alone, can bring "domestic" tranquility" in Haiti or the black war zones in America.

(4) Involve our historically black colleges and universities in the funded task of training and re-training Haiti's wretchedly poor people in the skills required for the above-referenced "infrastructure building projects" that must be funded by the international community

(5) To make sure that the money stays there and does not come in and go out in the hands of the Halliburtons and Bectels of the world, a concerted effort needs to be made at putting together joint ventures between experienced and technically competent Haitian businesspersons and African American businesses that will go in to establish the businesses for which the gun totting combatants and millions of unemployed Haitians will be trained to perform.

(6) The interim government officials and the international donor nations and groups have got to be disciplined not to fall back into the sloppy accounting, the lack of transparency and corruption that made so many government operatives in third world countries "predators" instead of enablers of the spread of income, education, healthcare, housing and justice to the masses of their people.

(7) And finally, the US government must assume the role of coordinating and concentrating all international public and private aid sent to Haiti so that there will no debilitating duplication of services and, most important, no loss of focus on getting to the bottom of the corruption that has and continues to thwart well-meaning efforts to improve the quality of life for the Haitian masses.

U.S. AGENCY FOR INTERNATIONAL DEVELOPMENT—FACT SHEET

HUMANITARIAN ASSISTANCE TO HAITI

FEBRUARY 23, 2004

On Tuesday, February 24, 2004, USAID will dispatch a three-person team to Haiti. The team will work closely with the Embassy, USAID Mission, and non-government organization (NGOs) partners to assess humanitarian conditions and monitor and coordinate the provision of humanitarian assistance.

The ongoing political turmoil and economic instability in Haiti have created a potential humanitarian crisis, and have affected numerous aspects of development such as food security, health, nutrition, water and sanitation. While sufficient food stocks are currently in-country and no immediate food crisis exists at present, this could change quickly in coming weeks, especially in the north, due to insecurity and disruptions of transport and distribution. The U.S. Agency for International Development (USAID) has more than 11,000 metric tons of food for direct distribution in country for food assistance development programs.

The U.S. Government through USAID is Haiti's largest bilateral donor. In 2003, USAID contributed $71 million. Through fiscal years 1995–2003, USAID provided a total of $850 million in direct bilateral assistance. For FY04, USAID has planned $52 million in assistance to programs ranging from health, democracy and governance, education and economic growth. To ensure that assistance goes to those Haitians most in need, USAID assistance is channeled principally through NGO's. The U.S. provides food and food-related assistance directly and indirectly to 650,000 poor Haitians.

USAID is the lead donor in providing assistance to combat the spread of HIV/AIDS in Haiti by working through U.S. private health organizations and Haitian NGO's. Haiti has also been singled out by President George W. Bush as a priority country for preventing Mother to Child Transmission of HIV/AIDS, resulting in several million dollars more each year of funding to help mothers and children. U.S. assistance works to alleviate poverty, illiteracy, and malnutrition and promotes respect for human rights and the rule of law.

A major humanitarian concern at present is the breakdown in the provision of basic health services, particularly in the north. The two main hospitals in Port-au-Prince lack supplies and drugs and are barely functioning. Similar disruptions are occurring in Gona?s, Haiti's fourth largest city, and other areas.

CARE, a USAID recipient, has distributed 520 metric tons (MT) of food commodities to the population of Gona?s. The International Committee of the Red Cross (ICRC) and CARE have negotiated limited safe passage to Gona?s. World Vision International (WVI) reports that there is no food emergency in Hinche, due to a good December harvest. Scarcity of fuel is a major problem in many areas and has hindered humanitarian operations, mainly in the north.

CARE reports that there is a potable water crisis in Gona?s due to the lack of fuel. The Haitian electrical company does not have enough fuel to continue to supply Gona?s with potable water. Although CARE has food stocks in the port of Port-au-Prince, the organization lacks fuel for transportation, particularly for food distributions in the north.

On February 18, 2004, U.S. Ambassador to Haiti James B. Foley issued a disaster declaration due to the ongoing complex humanitarian emergency in Haiti. USAID provided $50,000 to support the transport and distribution of emergency relief supplies, including 12 medical kits and three surgical kits, valued at approximately $87,000. Each medical kit is equipped to serve 10,000 people for approximately three months.

In addition, USAID approved $400,000 in funding for the Pan American Health Organization (PAHO) to purchase additional medical supplies and to conduct emergency relief activities in Haiti. To date, a total of $537,000 has been allocated for transport and distribution of medical supplies, as well as the purchasing of medical equipment and emergency health activities.

For more information about USAID's ongoing efforts in Haiti, visit www.usaid.gov/haiti.

United States General Accounting Office

GAO

Testimony

Before the Committee on International Relations, House of Representatives

For Release on Delivery
Expected at
10:00 a.m., EDT
Tuesday,
September 19, 2000

FOREIGN ASSISTANCE

Lack of Haitian Commitment Limited Success of U.S. Aid to Justice System

Statement of Jess T. Ford, Associate Director, International Relations and Trade Issues, National Security and International Affairs Division

GAO

Accountability * Integrity * Reliability

GAO/T-NSIAD-00-257

Mr. Chairman and Members of the Committee:

I am pleased to be here today to discuss the preliminary results of our review of U.S. assistance provided to Haiti's justice system.

In September 1994, the United States and other countries intervened militarily in Haiti to restore the democratically elected government that had been overthrown by the Haitian military in September 1991. Before this intervention, the Haitian military controlled the police and the judicial sector. Military and political cronyism dominated these institutions, and the military influenced the appointments of magistrates and the decisions made by them. These justice institutions were widely regarded as ineffective and corrupt.

After the intervention, the United States stepped in to provide assistance to the Haitian justice system -- both the police and the judicial sector -- aimed at developing a professional civilian police force, enhancing the effectiveness of existing judicial organizations, and improving the Haitian people's access to justice. This assistance also aimed at supporting a broader reform of the judicial sector that the Haitian government intended to pursue over time. The objectives of this assistance program were consistent with U.S. justice assistance objectives in other countries in Latin America.[1]

As you know, U.S. assistance to the judicial sector was suspended in July 2000, because the United States was not able to negotiate an agreement with the Haitian government for continuing these assistance efforts. As of September 2000, most of the U.S. assistance to the Haitian police has stopped, due to congressional concerns related to events surrounding the May 2000 Haitian parliamentary and local elections. The U.S. Department of State is currently reassessing several aspects of the U.S. relationship with Haiti, based on concerns about how votes were counted in Haiti's May 2000 parliamentary and local elections.

My statement today is based on work we are currently concluding for your committee and the Senate Foreign Relations Committee. First, I will discuss the results of the U.S. assistance provided to the Haitian police and judicial sector and the major problems that continue to affect these justice institutions. Second, I will discuss the primary factors that have affected the success of the assistance.

Our work is based on meetings with officials of the U.S. Departments of State and Justice, the U.S. Agency for International Development (USAID), the U.S. Coast Guard, and other U.S. agencies. To examine the results of assistance provided, in June 2000, we went to Haiti, where we met with officials of the Haitian government, other donor countries (Canada and France), the United Nations, nongovernmental organizations, and

[1] See Foreign Assistance: Rule of Law Funding Worldwide for Fiscal Years 1993-98 (GAO/NSIAD-99-158, June 30, 1999); Foreign Assistance: U.S. Rule of Law Assistance to Five Latin American Countries (GAO/NSIAD-99-195, Aug. 4, 1999); and Foreign Assistance: Status of Rule of Law Program Coordination (GAO/NSIAD-00-8R, Oct. 13, 1999).

U.S. contractors. We also performed an extensive review of program documents. We expect to issue our report in October 2000.

SUMMARY

Over the last 6 fiscal years, the United States provided about $97 million in assistance to help Haiti establish its first civilian-controlled police force and improve aspects of its judicial sector, which includes various judicial institutions, procedures, and legal codes. About $70 million in U.S. assistance helped Haiti recruit, train, organize, and equip a basic police force, including specialized units, such as an antinarcotics unit, a special investigative unit, and the Haitian Coast Guard. During the same period, the United States provided about $27 million in assistance that led to improvements in training magistrates and prosecutors, management practices of judicial institutions, and in the access of the Haitian people to justice services. However, despite these achievements, the police force has not effectively carried out its basic law enforcement responsibilities, and recent events suggest that politicization has compromised the force, according to U.S. and other donor officials. The judicial sector also has serious weaknesses, according to U.S. and other donor officials. The sector has not undergone a major reform and, as a result, lacks independence from the executive branch and has outdated legal codes and cumbersome judicial proceedings. Further, the judicial institutions have personnel shortages; inadequate infrastructure and equipment, such as shortages of vehicles and legal texts; and an ineffective internal oversight organization unable to stem corruption. Overall, these institutions provides justice services to only a small segment of the population, because the institutions rely heavily in judicial proceedings on the use of French rather than Creole—the language of the majority of the population.

The key factor affecting the lack of success of U.S. assistance has been the Haitian government's lack of commitment to addressing the major problems of its police and judicial institutions. U.S. assistance to the police has been impeded because the Haitian government has not acted, for example, to (1) strengthen the police organization by filling currently vacant key leadership positions, such as the Inspector General; (2) provide the human and physical resources needed to develop an effective police force; (3) support vigorously police investigations of serious crimes; and (4) keep the police force out of politics. U.S. assistance to the judicial sector has been largely undercut because the Haitian government has not, for instance, (1) followed through on implementing the broad reforms needed to address its major problems, (2) assumed responsibility for adopting many of the improvements made possible by U.S. assistance, and (3) provided the physical and human resources needed to operate effectively.

BACKGROUND

The U.S. Agency for International Development (USAID) and two organizations within the Department of Justice's Criminal Division--the International Criminal Investigative and Training Assistance Program and the Office of Overseas Prosecutorial Development, Assistance, and Training--implemented the majority of assistance provided to the Haitian police and judicial sector. The Department of State has overall responsibility for coordinating this assistance. It also funds training programs implemented by U.S. law enforcement agencies and, immediately after Haiti's return to democracy in 1994, carried out some training programs, mainly in support of the Presidential Palace Guard, which protects the Haitian President.

Several other U.S. agencies have also been involved in supporting the Haitian police. For example, the U.S. Coast Guard and the Department of Defense played key roles in helping to build the Haitian Coast Guard—a main component of the Haitian National Police. Also, the Drug Enforcement Administration helped to support the police's antinarcotics unit. In addition, the U.S. Customs Service helped to train Haitian customs and police officers on countersmuggling techniques.

U.S. ASSISTANCE HELPED IMPROVE THE POLICE AND JUDICIAL SECTOR, BUT MAJOR SHORTCOMINGS PERSIST

U.S. assistance to Haiti's justice sector totaled about $97 million since fiscal year 1995, with about $70 million going to help build a civilian-controlled police force and about $27 million going to improve certain aspects of Haiti's judicial system, such as case registration and tracking systems. Appendix I provides a breakdown of U.S. assistance to the Haitian police and justice sectors.

U.S. Assistance Helped Build a New Haitian Police Force

U.S. assistance was intended to help Haiti create and strengthen a civilian-controlled police force that would be professional and respect the rights of the population. The assistance was used to recruit, train, organize, and equip a new police force and was administered under the Department of Justice's International Criminal Investigative Training and Assistance Program.

The U.S. assistance helped Haiti

- recruit an interim police force of about 4,000 police officers and U.N. police monitors to work with this force;
- establish and equip a new civilian-controlled police organization and several specialized units, such as an investigative division and its antinarcotics and forensics units, the special investigative unit,[2] the crowd control unit, the special weapons and tactics unit,[3] and the Haitian Coast Guard;
- create a police academy and recruit and train a new police force of about 6,500 police officers;
- train police officers for the specialized units;
- develop managerial and supervisory skills at all levels of the police force; and
- establish an Inspector General's office for monitoring the police force.

---

[2] This unit has focused on investigating high profile crimes, including extrajudicial killings. The U.S. assistance's long-term goal is to help integrate this unit into the mainstream judicial police.

[3] The special weapons and tactics unit responds to crises in the Port-au-Prince area. This unit receives orders directly from the Director General of the police.

Other U.S. agencies, including the U.S. Coast Guard, the U.S. Drug Enforcement Administration, and the U.S. Customs Service, provided some assistance. For example, the U.S. Coast Guard provided over $4.6 million to help organize, train, and equip the Haitian Coast Guard. This assistance helped Haiti establish one Coast Guard base in Port-au-Prince, refurbish three vessels, maintain equipment, and develop capabilities for dealing with drug smuggling and illegal migration, for example.

Major Weaknesses Persist in the Police Force

Despite some initial achievements made possible by U.S. assistance, the current Haitian police force has major deficiencies and is considered by many U.S. and other donor officials as a largely ineffective law enforcement body. According to these officials, the police force suffers from organizational weaknesses, shortages of personnel and training, shortages of vehicles and equipment, and limited investigative capabilities. Over the past year, particularly, U.S. and other donor officials have expressed concern over the Haitian police's crippled internal oversight organization, continued corruption, and increased signs of politicization related to recent Haitian elections.

Starting in late 1994, the United States helped Haiti organize its police force so as to have the major components of a modern civilian police organization. However, the current organization of the Haitian police is weak, according to U.S. and other donor officials. For example, several key police units are not fully operational, such as the Maritime, Air, Border, Migration, and Forest Police Directorate. Also, a few individuals manage the police organization in a highly centralized manner, delegating little authority from headquarters to the field and within the police institutions in the field. As a result, the police force in the field shows little initiative, tending to be reactive rather than actively patrolling the community. Furthermore, the police force has not yet developed a strong esprit de corps and discipline. During our visits to several police units, we saw that many lower ranking police officers did not show much respect for high-ranking officers and were milling around police facilities, reading newspapers, or watching soccer games on television.

Initially, the United States sought to help Haiti recruit and train police officers, and by 1998 the police force had reached a peak of about 6,500 officers. However, shortages of personnel plague the current police force. According to U.S. and other donor officials, the current police force is estimated to range between 3,500 and 4,500 police officers. Compared with a country like El Salvador, with 19,000 police officers serving about 6 million people, Haiti – with its approximately 8 million people – has a relatively small police force. In addition, the Haitian police has a shortage of qualified commanders and supervisors.

According to U.S. officials, there has been serious attrition in police ranks, partly as a result of the police's failure to provide professional opportunities, to implement a work schedule better than the current schedule of 12 hours a day 6 days a week, and to provide work opportunities in locations near the officers' families. U.S. officials noted that police officers have also left the force to join the growing private security industry, which offers fewer risks and better pay and working conditions. Also, more than 1,100 police officers were dismissed from the force since 1995, as a result of the police Inspector General's investigations into police misconduct. In addition, the police's failure to recruit new officers regularly has exacerbated the attrition of the police force. Initially, the United States placed great emphasis on training the new force and setting up the police academy to continue such training. However, most of the current police force has received only basic training. For instance, police officers attend an initial 6-month training course at the academy, but they receive very little or no follow-on training unless they are assigned to a specialized unit. Although officers in the specialized units receive more training, they still have limited technical capabilities to prevent or investigate crimes. Most police officers do not get regular qualification training in firearms use, and, as a result, many officers are not qualified to use their weapons and cannot properly maintain their firearms, according to U.S. officials.

U.S. assistance helped Haiti equip its police force by supplying police vehicles, communications systems, and other equipment and supplies. However, the Haitian police force still faces severe shortages of all these items. For instance, during our visits to Saint-Marc and Jacmel, we noticed that the police stations had few vehicles, communications equipment, and other police equipment to service the large populations and territories under their jurisdictions. Moreover, U.S. officials told us that the special weapons and tactics unit could not train with its issued weapons because it did not have enough ammunition. According to U.S. officials, the effectiveness of Haitian Coast Guard is seriously constrained by its lack of bases, personnel, and equipment, particularly in the southern part of the country where the main cocaine trafficking routes are located. As a result, this unit has a limited capability to stop vessels suspected of carrying illegal cargo and emigrants.

The United States sought to help Haiti improve the investigative capabilities of its police force by providing training, technical assistance, and donations of equipment. However, the current force has made little progress in improving its investigative capabilities. For instance, U.S. officials indicated that the judicial police does not have enough trained officers to investigate crime—its primary mission—and the antinarcotics unit is too small to carry out major drug investigations. The antinarcotics unit also has limited investigative capabilities; it was until recently without a leader for months; and it consists of only 28 officers. According to an assistance agreement between the United States and Haiti, this unit was to have had about 75 officers.

Recent Problems Raise Particular Concerns About the Haitian Police

Over the past year, several problems have arisen with the Haitian police force that have raised particular concern for U.S. and other donor officials. These concerns relate to (1) the weakened position of the police Inspector General's unit, (2) the inability of the police to deal with the growing drug-trafficking threat, and (3) the signs of politicization of the police force during this past year's extended election period.

In 1995, the United States helped Haiti establish an oversight structure to monitor the conduct of its police. However, over the past year the police oversight structure has been crippled by the unexpected departures of the Secretary of State for Public Security and the Inspector General of the police, according to U.S., Haitian, and other donor officials. These two positions are key to ensuring the internal accountability of the police force. The U.S. Department of State noted that groups reportedly associated with former President Aristide's political party mounted a public campaign calling for the resignation of the Secretary of State for Public Security. On October 7, 1999, the Secretary resigned from his position, which remains vacant, and left the country. According to U.S. officials, the Inspector General–who was conducting investigations into human rights violations, narcotrafficking, corruption, and other offenses allegedly committed by police officers--unexpectedly left the force in April 2000 and has not been permanently replaced. According to U.S. and Haitian officials, the Inspector General's investigations had led to the dismissal of over 1,100 police officers for misconduct. As reported by the Department of State, at least 58 police officers were in prison as of September 1999 on a variety of charges. The Department noted that the police more often simply discharged officers caught committing flagrant abuses, rather than initiating legal proceedings against them. Since the departure of the Inspector General, investigations of police misconduct have dramatically decreased, opening the door to increased corruption within the force, according to U.S. and Haitian officials.

The United States also helped establish the antinarcotics unit and the Haitian Coast Guard to address the growing drug trafficking problem. U.S. estimates indicate that the percentage of cocaine coming into the United States through Haiti increased from 10 to 14 percent from 1998 to 1999. However, the Haitian police has been generally ineffective in countering the growing drug threat, due to the limited capabilities and resources of its antinarcotics unit and Coast Guard. As a result, the police has conducted few major drug-related investigations successfully. Moreover, the Haitian police does not have the resources to stop airdrops of cocaine loads to waiting land vehicles or maritime vessels.

The United States sought to help Haiti establish a professional and impartial police force. However, events over the past year have raised serious concerns about the impartiality of the force. In addition to concerns over the weakened role of the police oversight structure, as noted earlier, U.S. and other donor officials have serious concerns over the partisan role played by the police during the May 2000 parliamentary and local elections. During the extended election period, for example, the police on occasion failed to protect legal demonstrations by the opposition. According to U.S. officials, the police also arrested some opposition candidates after the elections and failed to successfully investigate major killings, including political assassinations, committed before the elections.

Assistance Helped Improve Certain Aspects of the Judicial Sector

From fiscal years 1993 through 2000, the United States provided about $27 million to support Haiti's judicial system. The aid was intended to help Haiti improve the effectiveness of existing judicial organizations and enhance the access of the population to justice. It also was intended to help Haiti develop and implement a broad reform of the judicial sector that would enhance its independence, modernize criminal codes, and restructure judicial organizations and processes.

USAID, its contractors, and the Department of Justice's Office of Overseas Prosecutorial Development, Assistance and Training provided most of this assistance under the USAID Administration of Justice Program. The bulk of the assistance, about $23 million, funded (1) administrative enhancements for judicial institutions, such as case registration and tracking systems; (2) judge and prosecutor training; and (3) the establishment and operation of the magistrate school. The remaining assistance, $4 million, funded legal assistance and education as a means of improving the access of the population to justice.

Serious Problems Remain in the Judicial Sector

Despite U.S. assistance, the Haitian judicial sector continues to exhibit major shortcomings. This sector has not undergone a major reform, and, as a result, it has outdated legal codes and cumbersome judicial proceedings. Also, it has inadequate infrastructure and shortages of personnel and equipment, and limited investigative capabilities. Furthermore, it suffers from corruption and a lack of effective internal oversight, and it serves only a small portion of the population.

Despite the constitutional mandate for an independent judicial sector, the executive branch, through the Ministry of Justice, continues to control the judicial sector, including the judicial budget and judicial appointments, training, evaluation, and removal. The lack of independence compromises the impartiality of the judicial sector, according to U.S., Haitian, and other donor officials. For instance, the Haitian government has not vigorously supported investigations and prosecutions of major crimes, including drug trafficking, major killings, and political violence. Investigations and prosecutions have moved slowly and produced very limited results, according to U.S. officials.

The judicial system is characterized by outdated legal codes and complex, time-consuming procedures. In criminal cases, many people are put behind bars in preventive detention. Some judicial institutions have large case backlogs, and criminal courts hold few jury trials every year.[4] During our visits to judicial facilities in Port-au-Prince and Jacmel, judicial officials emphasized the urgent need for developing and implementing a comprehensive reform of the judicial sector to modernize legal codes and streamline judicial proceedings.

The judicial sector receives only 11.5 percent of the Ministry of Justice budget, and as a consequence, the sector has serious personnel shortages and inadequate infrastructure. For example, during our visits to judicial institutions in Port-au-Prince and Jacmel, Haitian officials emphasized that their institutions did not have enough personnel to conduct business adequately, given the size of the populations and territories they had to serve. We also found that prosecutors' offices, justice of the peace courts, and other courts had very basic infrastructure. One of the courts that we visited had no doors, windows, bathrooms, running water, or electricity. The courts also had serious supply shortages, including vehicles, legal texts, telephones, and office supplies. Haitian officials noted that the dire conditions of judicial facilities such as this one projected a bad image

[4] Juries are convened only for serious criminal offenses, such as murders.

and did not inspire respect for their institutions, seriously undermining the people's confidence in the judicial sector.

The judicial sector also has limited capabilities to investigate and prosecute cases. Judicial officials have received little professional training; have minimum resources to conduct investigations, prosecutions, and trials; have received limited support from specialized units, such as the judicial police and forensics unit; and do not have many incentives to solve major crimes. In addition, some judicial officials stated that, because they have little personal protection, they fear for their personal safety when dealing with high-profile cases, such as drug trafficking and political assassinations.

In addition, the judicial sector suffers from corruption and lacks adequate oversight to monitor the behavior of judicial officials. For instance, U.S. officials noted that the cumbersome and lengthy judicial proceedings create opportunities for corruption among judicial officials willing to accept bribes in return for advancing cases in their offices. Also, according to these officials, the Ministry of Justice has a judicial inspection unit that has limited capabilities and has done little to address corruption and other major problems of the judicial sector. Despite efforts to enhance this unit, it remains largely ineffective, according to U.S. officials.

The judicial sector continues to provide only limited access to justice for the majority of the Haitian population. For example, by not having a public defender's office, by not systematically providing legal assistance to the population, and by conducting most of its business through written procedures in French, the judicial sector remains unavailable to the majority of the population, which is poor and illiterate and speaks only Creole.

KEY FACTOR AFFECTING SUCCESS OF U.S. ASSISTANCE IS THE HAITIAN GOVERNMENT'S LACK OF COMMITMENT TO STRENGTHENING JUSTICE INSTITUTIONS

The primary factor affecting the success of U.S. assistance has been the Haitian government's lack of clear commitment to supporting the police and judicial sector and dealing with the main problems affecting these institutions.

The Haitian Government Lacks Strong Commitment to Strengthening the Police Force

U.S. assistance to the police has been undermined because the Haitian government--after showing a strong initial commitment to establishing a civilian-controlled police force--failed to (1) strengthen the organizational capabilities of the force, (2) support investigations of police corruption and serious crimes, and (3) keep the police out of politics, particularly during the past election year.

The Haitian government's failure to strengthen the organizational capabilities of the police has hindered U.S. efforts to improve the capabilities of the force, according to U.S. officials. Although the Haitian government has allocated the bulk of the Ministry of Justice budget to the police and prisons--about 83 percent of the 1996-97 budget--the government has weakened the police by not filling key leadership positions, such as the Inspector General and the head of the antinarcotics unit, and by not strengthening key units. For instance, since the unexpected departure of the Inspector General, his office has stopped vigorously investigating police misbehavior, including corruption. Also, some key police units, such as the antinarcotics unit, have limited capabilities because the government has not provided needed resources and personnel. According to the Department of State, the Haitian government failed to increase the size of the antinarcotics unit, as had been agreed to by the U.S. and Haitian governments.

U.S. assistance to improve the investigative capabilities of the police has been constrained by the failure of the Haitian government to support investigations of police corruption and serious crimes, including drug-related crimes and political assassinations. In March 2000, the State Department reported that the Haitian government had failed to investigate drug-related corruption involving police officers. The State Department also reported that little progress had been made in bringing to justice persons responsible for major killings, such as political killings, in Haiti. U.S. officials are concerned about the Haitian government's lack of support for the police's special investigations unit, which is responsible for investigating major killings. This unit's human resources have declined by about 80 percent since 1997.

U.S. assistance to the Haitian police has also been undermined by the Haitian government's failure to keep the police out of politics during this past election year. The force's inaction during several violent campaign incidents and its arrests of several political candidates seriously compromised the perception of police impartiality.

Haitian Government Lacks Strong Commitment to Improving the Judicial Sector

U.S. assistance to the judicial sector has been undercut because the Haitian government, after initially supporting the assistance effort, failed to follow through in implementing broad reform of the judicial sector, adopt and institutionalize many of the improvements made possible by the assistance, provide the resources needed to operate the sector adequately, build an oversight capability to monitor the sector, and vigorously support the prosecution of major crimes.

The Haitian government did not follow through in implementing a broad reform of its legal codes and judicial organization and processes -- some of the measures that donors consider key to addressing the main problems of the judicial sector. The Haitian government has taken some steps since 1995 that may eventually lead to the implementation of a broad reform of the judicial sector. These steps include enacting judicial reform-related legislation in 1998, increasing judicial salaries, and pursuing further reform plans, such as expanding the use of Creole in judicial proceedings. However, none of these steps has moved significantly toward addressing the main shortcomings of the judicial sector.

Many improvements to the judicial sector made possible by the U.S. assistance have not been institutionalized because the Haitian government did not adopt and fund them.

Although the Haitian government assumed responsibility for most of the funding for the magistrate school that was created with U.S. and other donor support, the government did not assume ownership of the improvements, such as case registration and tracking systems, made possible by U.S. assistance in the justice of the peace courts and prosecutors' offices. As a result, according to U.S. officials, after USAID stopped its assistance to the justice of the peace courts, the improvements made by this assistance disappeared.

The Haitian government has not provided the resources needed to operate judicial institutions. During our visits to judicial institutions in Port-au-Prince, Saint-Marc, and Jacmel, we saw that the judicial institutions were overwhelmed by the lack of personnel and equipment and by their poor physical conditions.

The improvements to the judicial sector made possible by U.S. assistance have also been limited because the Haitian government has not put in place an effective oversight capability to monitor the judicial sector. The Ministry of Justice has a judicial inspection unit that has limited capabilities and physical and human resources to deal with the problems of the sector, such as judicial corruption.

The Haitian government's failure to vigorously support investigations and prosecutions of serious crimes, such as drug-related crimes and political assassinations, has hindered the improvements in the prosecutorial capabilities of the judicial sector made possible by the U.S. assistance. According to U.S., other donor, and Haitian officials, prosecutors and investigating magistrates do not have an incentive to investigate and prosecute major criminal cases and, if they do investigate, they do it with the knowledge that they are risking their personal security.

Mr. Chairman and Members of the Committee, this concludes my prepared remarks. I would be happy to respond to any questions you may have.

Contact and Acknowledgments

For future contacts regarding this testimony, please call Jess T. Ford at (202) 512-4128. Individuals making key contributions to this testimony included Virginia Hughes, Juan Tapia-Videla, David Bernet, Lee Kaukas, Richard Seldin, Steve Iannucci, Douglas Ferry, and Rona Mendelsohn.

U.S. ASSISTANCE TO THE HAITIAN POLICE AND JUSTICE SECTOR, FISCAL YEARS 1995-2000

Table 1 shows U.S. assistance to the Haitian police force.

Table 1: International Criminal Investigative Training Assistance Program Assistance to the Haitian Police, Fiscal Years 1995-1999

Activity	Amount
Police training and donations of equipment	$34,402,963
Construction of police academy	18,680,474
Program headquarters expenses	6,357,274
U.S. embassy support and program expenses	2,477,990
Staff salaries and benefits	1,838,928
Staff travel expenses	967,604
Antinarcotics training	347,029
Program audits	221,738
Total	**$65,294,000**

Source: International Criminal Investigative Training Assistance Program.

Table 2 shows the overall assistance provided to Haiti's judicial system under the USAID Administration of Justice Program.

Table 2: USAID Administration of Justice Program Assistance to Haitian Judicial Sector, Fiscal Years 1993–2000

Dollars in millions

Organization and activity	Amount	
USAID	$5.4	
Direct aid to Ministry of Justice		2.4
Other technical and equipment assistance		0.8
USAID management		2.0
Audit of Checchi		0.2
RONCO Consulting Corporation	2.8	
Interim Administration of Justice Program		
Checchi & Company Consultants, Inc.	11.5	
Legal assistance and education		4.0
Case registration and court management		3.2
Judicial mentoring		1.8
Other technical and equipment assistance		2.5
Department of Justice's Office of Overseas Prosecutorial Development, Assistance and Training	7.0	
Magistrate school		2.1
Case tracking system		0.5
Model jurisdiction program and related assistance		4.4
Total	**$26.7**	

Source: GAO analysis of USAID data.

USAID provided $2.4 million in direct aid and $0.8 million in technical and equipment assistance to the Haitian Ministry of Justice in fiscal years 1993-2000 and incurred $2.2 million in management costs for its Administration of Justice Program.

RONCO provided $2.8 million in aid from June 1995 to July 1996. This contractor primarily focused on refurbishing, equipping, and providing administrative and logistical support to the magistrate school established in 1995.

Checchi provided $11.5 million in assistance August 1995 to August 1999. Under its contract with USAID, Checchi focused its efforts on three activities: legal assistance and education, case tracking and court management, and judicial mentoring.

(711564)

ORDERS BY INTERNET

For information on how to access GAO reports on the INTERNET, send an e-mail message with "info" in the body to

Info@www.gao.gov

or visit GAO's World Wide Web Home Page at

http://www.gao.gov

TO REPORT FRAUD, WASTE, AND ABUSE IN FEDERAL PROGRAMS

Contact one:

- website: http://www.gao.gov/fraudnet/fraudnet.htm
- e-mail: fraudnet@gao.gov
- 1-800-424-5454 (automated answering system)

United Nations A/55/618

General Assembly

Distr.: General
9 November 2000

Original: English

Fifty-fifth session
Agenda item 48
The situation of democracy and human rights in Haiti

United Nations International Civilian Support Mission in Haiti

Report of the Secretary-General

I. Introduction

1. The present report is submitted pursuant to General Assembly resolution 54/193 of 17 December 1999, in which the General Assembly established the International Civilian Support Mission in Haiti (MICAH) in order to consolidate the results achieved by the Organization of American States (OAS)/United Nations International Civilian Mission in Haiti (MICIVIH), the United Nations Civilian Police Mission in Haiti (MIPONUH) and previous United Nations missions. In paragraph 12 of the same resolution, the General Assembly requested me to submit a report to the General Assembly every four months. The present report covers developments in the mission area since the submission of my previous report to the Assembly, on 17 July 2000 (A/55/154).

II. Political situation and elections

2. Since mid-July, Haiti's political and electoral crisis has deepened, polarizing its political class and civil society, jeopardizing its international relations, sapping an already declining economy and adding to the hardship of the impoverished majority.

3. Disregarding all calls for rectification of the method of calculation of the Senate results and certain other irregularities in the 21 May legislative and municipal elections, and with the opposition maintaining its boycott, the authorities completed the drawn-out electoral process, promulgated the final results and seated a new Parliament. The ruling Fanmi Lavalas party of former President Aristide took 18 of the 19 contested Senate seats and 72 of the 83 seats in the Chamber of Deputies. Without consulting the opposition, President Préval named three new members to the Provisional Electoral Council (CEP) to replace its President, who had fled the country in June, and two opposition representatives who had previously resigned. He then empowered the contested CEP to organize elections for president and the remaining one third of the Senate seats on 26 November.

4. Most of the opposition, grouped in a tactical alliance, first known as the Groupe de convergence and currently as the Democratic Convergence, adhered throughout most of this period to the position that the 21 May elections were so fraudulent that they should be annulled and held again under a new CEP, but only after President Préval had stood down and been replaced by a provisional government. In the meantime, the opposition ruled out any participation in the November elections. This position was promoted through the media and in a series of rallies in provincial towns, of which the largest drew a crowd of

00-74167 (E) 211100

5,000. The campaign failed in every way to deter the Government and Fanmi Lavalas.

5. While not backing the opposition call for the complete annulment of the elections, civil society organizations — private sector groups, churches, labour unions, intellectuals — all urged the authorities to address the serious electoral irregularities in order to avoid exacerbating the political crisis and jeopardizing much-needed international assistance. Groups of intellectuals, including some who had once supported former President Aristide's Lavalas movement, issued a series of petitions voicing concern about the perceived totalitarian tendencies of Fanmi Lavalas and the possible emergence of a one-party state. For the most part, Fanmi Lavalas dismissed these civil society organizations as representing only the elite of Haitian society and as being disconnected from the overwhelming majority of the people.

6. The international community always held that the errors of the 21 May elections could be rectified, although its appeals to this end at every stage in the process had no effect. Its chief concern was the flawed method of calculating the Senate results, in which all of the front-runners won outright in the first round, regardless of whether they had the absolute majority required by the electoral law or just a plurality. According to the OAS Electoral Observation Mission, there should have been run-offs for 10 of the 19 Senate seats. Concern was also voiced about the significant, unexplained differences between the final figures of CEP and those previously posted by the regional electoral offices, and the failure of CEP to deal with the complaints filed by candidates challenging voting procedures and results.

7. After the mission led by OAS Secretary-General César Gaviria in mid-August and several visits by envoys of the Caribbean Community (CARICOM) and the United States of America had failed to stop the seating of the new Parliament on 28 August, Haiti's main bilateral donors announced the end of "business as usual". They would not finance the November elections or any electoral observer missions, they would not recognize the new Parliament, and they would henceforth provide little or no assistance to the Government of Haiti, channelling it all through non-governmental organizations. The United States Administration also stated that it would consider opposing Haitian loan requests from international financial institutions. All this was to stay in effect until an independent and credible CEP was established; there was some accommodation on the 21 May elections, especially the contested Senate seats; and a dialogue was started with the opposition on ways to strengthen Haitian democracy. Meanwhile, the European Union, which had already suspended some projects in July, took steps to invoke a provision of the Lomé Convention which could lead to the suspension of its assistance.

8. At a ministerial-level meeting held in New York on 13 September, the Group of Friends of the Secretary-General for Haiti (Argentina, Canada, Chile, France, the United States of America and Venezuela) voiced profound disappointment and deep concern at the failure of the Haitian authorities to rectify the flaws of the 21 May elections. At the Government's invitation, OAS Assistant Secretary-General Luigi Einaudi led a new mission to Haiti one week later, with the aim of facilitating a dialogue between Fanmi Lavalas and the opposition. President Préval pledged to implement any accord resulting from the dialogue, provided it "did not violate the Constitution" or delay the handover to a new President on 7 February 2001. Fanmi Lavalas was ready to take part in the dialogue although it reiterated that it was not prepared to consider any revision of the 21 May election results. The Democratic Convergence, for its part, published a set of conditions for its participation in the dialogue which included the suspension of the activities of all parliamentarians, mayors and local officials elected in May, the cessation of the activities of CEP and its replacement, and an end to all repression and acts of intimidation against the opposition.

9. In the event, no face-to-face dialogue took place, and Mr. Einaudi instead spent a week of shuttle diplomacy between the two sides. OAS made a third attempt at mediation, from 13 to 21 October, and was successful in convening direct talks witnessed by some representatives of the international community. While there was an exchange of position papers and some progress made, the talks ultimately failed to produce an agreement that could serve as a foundation for proceeding with presidential and senatorial elections that would include candidates from across the political spectrum. Based on his bilateral consultations, Mr. Einaudi prepared a six-point document that contained elements for a national accord, covering public security in the electoral context, issues outstanding from the 21 May 2000 elections, the

elections planned for 26 November 2000, restructuring of the electoral council, strengthening democracy, and the role of the international community. For his part, Mr. Aristide, citing security concerns, agreed to meet with the Democratic Convergence only if its leaders came to his home.

10. On 23 October, Mr. Einaudi reported to the Permanent Council of OAS that appreciable progress had been made towards breaking the logjam but that very substantial differences persisted, primarily concerning the contentious 21 May elections. On that occasion, CARICOM indicated its intention to field observers for the presidential elections.

11. Late in September, the Department of Political Affairs dispatched an electoral expert to consider United Nations electoral assistance in the light of the current political stand-off. The expert consulted with the international community, including donors, the Government and opposition, and sought to assess the technical capacity of CEP to stage free and fair elections. The mission coincided with a round of OAS mediation, providing an opportunity for consultation with representatives of OAS which has been extensively involved in the Haitian elections. After meeting with a wide range of actors, the expert found that, assuming the necessary political will, the Council's preparedness was adequate. The United Nations, meanwhile, decided that, in the present circumstances, it was not in a position to continue its technical assistance to CEP in its preparations for the November elections. As a result, the United Nations technical assistance team — deployed under the auspices of the United Nations Development Programme (UNDP) — left the country on 15 October.

12. The deepening political crisis and the continued suspension of much financial assistance by international financial institutions precipitated a fall in the Haitian gourde, from 18 to the United States dollar in May to around 25 at present. This has provoked a surge in the price of basic commodities in a country in which the majority lives in great poverty. An additional spur to inflation came from a 44 per cent hike in the price of fuel, which the Government was obliged to introduce on 2 September because of the increase in world oil prices. This has already prompted a one-day general strike backed by the opposition and a three-day closure of petrol stations, and is expected to lead to further protests. The constraints on Government spending exacerbated by the need to finance the November elections from its own resources have given rise to unrest in the public sector. In the meantime, the expectations of the so-called popular organizations that they would be rewarded with jobs for supporting Fanmi Lavalas (by means of the violent street demonstrations held during the electoral period) have emerged as an additional source of pressure on the Government and Fanmi Lavalas.

13. Since July, there has been an increase in violent crime that may be linked to the worsening political and social situation. The victims of fatal shootings include a MICAH staff member who was shot while behind the wheel of a clearly marked United Nations vehicle near the head office of MICAH on 7 August. Another MICAH international staff member in a marked United Nations vehicle was the target of an attempted car hijacking by two gunmen near a well-known hotel in September. There have been worrying allegations of police involvement in robbery, extortion and abduction, as well as drug trafficking, together with reports of anarchic tax collection by newly elected local officials, and the involvement of popular organizations in protection rackets.

14. Political pressures on the Haitian National Police (HNP), together with such incidents as the attempted lynching of a police commissioner during a pro-Aristide demonstration on 2 October, have contributed to the demoralization of HNP and eroded its operational capacity and credibility. Reports that its effective strength has fallen to alarmingly low levels have fuelled fears of a breakdown in public order.

15. These fears were exacerbated on 18 October when the Government alleged that several ranking local police chiefs (commissaires) were plotting to seize state power. As a result, two agents were arrested, seven fled the country and have applied for political asylum in the Dominican Republic, and two others have sought the protection of the Dominican embassy in Port-au-Prince. Some of those implicated have stated publicly that the coup plot was fabricated by Fanmi Lavalas members who wish to assume control of HNP. They mentioned specifically Senator Danny Toussaint, President of the Senate's Permanent Commission for Justice and Public Security, who issued a report on 12 September alleging the presence of criminals within HNP and proposing that it be purged. They also claim that Fanmi Lavalas interfered inappropriately in security matters related to the May election and was involved in illegal acts.

16. A degree of hostility towards the international community was sustained by talk in the media of international sanctions, and statements by the President and Prime Minister in July. They called upon Haitians to tighten their belts, likening the situation to 1804 when Haiti won its independence on the battlefield. Intermittent street demonstrations, for the most part non-violent, continued outside embassies and offices of the United Nations and OAS, albeit with less frequency than in June and early July. On 27 July, a grenade was thrown at the Canadian Ambassador's residence and, on 11 August, a Molotov cocktail was tossed at the home of a European Union official. No one was hurt in either incident and damage was considered minimal. Unexploded grenades were also found at the building that used to house MICIVIH and at a French-run private school. Requests for increased police protection by the international community in Haiti for the most part did not result in any significant measures.

III. Deployment and operations of the International Civilian Support Mission in Haiti

17. It is recalled that the recruitment of substantive staff of MICAH was delayed because of financing problems and that the first advisers did not begin to arrive in Haiti until mid-June 2000. Thereafter, staff were progressively recruited and deployed and, by mid-October, the three pillars of MICAH justice, police and human rights — had a total of 68 advisers assigned to the Ministry of Justice, HNP, the Prison Authority, the Judges School and the Office of the Ombudsman, as well as to MICAH regional offices, a human rights verification unit and units working with civil society partners.

18. MICAH worked with UNDP and bilateral donors involved in the areas of justice, police and human rights to identify short-term projects that would best be undertaken by the Mission. When issues concerned more than one of the MICAH pillars, joint approaches were made to the authorities. MICAH took part in a discussion with all the United Nations agencies on the common country assessment conducted throughout June 2000, and on the methodology and joint initiatives being undertaken to prepare the United Nations Development Assistance Framework for the period 2002-2006.

IV. Justice

19. The justice pillar of MICAH, which had 17 advisers by mid-October, provided logistical and organizational support for a process of discussion and revision of five newly prepared draft laws, three concerning the organization and independence of the judiciary, one concerning drug trafficking and one concerning money-laundering. The process began with discussions with judicial officials and lawyers in each of Haiti's five appellate courts. It was followed by a five-day national forum at the Judges School, organized jointly by the Ministry of Justice and the MICAH justice pillar, which brought together all of the actors in the justice sector to discuss the five draft laws, with the participation of three United Nations international experts.

20. There were two trials held during this period that were landmarks in the fight against impunity and in efforts to improve due process during criminal trials. One was the three-week trial of a group of police officers accused of 11 executions in 1999 in the Port-au-Prince district, Carrefour-Feuilles. The other was the trial of 22 former army officers, soldiers and civilians accused in a 1994 massacre in the Gonaïves district of Raboteau, which began on 29 September. MICAH monitored the Raboteau trial and provided technical assistance to those planning security. UNDP also facilitated the testimony at trial of five military experts and legal anthropologists.

21. Building on the work of UNDP, the justice pillar helped to reorganize the Prison Authority and began a programme of training in prison and personnel management for the Prison Authority's trainers and wardens. Together with UNDP and the International Committee of the Red Cross, it supported the Prison Authority's attempts to address problems in prison conditions, including inadequate food, medical treatment, sanitary conditions and recreation time outside cells. MICAH voiced its concern to the authorities about the continued detention, without legal basis, of nearly 300 deportees in the National Penitentiary and in Port-au-Prince police stations after their repatriation from the United States upon completion of prison sentences. The authorities, who reluctantly resumed accepting deportees in June, acknowledged that such detentions were not legal but maintained that public security concerns and the lack of facilities for social rehabilitation and reintegration

prevented their immediate release. A female deportee died in hospital in September after falling ill in police custody.

22. The justice pillar also gave juridical and technical support to non-governmental organizations providing legal aid for the poor, and took on the publishing of a French-Creole lexicon of legal terms, together with the Ministry of Justice, the State University of Haiti, the Port-au-Prince Bar and the jurists' association. Advisers were also assigned to provincial courts to help speed up the processing of detainees, assist with judicial control over the police, and improve the work of court and prison clerks.

V. Haitian National Police

23. The police section of MICAH had 24 advisers by mid-October, assigned to the directorates and central offices of HNP in Port-au-Prince — including the General Directorate, the Inspectorate General, the Administrative Police, the Judicial Police Directorate, the Bureau for Criminal Affairs and the Centre for Information and Operations — and the nine Police departmental directors.

24. The equipment and materiel necessary for the police to operate were found to be in extremely short supply in most units. Some police officers of all ranks were reported to be demoralized and unmotivated. In addition to the tough conditions and shortage of equipment, the reasons for demoralization included the negative impact of instances of corruption and drug trafficking, accompanied by attempts by a faction of Fanmi Lavalas to gain control of the force. After the installation of the new Parliament, several Fanmi Lavalas senators embarked on a campaign of almost daily criticism of the police, accusing the service of incompetence and inactivity in the face of soaring crime and of having corrupted elements within its ranks. Expectations that many police officers would be replaced after the change of Government contributed to a wait-and-see attitude, in particular in view of the arrest of several high-ranking officers on suspicion of plotting a coup d'état, a charge for which there was seemingly little evidence.

25. During this period, the police section organized a one-day seminar which brought all of its advisers together with 26 senior HNP officials and representatives of bilateral and multilateral donors working in the police and justice areas. The Director General of HNP also attended the seminar, which was aimed at explaining the nature of MICAH technical assistance to the police and encouraging receptivity, as well as providing a forum for a free exchange of ideas. A nationwide police recruitment drive was launched on 2 October with the support of MICAH.

VI. Human rights

26. The human rights section of MICAH had 27 advisers by the start of October, with teams deployed to Cap Haïtien, Gonaïves and Les Cayes as well as Port-au-Prince. Advisers began assignments at the Office of the Ombudsman (Office de la Protection du Citoyen) and at the Inspectorate General of the Police. A four-day training programme was developed for human rights instructors at the Police Academy, in order to reinforce their knowledge of human rights issues, Haitian law and good police practice. A team also initiated human rights training for new prison guard recruits with the eventual aim of training trainers at the Prison Authority to take over the module.

27. International Peace Day (19 September) was used as a vehicle to promote the values of a culture of peace through the media, round-table meetings and other activities organized jointly with the United Nations Educational, Scientific and Cultural Organization (UNESCO). MICAH planned other events in the context of the International Year for the Culture of Peace, including supporting a nationwide writing competition for young people organized by radio journalists. A seminar on the complaints mechanism of the Inter-American Commission of Human Rights was held with members of the Commission in August for Haitian human rights organizations.

28. Although on a lesser scale than its MICIVIH predecessor, the human rights section began carrying out verification activities, following up primarily incidents of violence which could be of a political nature and a number of allegations of serious abuse. Incidents of violence linked to the 21 May electoral process subsided as the process slowly concluded. There were, however, sporadic reports of groups of sometimes heavily armed men accompanying Fanmi Lavalas officials and acting in an intimidatory fashion. Likewise, the continued failure to punish individuals linked to certain pro-Fanmi Lavalas organizations allegedly responsible for violent and threatening

behaviour compounded the perception that institutions responsible for guaranteeing law and order and protecting human rights were increasingly subordinated to the dominant power group. Following the installation of the new municipal councils, security agents attached to town halls assumed policing functions, posing a threat to the protection of human rights, given the lack of controls or a legal framework for their activity.

29. Respect of the rights to individual liberty and a fair trial within a reasonable time limit continued to be the most frequent human rights violations, in particular in Port-au-Prince where there are detainees held since 1995 and 1996 without trial, some of them with release orders. Political considerations would still appear to dominate in some cases. Poor record-keeping in both prisons and courts compounded the difficulties of tracking cases and facilitated such violations. These problems were referred to the MICAH justice section for follow-up through its technical support at the Prison Authority and in certain jurisdictions. Local police authorities in Port-au-Prince began taking action in response to concerns expressed about prolonged detention in police custody and sharply deteriorated conditions which were jeopardizing the health of detainees. The human rights section also monitored the Carrefour-Feuilles trial of six police officers, four of whom were convicted of murder.

VII. Development activities

30. Representatives of the United Nations system in Haiti have continued their efforts to implement the reform programme of the Secretary-General. After almost one year of dialogue, consensus-building and formulation involving all key development partners, and following a thorough validation process, the common country assessment document was finalized and officially released on United Nations Day. Building on the consensus that emerged from the assessment, and in line with Economic and Social Council resolution 1999/11 of 27 July 1999, in which the Council called for the development of a long-term strategy and programme of support for Haiti, the United Nations system is engaged in the formulation of a United Nations Development Assistance Framework for Haiti, which is expected to be finalized in January 2001. To launch the process, two workshops were organized for all United Nations agencies, with the participation of representatives of the United Nations Development Group Office at UNDP. Three broad, transversal themes were adopted in the preparation of the Framework: (a) education for all, enhancement of human resources and access to social services; (b) governance and rule of law; and (c) food security and rural development.

31. Pursuant to an earlier agreement among the Government, the World Bank and the International Monetary Fund (IMF) on the preparation of an interim poverty reduction strategy paper, the Government formulated a preparatory document describing the underlying strategy. Meanwhile, an IMF mission visited Haiti in order to evaluate the status of the budget deficit and public finances and to devise a strategy to restore equilibrium to the budgetary accounts and control inflation.

32. In addition to the United Nations country team's intense mobilization around the assessment and Framework processes, agencies have continued to develop and implement their own programmes within their mandated areas. UNDP launched its justice programme, after in-depth discussions held with the Ministry of Justice and MICAH. The programme is aimed at (a) reinforcing the leadership of the Ministry of Justice and its capacity to formulate a policy for the justice sector; and (b) promoting the participation of other actors, including civil society, in the debate on judicial reform. In the context of the employment programme of UNDP and the International Labour Organization, a presentation was made to introduce the broad lines of the national employment promotion policy. UNDP also supported the preparation of the first national plan for risk and disaster prevention and management.

33. In cooperation with relevant national and local authorities, the World Food Programme (WFP) provided special assistance to stabilize the food security situation in the drought-stricken north and north-eastern regions. WFP also undertook an inter-ministerial review of its programme in Haiti. In addition to its regular activities, the World Health Organization provided continuous support for vaccination campaigns against measles, together with the United Nations Children's Fund (UNICEF), and mobilized special resources to combat infant mortality. UNICEF also finalized its cooperation strategy with the Government for its next country programme and supported the Government in finalizing the national

report on the follow-up to the World Summit for Children. The Joint United Nations Programme on HIV/AIDS (UNAIDS) continued its public information campaign in 10 major cities, entitled "Artists and youth caravan against AIDS". In collaboration with UNICEF and UNESCO, the United Nations Population Fund supported a youth national congress. It also launched a project on HIV/AIDS prevention and provided support to the Haitian delegation attending the five-year follow-up to the Fourth World Conference on Women. The Food and Agriculture Organization of the United Nations supported a series of activities for World Food Day and aided in the preparation of an agricultural policy document and action plans for the fisheries and aquaculture sectors. The International Organization for Migration organized a series of workshops on migration issues and provided support for the drafting of a migration law. The United Nations disaster management team reacted swiftly to Hurricane Debby, facilitating several coordination meetings with all concerned actors so that preparatory measures were taken.

VIII. Observations

34. The political polarization of Haiti was highlighted by the Inter-American Commission of Human Rights, which visited Port-au-Prince from 21 to 25 August. In a statement issued at the end of the visit, the Commission stated that the most critical and worrying aspect of the current human rights situation in Haiti was the deterioration of the political climate to such a point that no consensus seemed to exist about the ways in which to consolidate the country's fledgling democracy. In his most recent report, the independent expert of the Commission on Human Rights on the situation of human rights in Haiti pointed out that Haiti suffered from an enormous lack of a culture of democracy, which must be reduced if democracy were truly to be strengthened and political stability ensured in that country, which seemed to have gone from one crisis to another since the restoration of democracy (A/55/335, para. 29).

35. A disturbing element of this polarization is the widely held perception among opponents of Fanmi Lavalas shared by many former supporters that the party might establish a dictatorial and repressive regime if, as is widely expected, Mr. Aristide once again assumes the presidency. On the other hand, it is very evident that Mr. Aristide enjoys the loyalty of broad sectors of the urban and rural poor. The disinclination of the parties to work towards a compromise is a fundamental cause of the polarization.

36. The negative perception of Mr. Aristide's party seems to be a factor in the opposition's reluctance to enter into a dialogue. Many in the opposition seem to hope that, under the pressure of international isolation and internal unrest, Fanmi Lavalas will somehow disintegrate and that compromise is therefore unnecessary. The consequences of this attitude can be seen in Haiti's political stalemate, soon to enter its fourth year. Its costs can be witnessed in the increasingly desperate situation of the country's poor, unprotected from the impact of external factors, such as rising oil prices and some aspects of globalization.

37. In my previous report, I stressed the fact that Haitian authorities had flouted the views of OAS, the International Organization of la Francophonie, CARICOM, bilateral partners, domestic electoral monitors and other civil society groupings, as well as the United Nations, in particular the concern of members of the Security Council. In refusing to recalculate the erroneous Senate results, some Haitian leaders have violated basic norms of democratic governance and fair play. In recent weeks, as opportunity after opportunity to reach common ground has been missed, there have been suggestions by critics that these leaders are further isolating Haiti, and ensuring it pariah status. This isolation is apt to grow, as a Parliament has been seated whose legitimacy is in doubt, rendering unlikely the early resumption of international assistance.

38. A further indication of the deteriorating political situation is the charge that high-ranking officers within HNP were plotting a coup d'état, although evidence has not been presented. Already demoralized by poor working conditions and a climate of impunity, HNP is increasingly the target of those who would use the force for their own political ends. It bears recalling that public security is central to the lives of all citizens and that an independent police force, which respects the rights of citizens, is indispensable to any democratic society.

39. It was with considerable reluctance that the United Nations withdrew the team of experts which was providing technical assistance to CEP, after supporting for several years Haiti's efforts to ensure

conditions adequate to the free exercise of the franchise. This most recent technical assistance project began nearly one year ago, and was expected to last through the presidential elections scheduled for the end of 2000. It aimed also to train a new Permanent Electoral Council, which will be charged with organizing elections over the next decade. After intensive examination of Haiti's current electoral council and its practice, it was decided that requisite standards had not been met, necessitating the withdrawal of United Nations support.

40. While denying the Government direct international assistance, so as to send a political message, Haiti's bilateral donors hope to avoid hurting the Haitian population by channelling aid through non-governmental organizations. However, directly or indirectly, the Haitian economy and population will inevitably suffer. The swings of international assistance from government to non-governmental organizations and back, according to the legitimacy of the government of the day, have disrupted long-term development in the past. Assistance provided through non-governmental organizations may partially alleviate hardship but the Government is a necessary partner for poverty reduction and health programmes. Likewise, the kinds of programmes needed to revive development — such as infrastructural projects and schemes to reinforce the police and overhaul the judicial system — require strong, governmental measures. Furthermore, the failure of the Haitian authorities to address the concerns of the political parties and the international community has so far prevented Haiti from regaining access to the international financial assistance that has been suspended for the past three years. These factors, and the overall political crisis, have been largely responsible for the fall in the gourde, which has hit the poor hard by triggering a rapid rise in the price of foodstuffs and other basic commodities.

41. In the absence of any solution to the crisis, popular discontent seems likely to mount in response to the rising prices and increasing poverty, and may lead to further turmoil. A combination of rampant crime, violent street protests and incidents of violence targeted at the international community could severely limit the ability of MICAH to fulfil its mandate. Its capacity to function effectively has already been adversely affected by the withdrawal or reduction of once-important bilateral programmes of assistance in the areas of justice and public security. At bottom, MICAH support is contingent upon legitimate counterparts who enjoy the esteem of the Haitian people and that of the international community.

42. In this climate of political turmoil and instability, and with national counterparts often lacking or distracted by political concerns, it will be necessary to devise new forms of technical assistance that might better allow the United Nations system to continue supporting the Haitian people. It is my view, therefore, in the light of the conditions in Haiti, that a renewal of the mandate of MICAH is not advisable, and it is with regret that I recommend that the Mission be terminated when its mandate draws to an end on 6 February 2001. In preparation, discussions have already commenced among UNDP, MICAH and the Friends of the Secretary-General for Haiti, in consultation with other members of the United Nations system, with the aim of designing a programme of assistance to the Haitian people that is commensurate with the country's political realities and absorption capacity.

43. Overall, it is imperative that the country's political leaders and civil society engage in a constructive dialogue so as to address the needs of one of the most impoverished populations in the world and create an enabling environment for international financial and developmental assistance. I hardly need emphasize that a well-functioning, multi-party system is essential to democratic governance. Political turmoil has produced plummeting economic indicators, which in turn has led to a deteriorating security situation. Firm action to stop this downward spiral is long overdue. It should be emphasized that, in the absence of such steps, the misery of Haiti's long-suffering poor majority will only be exacerbated.

44. The Friends of the Secretary-General for Haiti deserve gratitude for their advice and cooperation, which have been a key element throughout United Nations activities in Haiti. I shall count on their counsel in the future. I am grateful to the Member States which have contributed to the Trust Fund for MICAH — Canada, Norway and the United States of America. I would like to commend the efforts of my representative, Alfredo Lopes Cabral and all MICAH personnel, for their work in difficult and challenging circumstances.

United Nations S/RES/1529 (2004)

Security Council

Distr.: General
29 February 2004

Resolution 1529 (2004)

Adopted by the Security Council at its 4919th meeting, on 29 February 2004

The Security Council,

Recalling its previous resolutions and statements by its President on Haiti, in particular the statement of 26 February 2004 (S/PRST/2004/4),

Deeply concerned by the deterioration of the political, security and humanitarian situation in Haiti and *deploring* the loss of life that has already occurred,

Expressing its utmost concern at the continuing violence in Haiti, as well as the potential for a rapid deterioration of the humanitarian situation in that country, and its destabilizing effect on the region,

Stressing the need to create a secure environment in Haiti and the region that enables respect for human rights, including the well-being of civilians, and supports the mission of humanitarian workers,

Commending the Organization of American States (OAS) and the Caribbean Community (CARICOM) for their lead efforts to advance a peaceful solution and for attempting to establish confidence among the parties, in particular through their Plan of Action,

Taking note of the resignation of Jean-Bertrand Aristide as President of Haiti and the swearing-in of President Boniface Alexandre as the acting President of Haiti in accordance with the Constitution of Haiti,

Acknowledging the appeal of the new President of Haiti for the urgent support of the international community to assist in restoring peace and security in Haiti and to further the constitutional political process now under way,

Determined to support a peaceful and constitutional solution to the current crisis in Haiti,

Determining that the situation in Haiti constitutes a threat to international peace and security, and to stability in the Caribbean especially through the potential outflow of people to other States in the subregion,

Acting under Chapter VII of the Charter of the United Nations,

04-25410 (E)

1. *Calls on* Member States to support the constitutional succession and political process now under way in Haiti and the promotion of a peaceful and lasting solution to the current crisis;

2. *Authorizes* the immediate deployment of a Multinational Interim Force for a period of not more than three months from adoption of this resolution:

(a) To contribute to a secure and stable environment in the Haitian capital and elsewhere in the country, as appropriate and as circumstances permit, in order to support Haitian President Alexandre's request for international assistance to support the constitutional political process under way in Haiti;

(b) To facilitate the provision of humanitarian assistance and the access of international humanitarian workers to the Haitian people in need;

(c) To facilitate the provision of international assistance to the Haitian police and the Haitian Coast Guard in order to establish and maintain public safety and law and order and to promote and protect human rights;

(d) To support establishment of conditions for international and regional organizations, including the United Nations and the Organization of American States, to assist the Haitian people;

(e) To coordinate, as needed, with the OAS Special Mission and with the United Nations Special Adviser for Haiti, to prevent further deterioration of the humanitarian situation;

3. *Declares* its readiness to establish a follow-on United Nations stabilization force to support continuation of a peaceful and constitutional political process and the maintenance of a secure and stable environment, and in this regard requests the Secretary-General, in consultation with the Organization of American States, to submit to the Council recommendations, preferably by 30 days from adoption of this resolution, for the size, structure and mandate of such a force, including the role of international police and means of coordination with the OAS Special Mission, and for subsequent deployment of the United Nations force not later than three months from adoption of this resolution;

4. *Welcomes* the Secretary-General's February 27 appointment of a Special Adviser for Haiti, and *requests* the Secretary-General to elaborate a programme of action for the United Nations to assist the constitutional political process and support humanitarian and economic assistance and promote the protection of human rights and the development of the rule of law;

5. *Calls on* Member States to contribute personnel, equipment and other necessary financial and logistic resources on an urgent basis to the Multinational Interim Force and invites contributing Member States to inform the leadership of the force and the Secretary-General of their intent to participate in the mission; and *stresses* the importance of such voluntary contributions to help defray the expenses of the Multinational Interim Force that participating Member States will bear;

6. *Authorizes* the Member States participating in the Multinational Interim Force in Haiti to take all necessary measures to fulfil its mandate;

7. *Demands* that all the parties to the conflict in Haiti cease using violent means, and reiterates that all parties must respect international law, including with respect to human rights and that there will be individual accountability and no

impunity for violators; *further demands* that parties respect the constitutional succession and the political process under way to resolve the current crisis, and enable legitimate Haitian security forces and other public institutions to perform their duties and provide access to humanitarian agencies to carry out their work;

8. *Further calls* on all parties in Haiti and on Member States to cooperate fully with the Multinational Interim Force in Haiti in the execution of its mandate and to respect the security and freedom of movement of the Multinational Interim Force, as well as to facilitate the safe and unimpeded access of international humanitarian personnel and aid to populations in need in Haiti;

9. *Requests* the leadership of the Multinational Interim Force in Haiti to report periodically to the Council, through the Secretary-General, on the implementation of its mandate;

10. *Calls upon* the international community, in particular the United Nations, the Organization of American States, and the Caribbean Community, to work with the people of Haiti in a long-term effort to promote the rebuilding of democratic institutions and to assist in the development of a strategy to promote social and economic development and to combat poverty;

11. *Decides* to remain seized of the matter.

THE NEW REPUBLIC

ISLAND OF DISENCHANTMENT (EXCERPTS)

CHARLES LANE

SEPTEMBER 29, 1997

This obscure underworld episode would be of no interest outside Haiti except for one fact: Eddy Arbrouet is also wanted for the August 1996 murder of Antoine Leroy and Jacques Fleurival, two right-wing opponents of the U.S.-backed Haitian government. A pile of evidence links Arbrouet to the murders—and other evidence suggests that he was acting in collaboration with senior officers of Haiti's Presidential Security Unit, the American-trained and—financed corps of official bodyguards who protect Haiti's president, Rene Preval. Haitian officials deny that any such conspiracy existed. But U.S. officials and other sources familiar with the incident say the killing was one in a series carried out by political hit men who appear to have been operating from within the National Palace.

Aristide promised the U.S. that "national reconciliation," not vengeance, would follow his return to office. But with Arbrouet still at large, and twenty-six political murders since 1995 still officially unsolved, that promise—and hence the promise of democratic rule—seems unfulfilled.

On August 19, the United Nations announced it would provide no further aid to elections in Haiti " until the credibility and transparency of the electoral process are re-established."

And then there are the political murders, for which no one has yet been convicted, or even formally charged, and which remain a source of quiet tension between the United States and Haiti. The Clinton administration has informed Preval that the Leroy-Fleurival investigation is a test case of Haiti's commitment to the rule of law; it has done so largely because Republicans in Congress have made clear they see Haiti's response to the murders as a test of the Clinton administration's policy

The trail of blood that leads to Eddy Arbrouet's hideout began at 3:45 in the afternoon of March 28, 1995, on a busy street in Port-au-Prince. Mireille Durocher Bertin and a client, Eugene Baillergeau Jr., were sitting in their car, stuck in a traffic jam, when two assailants opened fire on them with a 9 mm pistol and a 5.56 mm machine gun. Both died on the spot.

Coming soon after Aristide's restoration to power, the murder of Bertin and her associate sent a chill through Haiti: Bertin, an attorney for members of the traditional elite, was one of Aristide's leading critics. Shortly before her death, she had sent a letter to U.S. military authorities, who were in control of the island at the time. Written on behalf of the right-wing Mobilization for National Development Party (MDN), the letter accused an Aristide government intelligence operative named Patric Moise of being involved in a plot to kill 100 members of the right-wing elite.

nine days before the killing, a Haitian employee of the U.S. forces had made a startling statement to his American boss: Moise had asked him to assist in a plan to kill Bertin. Mondesir Beaubrun, then Aristide's minister of interior, had purportedly offered Moise $5,000 to carry out the hit. The U.S. Army immediately arrested five suspects, including Moise, catching four of the alleged conspirators in an Isuzu Trooper owned by the Ministry of Interior, a car Moise said Minister Beaubrun had lent to him.

But then U.S. officials made a strange decision. Rather than warn Bertin about the plots directly, they asked Aristide and his Minister of Justice, Jean-Joseph Exume, to warn Bertin. (Some U.S. embassy officials had argued that U.S. officials should warn Bertin directly, but they were overruled by the U.S. Ambassador, William Swing, according to a General Accounting Office report about the affair.)

Whatever the case, U.S. officials were palpably alarmed when Bertin showed up dead despite what they thought was a good-faith understanding that Aristide and his justice minister would protect her. With President Clinton set to arrive for a triumphal visit to Haiti on April 1, Ambassador Swing asked Aristide to invite FBI agents to help crack the case.

The FBI quickly discounted theories that the murders had been related to a robbery, drug trafficking or a family dispute. Instead, the investigators said, the most likely scenario was that a second group of government hit men had taken over after the U.S. nipped the Beaubrun-Moise plot in the bud. Among the leads were radio conversations intercepted by the U.S. military the day of the killing, in which two men appeared to be talking about following Bertin's car. The two men were Joseph Medard, then the deputy chief of Aristide's bodyguards, and Lieutenant Pierre Lubin of the Interim Public Security Force (ipsf), the police force that Aristide selected—and financed with U.S. money—to help American troops keep order during the transition. The FBI began trying to question Medard, Lubin and several other officials of the ipsf and the National Palace.

1. Suddenly, FBI agents found themselves in the position of having to investigate the very government officials who were supposed to help them solve the case. The Haitians were not accommodating. Haitian officials told the FBI agents they could not investigate the Bertin case unless they also agreed to investigate twenty killings by the ousted military regime. In May, FBI agents saw Haitian government vehicles parked menacingly near the home of a key witness. Witnesses told of threats from the ipsf.

Ambassador Swing sent the State Department a cable saying that "the FBI investigation of the Bertin assassination is at a standstill due to lack of Haitian government cooperation."

After the FBI quit, the Bertin case was assigned to the Haitian police force's new Special Investigations Unit. The unit consists of a small U.S.-funded team of Haitians working under the direction of an American adviser with forensic support from the FBI. At Haitian insistence, the unit is also looking into killings by the ousted military regime; but it has had plenty of new business. Indeed, the suspicious killings continued while the FBI was still in town.

1. Michel Gonzales, a prominent Haitian airline executive, lived with his horses on forty acres in the Port-au-Prince exurb of Tabarre.

Gonzales's next-door neighbor was a powerful Haitian, too: Aristide. On two occasions around the time of Aristide's return to Haiti, Aristide's advisers, Jean-Marie Cherestal and Leslie Voltaire, asked U.S. officials to obtain the land for Aristide's use, according to two U.S. sources familiar with the events. The request was refused.

At that point, Gonzales's friends say, visitors began arriving and telling Gonzales pointedly to get out. He didn't. On May 22, 1995, two men on a motorbike shot Gonzales dead in front of Aristide's place, while Gonzales's wife and daughter—both American citizens—looked on in horror.

Two days after the cops found Gonzales dead, Michel-Ange Hermann, a former colonel in the fadh, was gunned down. And in the run-up to the national elections, assassins felled two minor Senate candidates: Leslie Grimar, an auto parts dealer, and Max Mayard, a former general with the fadh. An FBI inspection of shell casings found at the Bertin, Hermann, Mayard and Grimar murder scenes has established that the bullets were all fired from the same gun. They also match shell casings found at the Leroy-Fleurival homicide scene. Which brings us back to the case

Two days after the cops found Gonzales dead, Michel-Ange Hermann, a former colonel in the fadh, was gunned down. And in the run-up to the national elections, assassins felled two minor Senate candidates: Leslie Grimar, an auto parts dealer, and Max Mayard, a former general with the fadh. An FBI inspection of shell casings found at the Bertin, Hermann, Mayard and Grimar murder scenes has established that the bullets were all fired from the same gun. They also match shell casings found at the Leroy-Fleurival homicide scene. Which brings us back to the case

Two days after the cops found Gonzales dead, Michel-Ange Hermann, a former colonel in the fadh, was gunned down. And in the run-up to the national elections, assassins felled two minor Senate candidates: Leslie Grimar, an auto parts dealer, and Max Mayard, a former general with the fadh. An FBI inspection of shell casings found at the Bertin, Hermann, Mayard and Grimar murder scenes has established that the bullets were all fired from the same gun. They also match shell casings found at the Leroy-Fleurival homicide scene. Which brings us back to the case

The summer of 1996 was a politically tense period in Port-au-Prince. U.S. intelligence developed reliable information that Haitian rightists and ex-fadh officers were arming for a coup against President Preval. Shots were fired at the National Palace. On August 17, Preval's police tackled the threat by rounding up nineteen former fadh members at the headquarters of the same party with which Bertin had been associated, the MDN. Three days after that, Leroy and Fleurival were killed.

Within hours of the shooting, the U.S. Embassy in Port-au-Prince had convincing evidence that several presidential bodyguards had been present at the crime. (The Los Angeles Times has reported that the evidence consisted of intercepted radio conversations among the bodyguards.) Police found a Taurus 9 mm pistol next to Leroy's body. The serial number on the Taurus identified it as property of the presidential bodyguards.

Even more damning evidence about Arbrouet's ties to the National Palace has emerged since then. Arbrouet was a paid informant for the presidential bodyguards, working directly for the top officer, Joseph Moise. Arbrouet had both an entry pass to the National Palace and a government-issued gun.

The Clintonites tried to handle the dilemma by dispatching forty-six American bodyguards to watch Preval's back while he began the delicate process of removing the ten bodyguards who were suspected of having knowledge of, or a role in, the killings. Moise, the top officer, was one of the first to be suspended at U.S. insistence. But Preval dragged his feet about firing the men, and delays cropped up in the Haitian investigation.

○

APEX
TP
9780160718847
76901945 – 94

APEX
TP
9780160750595
76901953 — 77